THE WOMEN OF 1798

THE WOMEN
OF 1798

Dáire Keogh & Nicholas Furlong

EDITORS

FOUR COURTS PRESS

Set in 10.5 on 12.5 point Ehrhardt for
FOUR COURTS PRESS
Fumbally Lane, Dublin 8, Ireland
e-mail: info@four-courts-press.ie
and in North America
FOUR COURTS PRESS
c/o ISBS, 5804 N.E. Hassalo Street, Portland, OR 97213.

© Four Courts Press and the various contributors 1998

A catalogue record for this title
is available from the British Library.

ISBN 1–85182–358–7 hbk
ISBN 1–85182–359–x pbk

Printed in Ireland by ColourBooks, Dublin.

Contents

7
PREFACE

9
Liberty, Hibernia and Mary Le More:
United Irish images of women
Mary Helen Thuente

26
Matilda Tone and virtuous republican femininity
Nancy J. Curtin

47
Mary Anne McCracken:
Belfast revolutionary and pioneer of feminism
John Gray

64
Bearing witness: Female evidences in courts martial
convened to suppress the 1798 rebellion
Thomas Bartlett

87
Bridget 'Croppy Biddy' Dolan: Wicklow's anti-heroine of 1798
Ruan O'Donnell

113
Protestant women of county Wexford
and their narratives of the rebellion of 1798
John D. Beatty

137
Mary Shackleton Leadbeater: Peaceful rebel
Kevin O'Neill

Contents

163
Lord Edward's aunt: How Louisa Conolly and her sisters
faced the rebellion
Eleanor Burgess

177
'The Noggin of Milk': An Old Testament legend
and the Battle of Ballinamuck
Maureen Murphy

187
Nineteenth-century perspectives:
The women of 1798 in folk memory and ballads
Anna Kinsella

200
SELECT BIBLIOGRAPHY

202
LIST OF CONTRIBUTORS

203
INDEX

Preface

When the tyrant's hand was laid
Upon the true and brave,
In the tender pride of womanhood
The true rose to help and save.
                    'Leo' (John Keegan Casey, 1846-70).

No aspect of the 1798 rebellion has been so neglected as that of the
women's role in the events of that year. Contemporaries drew upon
their experience, but for the most part the women's voice was smothered beneath the partisan priorities of the commentators. There was little enthusiasm in the immediate aftermath of the rebellion for an
accurate record of events since both loyalists and the vanquished
attempted to play down the politicisation of the 1790s. The former
sought to interpret the rising as a *jacquerie* or popish plot, while the latter attempted to minimise their culpability, presenting themselves as
'reluctant rebels' or moderating elements in a spontaneous rebellion
provoked by unrelenting terror.

Within this scenario it was difficult to accommodate the women's
contribution and such priorities contributed to the reduction of their
role to that of victim: the mourner, the suffering loyalist of Musgrave's
depositions or the avenging 'woman raped'. Such interpretations, however, were due in part to the broader context of the period and to eighteenth-century society which drew a rigid distinction between male and
female roles. It is an irony of the Enlightenment that the *philosophes*
through their reflection on the question of gender perpetuated the
notion of women as inferior to men. Definitions of femininity were
altered, but the effect remained constant: women were excluded from
the public realm. Mary Wollstonecraft compared this denial of rights to
the condition of slaves; yet the United Irishmen, for all their lofty talk
of liberty, refused to entertain the possibility of the admission of women
to the body politic.

Despite their exclusion from the United Irish programme, unlike
France where women's participation was necessary to the success of the
revolution, the 'rebel daughters' played an active role in Ireland's rebellion. After the event, however, this was largely ignored; as Bartlett
observes below, 'women could be symbols or model or victim but ... the
role of actor, activist or combatant – *in a political context* – was denied
them'. Nor would the passage of time be kinder to their memory,

7

indeed the applicability of the title of this volume, *The Women of 1798*, is itself an indication of their neglect.

One hundred years ago, during the centenary, gestures were made to incorporate the women of '98 in the rash of literature and ballads which marked the celebrations. However, the temper of the time and the Catholic Nationalism which dominated the commemorations reinforced earlier accounts which had stressed their femininity and confined women's participation to a supporting role. This process reached its climax with the publication of Helena Concannon's *Women of 'Ninety-Eight* (1919), written in the context of the Anglo-Irish War, which dealt with 'The Mothers of '98', 'The Wives of '98' and other similar headings which was as likely to have been intended as an inspiration to her contemporaries than a history of the rebellion. Yet, for all this, Concannon's work has remained the unique study of the subject.

It is the intention of *The Women of 1798* to redress this neglect – to bring a new light to bear on the subject in the hope of creating an accurate assessment of the role of women in 1798. The conclusions of the ten scholars below, working from diverse and complementary disciplines, have combined to present the complexity of the subject and to show the women in their many roles, not alone as symbol, victim and observer, but as activist and combatant. The editors present these papers not by way of conclusion, but rather as a statement of the current research and as an aid to further study.

The editors are indebted to many who have facilitated this publication. In the first instance, we would like to express our gratitude to the contributors but also to Walter Forde and the committee of Gorey's Byrne-Perry Summer School upon whose initiative this project began. It is imperative, too, that we thank Bernard Browne, the Board and the Historians-Librarians advisory committee of Comoradh '98. Many others deserve our gratitude: James Kelly, Mark Woods, James Quinn, Dick and Lise Aylmer, Trevor Parkhill, Alice Kearney, Kate Bateman, Kevin Whelan, Pauric Travers and Susan Hood. Finally, we would like to thank Michael Adams and his staff at Four Courts Press for their customary courtesy and efficiency.

Liberty, Hibernia and
Mary Le More:
United Irish images of women

Mary Helen Thuente

The warning that 'we have to remember that what we call our country is not a poetical abstraction', voiced by Eoin MacNeill as nationalist iconography about women was inspiring the events of 1916, was reiterated by Sean O'Faolain in *The Bell* in the 1940s and more recently by writers on both sides of the scholarly battles about revisionism who have called for the deconstruction of the trope of the idealised woman as suffering Ireland.[1] The tropes of women that are so fundamental to modern Irish nationalism originated in the United Irish movement in the 1790s. United Irish verse, particularly the four songbooks that the United Irishmen published under the title *Paddy's Resource* in 1795, 1796, 1798, and 1803, presented their major tropes of women – goddesses, mothers, maidens, and maniacs. The United Irishmen's iconography of women is a tapestry of interrelated images much richer and more complex than the stereotypical sorrowing mother or maiden symbolising Ireland's political oppression and sufferings.

The authority and power of United Irish images of women derived from multiple traditions within and outside of Ireland: classical and medieval allegory; English, Irish, French, and American literature; and religious and political iconography. Therefore, calls for the deconstruction of the trope of idealised woman as suffering Ireland must recognise, not only that the tropes are cultural constructs and political myths, but

---

1 D. Cairns and S. Richards, 'Tropes and Traps: Aspects of Women and Nationality in Twentieth-Century Irish Drama', in T. O'Brien Johnston and D. Cairns (eds), *Gender in Irish Writing* (Philadelphia, 1991), pp 131-3, 137. For background about images of women see the following: M. Warner, *Monuments and Maidens: The Allegory of the Female Form* (New York, 1985); B. Loftus, *Mirrors: William III and Mother Ireland* (Dundrum, 1990); H. Concannon, *Women of 'Ninety Eight* (Dublin, 1919); N. Curtin, 'Women and 18th Century Irish Republicanism', in M. MacCurtain and M. O'Dowd (eds), *Women in Early Modern Ireland* (Edinburgh, 1991), pp 133-44.

that suffering-mother/maiden-Ireland is only one of many such tropes whose meanings, and hence whose strength and authority, are rooted in a complex intersection of venerable and powerful images of women. This essay will focus on the origin, meaning, interrelationships, and development of several major images of women in United Irish iconography: Liberty and Hibernia; the portrayal of women as maidens, mothers, and maniacs; the maiden harp and the 'genius of Ireland'.

The heroic tropes of the maiden harp and the 'genius of Ireland' have all but disappeared in nationalist iconography of women and demand some explanation. The maiden harp, with a forepillar of a winged figure who was a naked woman from the waist up and a fish from the waist down, had been used as a visual symbol of Ireland since the seventeenth century.[2] The maiden harp was a popular United Irish motif, appearing on the United Irish seal and membership certificates, on the mastheads of two United Irish newspapers, the Belfast *Northern Star* and the Dublin *National Journal*, and as the insignia on Wolfe Tone's design for an Irish flag and Robert Emmet's design for a seal.[3] Its exact meaning has been lost, but it is clearly connected with classical, medieval, and Irish traditions. The angelic female figure referred to as 'the genius of Ireland' in United Irish verse evidently had wings because William Drennan's poem on the harp claims 'angelic ERIN brush'd it with her wings'.[4] Another clue to the maiden harp's meaning comes from Thomas Moore's 'The Origin of the Harp', in the third number of his *Irish Melodies*. Moore, who had published verse in United Irish newspapers in the 1790s, describes how a 'Siren of old, who sung under the sea', abandoned by her love who had 'left her to weep', was transformed into a harp with 'the sea-maiden's form' on which 'her sea-beauties gracefully curled round the frame' and her hair became the harp strings. Daniel Maclise's illustration for this song, supposedly based on a United Irishman's drawing on his prison wall, shows a woman whose long hair is entwined with flowers rising from the sea.[5]

Moore's association of the maiden on the harp with the sirens of Greek mythology, winged sea nymphs whose alluring music enchanted men and who are depicted as mermaids in heraldry, is appropriate because once Hibernia's harp was 'new strung,' her music was intended to inspire patriot Volunteers and then United Irishmen to die for her.

2 G.A. Hayes-McCoy, *A History of Irish Flags from Earliest Times* (Dublin, 1979), pp 22-3, 46-7. 3 Ibid., pp 111, 121; C. MacLeod, 'Irish Volunteer Glass', *The Irish Sword*, vol. vii, no. xxviii, pp 241-55. 4 W. Drennan, *Fugitive Pieces in Verse and Prose* (Belfast, 1815), p. 152. 5 T. Moore, 'The Origin of the Harp', in *Moore's Irish Melodies* (London, 1866), pp 60-1.

Two emblematical figures from Cesare Ripa's influential late sixteenth-century *Iconologia* are also relevant. The 'Rational Soul' is a female figure draped in white with wings, while the image of 'Pleasure' is a winged young woman crowned with flowers who is about to play a harp in concert with a siren in the background. Commentary describes the sirens as water goddesses celebrated for their sweet voices and skill in music whose upper parts were beautiful women who were fishes or birds below the waist.[6] The concept of a 'genius' goes back to the Roman belief that each person was accompanied through life by a protecting spirit or genius (similar to Greek daimons and Christian guardian angels) who provided comfort in sorrow and inspiration to noble deeds. Male genii were often depicted as winged youths. The Greek image of winged victory is no doubt also relevant, as are depictions of angels as creatures of celestial light and as winged messengers from the heavens. The 'genius of Ireland' also bears noteworthy resemblance to the 'speirbhean' or sky-maiden of the native Irish aisling tradition.[7]

A poem entitled 'The Grave of Russell' typifies the United Irish use of the motif: 'From the sky, like an angel of light,/The genius of Erin, in glory arrayed' visits Thomas Russell's grave where 'The voice of her harp, that to sorrow was strung' praises his heroism and promises him fame.[8] The heroic dimensions of the 'genius of Erin' trope are also apparent in a song in the 1798 *Paddy's Resource* describing 'Ierne's Genius' hovering over the bodies of two executed United Irishmen and declaring they should not be mourned 'For happy he, who sheds his blood,/In Freedom's glorious cause!'[9] Robert Emmet wrote a poem entitled 'Genius of Erin' calling upon her to 'tune thy harp'.[10] One of the latest examples of the motif is a poem called 'Carolan's Receipt', written by United Irishman John Daly Burk after he came to America in 1798, which describes a 'genius of Erin' clad in green with a half-strung harp and streaming hair amidst a storm.[11] Although Burk's image bears interesting similarities to the pathetic maniac-on-the-moor motif

6 C. Ripa, *Baroque and Rococo Pictorial Imagery* (1758-60; rept. ed. New York, 1971), figure 5; G. Richardson, *Icononolgy; or, A Collection of Emblematical Figures*, ii (London, 1779), pp 61-2, figure 293. 7 G. Murphy, 'Notes on Aisling Poetry', *Eigse: A Journal of Irish Studies*, vol. i (1939), pp 40-50. 8 R.R. Madden, *Literary Remains of the United Irishmen of 1798, and Selections from Other Popular Lyrics of Their Times* (Dublin, 1887), p. 289. 9 'Song to the Memory of Daniel Mahon, and Thomas Carty, Privates in the Kildare Militia, who were shot in the Phoenix Park, the 6th of June, 1797, for their Attachment to the Cause of Ireland', in *Paddy's Resource; or, The Harp of Erin Attuned to Freedom* (Dublin, 1798), pp 87-9. 10 R. Emmet, 'Genius of Erin', in T.A. Emmet, *Memoir of Thomas Addis and Robert Emmet* (New York, 1915), pp 16-17. 11 'Carolan's Receipt', in J. McCreery (ed.), *A Selection from the Ancient Music of Ireland* (Petersburg, 1824), pp 41-3.

popular in post-1798 United Irish songs, he portrays his 'genius of Erin' in an heroic not a pathetic mode. The trope's most notable nineteenth-century survival is Horatio's statement in Lady Morgan's *The Wild Irish Girl* (1806) that 'the genius of Glorvina has ever appeared to me as a light from heaven, an emanation of divine intelligence, which wants only a right direction'.[12] In 1809 James McHenry, who witnessed the events of 1798 as a young man in county Antrim and subsequently wrote fiction and verse about the United Irishmen, published a poem entitled 'The Bard of Erin' in which 'Erin's Genius' is described as a 'celestial maid' wandering over the plains with her 'pathetic Harp'. Her prophecy of the advent of 'a glorious age' in Ireland is introduced with this description:

> A Virgin harper of angel mein!
> With gold and purple were her temples crown'd,
> Beset with stars and flaming rubies round;
> Of heavenly mould the harp on which she play'd,
> In holy wreaths of shamrock green array'd!
> With joy, the Bard beheld th' impressive smile,
> That spoke the Genius of his darling Isle![13]

The most complete portrait of the genius of Ireland figure appeared in the most popular United Irish satire, Presbyterian minister James Porter's *Billy Bluff and the Squire*, a comic portrait of life in rural county Down in the 1790s. Billy Bluff describes a vision of 'The Genius of Ireland' as 'a beautiful Angel clad in robes of white', who 'came sailing through the air' and descends on a 'beautiful green hill' covered with shamrocks that was 'the center of Ireland' in the midst of a wide plain near Athlone. A bright light rising from the west rather than the east reveals crowds of people 'from all ranks, ages, and pro-fessions', the rich and the poor, walking on to the plain. Some can speak only English, others could speak only Irish, 'but the greatest number could speak both English and Irish'. The sky opens to reveal an 'angel clad in robes of white' carrying a large flag and an olive branch with which she beckons the people forward. The people link arms and clasp each other by the waist in contrast to the 'dignitaries of the church, the sages of the law, and the lords of the land' who had arrived in coaches and, instead of joining the people climbing the hill, were flying toward 'the dark cloud that still hung over the east' and had 'turned the color of clotted blood'. The Angel, carrying a large flag

---

12 S. Owenson, *The Wild Irish Girl* (London, 1986), p. 70. 13 J. McHenry, *The Bard of Erin and Other Poems* (Belfast, 1809), pp 1-9.

with gold letters declaring her to be 'THE GENIUS OF IRELAND', announces 'with a voice exquisitely fine' that 'ravished' the listeners' ears, that the people 'are all my children', that 'This is the HILL OF UNION' and that the result of this meeting would be 'LIBERTY & PEACE' as she reveals those two words inscribed in great letters of gold on the flag and the vision vanishes.[14]

Although the vision's grandeur and serious symbolic meaning have only a weak connection with the satire's comic plot, Porter considered it a central scene because his December 1796 introduction to *Billy Bluff*, when it was published separately after being serialised in the *Northern Star*, included the following passage: 'With regard to the *Vision at Athlone*, those who do not understand it, need not be informed of its meaning – those who do, require no farther explanation. Let the Friends of *Peace*, *Virtue*, and *Union* endeavour to realise the fiction, and let every honest Man lend his assistance to erect a visible Monument to the Genius of Ireland.'[15] While no harp is associated with Porter's 'genius of Ireland', her ravishing voice recalls those of the sirens, her white dress and olive branch are reminiscent of the goddess Liberty, and her heavenly appearance suggests the Virgin Mary in Catholic tradition who is at once virgin and mother. Personifications of Liberty and Hibernia in United Irish verse embody a similar duality in that they are variously depicted as maidens inspiring their lovers or mothers exhorting their sons.

The iconography of women in United Irish songs must also be seen as part of trans-Atlantic and European traditions. Descriptions of Liberty and Columbia in eighteenth-century American political verse also parallel the various personifications of Ireland in their sky-goddess forms. Songs of the American Revolution described Liberty's 'celestial form' and 'her lyre to strains of seraphs strung' or portray her as a captive 'wailing in chains' until freed from her shackles by Washington, her favorite son.[16] Thomas Paine's famous song 'The Liberty Tree' described the goddess of Liberty in a 'chariot of light' bringing a 'fair budding branch' to plant as the liberty tree.[17] In a similar vein, Columbia was portrayed as 'queen of the world' and 'child of the skies,' while other late eighteenth-century American songs refer to the 'Genius of Masonry' descending from the heavens and the 'Genius of America' speak-

---

14 J. Porter, 'Billy Bluff and the Squire', in the *Northern Star*, 15 August 1796. 15 Porter, 'Preface', *Billy Bluff and Squire Firebrand: or, A Sample of the Times* (Belfast, 1797), p. 1. 16 *The American Songster; or Federal Museum* (Baltimore, 1799), p. 29; *The Skylark: or Gentlemen and Ladies' Complete Songster* (Worcester, 1797), p. 196. 17 *The Nightingale of Liberty: or Delights of Harmony, a Choice Collection of Patriotic, Masonic, and Entertaining Songs* (New York, 1797), p. 15.

ing to her sons.[18] French tropes of Liberty and the republic as majestic goddesses in the solemn mode of classical allegory also influenced the United Irish portrayal of Hibernia.[19]

The songs and visual images of the Irish Volunteer movement provided the richest and most immediate iconography of women to the United Irishmen. The goddess Liberty, who had frequently been depicted in popular emblem books of classical and medieval allegories, personifications, and symbols derived from Cesare Ripa's late sixteenth-century *Iconologia*, was a common image in eighteenth-century political verse in England and in Ireland, particularly in the songs of the Irish Volunteers. Many odes and songs addressing the heavenly goddess Liberty as a guardian spirit of Ireland or 'heaven-born maid' were published in Volunteer newspapers in Belfast and Dublin.[20] Three 'Volunteer' songs are appropriately included in R.R. *Madden's Literary Remains of the United Irishmen of 1798, and Selections from Other Popular Lyrics of Their Times*. In one typical song, 'fair Liberty' is described as coming 'from Sparta and Athens' to Britain from whence she was 'doom'd to exile' in Ireland where she is 'cherish'd and honour'd' by personifications of Ireland variously referred to as Hibernia, Ierne, and the 'Genius of Ireland', and her sons, the Volunteers.[21] In a song entitled 'Liberty', printed in the Dublin United Irish newspaper *The Press* on 15 February 1798 and in the *Paddy's Resource* songbook that year, Liberty is described as a religious and artistic muse, waking the soul to ecstasy and inspiring the poet's song.

While the goddess Liberty was invariably depicted in an heroic mode, the figure of Hibernia had generally been presented as pathetic in the seventeenth century, but by the mid-eighteenth century images of Hibernia seated or standing proudly with the cap and spear of Liberty began to appear. The Volunteers used both heroic and pathetic images of Hibernia. Two poems published privately in Belfast in 1789 are based on the popular Volunteer motif of Liberty coming to Ireland. *Libertas*, which recounts how Liberty inspired the heroic citizens of Derry to withstand the siege by King James' forces in 1688, opens with

---

18 *Nightingale of Liberty*, p. 29; *Skylark*, p. 285; G.B. Anderson, *Freedom's Voice in Poetry and Song: Political and Patriotic Lyrics in Colonial American Newspapers 1773-1783* (Wilmington, 1975), p. 202. The trans-Atlantic connection is also apparent in several early nineteenth-century American political songbooks that show a marked influence of United Irish tunes and lyrics due to the political activities of United Irishmen exiled to America after 1798. 19 M. Agulhon, *Marianne into Battle: Republican Imagery and Symbolism in France, 1789-1880* (London, 1991). 20 'Liberty, A Poem', in *The Belfast Mercury; or, Freeman's Chronicle*, 20 April 1784, p. 4. 21 'Volunteer Song', in Madden, *Literary Remains*, pp 233-4. 22 J. Glass, *Libertas, A Poem* (Belfast, 1789), pp 5-6.

the goddess Liberty with sword and shield appearing to 'Ierne', who is reclining in despair on a rock with her hair dishevelled and her harp unstrung, after which Liberty proceeds to Derry.[22] In *The Patriot Soldier*, which heroicised the Volunteer movement, the goddess Liberty, accompanied by a young Volunteer, urges a less pathetic and distraught Hibernia, called 'the lost Genius of our isle', who is sitting in a sylvan shade with her silent wolfhound, unstrung harp, and decaying shamrock crown by her side, to reclaim her 'long last fame'.[23] Similarly, what contemporary accounts described as a 'striking emblem' of a Volunteer presenting Liberty to a 'large figure of Hibernia in a reclining position' appeared on the 'Great Standard' elevated on a triumphal car at the Belfast Bastile Day 'Grand Procession' in 1791 and 1792.[24] A United Irish song entitled 'The Olive Branch' in the 1795 *Paddy's Resource* songbook describes a similar trope: 'Descend sweet Liberty, descend,/ On poor Hibernia's wretched Isle'.[25]

Goddess figures were prominent in United Irish iconography, particularly in their earliest propaganda. Often the figure has several possible interpretations. For example, a song celebrating the French Revolution in a United Irish songbook, published in conjunction with Belfast's celebration of Bastile Day in July 1792, describes how 'Sweet Peace from her sphere will descend,/When fiends of oppression have fled'.[26] This female figure could be any one of several goddesses or personifications of Erin or the Blessed Virgin. The most common United Irish image of a goddess, Liberty descending from the heavens as a goddess of light to inspire Irish heroes, is found in all four *Paddy's Resource* songbooks. Eight lines addressing Liberty as a 'goddess, heav'nly bright' from Joseph Addison's 'Ode to Liberty', although he is not identified as the author, are placed on or opposite the title page in the last three songbooks. Several songs in the 1795 songbook described Liberty as a powerful goddess descending from heaven and tuning Hibernia's harp to freedom. In the 1798 songbook both Liberty and Erin are portrayed as heavenly goddesses descended from those of Greece and Rome.

The masthead of the Belfast United Irish newspaper *Northern Star* depicted two goddesses, Justice and another figure who is probably

23 *The Patriot Soldier; or Irish Volunteer, A Poem* (Belfast, 1789), pp 5-7. 24 H. Joy, *Historical Collections Relative to the Town of Belfast: from the Earliest Period to the Union with Great Britain* (Belfast, 1817), p. 349. 25 'Olive Branch' in *Paddy's Resource: Being a Select Collection of Original and Modern Patriotic Songs, Toasts, and Sentiments Compiled for the Use of the People of Ireland* (Belfast, 1795), p. 80. 26 'Song on the French Revolution' in *Songs on the French Revolution that took place at Paris, 14 July 1789. Sung at the Celebration thereof at Belfast, on Saturday, 14 July 1792* (Belfast, 1792); published as 'The World Will Be Free' in *Paddy's Resource* (1795).

meant to be Hibernia. From the newspaper's founding in January 1792 through December 1792, the Justice (holding a sword and scales) and Hibernia (holding only the lictor rods generally associated with Concord, but associated with Hibernia on Volunteer flags and glassware), with no background details, upheld a shield depicting an unadorned harp in the midst of a sunburst (the emblem of the enlightenment of Liberty) with a crown on top. In January 1793 the crown disappeared and the following details were added to the masthead: a maiden harp between the two goddesses, a blindfold on Justice and an olive branch (a symbol associated with Concord, Hibernia, and the 'genius of Ireland') in the hand of Hibernia, plus a realistic backdrop depicting a town, hills, and a ship. After October 1793, the background was still realistic, but contained only distant trees. The masthead of the Dublin United Irish *National Journal*, published for about two months in the spring of 1792, portrayed a female figure, presumably Hibernia, in classical drapery seated next to a maiden harp and holding a spear, shield (inscribed with the words 'Unite and Be Free'), and a pen with which she is inscribing a pillar with the words 'Let the will of the people be the law of the land'. In United Irish verse Hibernia was simultaneously referred to as pathetically languishing in chains and heroically exhorting her sons to glory.

United Irish iconography also depicted various types of human women, most notably the mother, the maiden, and the maniac. United Irish references to Ireland as the poor old mother, usually called Granu or Granu Wale (the spellings of the name vary notoriously), ranged from pathetic images of her wailing in chains to stronger images of her ordering her sons to defend her. The legendary Grace O'Malley or Granuaile, the extraordinary sixteenth-century Mayo woman renowned for her courage and success on the high seas, exemplifies the protean quality of tropes of women. While the historical Grace O'Malley was a survivor who, after defying the English presence in Ireland for much of her life, in old age sought pardon from Queen Elizabeth to secure her rights, she was remembered in Irish tradition for her defiance.[27]

In July 1793 the Dublin magazine *Anthologia Hibernica* printed an engraving entitled 'Grana Uile introduced to Queen Elizabeth' depicting her legendary visit at age sixty-three to London in 1593 when, according to legendary accounts, she outshone Queen Elizabeth in dress and demeanor. According to the article accompanying the engraving, 'Tradition says that her piracies became so notorious and her power so dangerous, that she was proclaimed ... [and] the English power growing strong in Connaught', she went to London where she made peace with

27 A. Chambers, *Granuaile: The Life and Times of Grace O'Malley* (Dublin, 1983).

Queen Elizabeth. The following anecdote recounted in the article suggests that Granuaile made peace on her own terms: 'The court stared with surprise at so strange a figure, when one of the ladies perceived that Grana wanted a pocket handkerchief, which was instantly handed to her'. After she used several and threw each in the fire and was told to put it in her pocket, she declared 'that in her country they were much cleaner than to pocket what comes from their nostrils'.[28] In 1794 the *Anthologia Hibernica* published 'Granuweal – An Old Song' in which 'brave Granuweal' saucily refuses an English courtier who is attracted to her 'charms' and comes to court her in 'his Majesty's yacht', with the words:

> Says Granu, I always still lov'd to be free;
> No foe shall invade me in my liberty.
> While I've Limerick, Derry and the fort of Kinsale,
> I'll love and not marry, says Granuweal.[29]

With such legends and songs providing the context, United Irish allusions to Granu Wail could refer to the heroic pirate queen of Connaught who defied England in her old age or to the tropes of young or old women, whether vigorous or pathetic, who had assumed her name.

James Porter's *Billy Bluff and the Squire* presented the trope of the poor old woman in a ballad singer whom Billy Bluff brings to the Squire and describes as 'the old strumpet who was singing impudent sedition'. Her basket contains 'Grawny Wail's Address to the Potato Digger' which asks her 'dear children' to help their 'oppressed but affectionate Mother' reclaim her potato garden that has been trodden over and over by her neighbor's cattle. The Squire points out that 'Grawny Wail means Ireland' and orders Billy to throw the old woman into 'the black hole' without food, drink, coal, candle, or blanket. While Porter's ballad singer is a pathetic figure, the address from 'Grawny Wail' in her basket is less so.[30]

The poor old woman presented in the popular songs of the day about the Shan Van Vocht could be heroic or pathetic. A song called 'Adversity's Cot' in the 1795 *Paddy's Resource* songbook, with a realistic twist on the poor old woman motif, portrays a gray-haired mother's frantic grief for a son killed in Flanders.[31] By contrast, in the 1796 song-

---

28 *Anthologia Hibernica*, vol. ii (July 1793), p. 1. 29 *Anthologia Hibernica*, vol. iv (October 1794), p. 300. 30 Porter, 'Billy Bluff', *Northern Star*, 2 December 1796. 31 *Paddy's Resource* (1795), pp 81-3.

book, songs entitled 'Granu's Advice to Her Children' and 'Granu's Call' portrayed her as vigorously exhorting her sons to replace 'the willow' (passive suffering) with the 'pike and gun'.[32] At the end of the decade, United Irish songs portrayed heroic mothers who urged their United Irish sons to accept execution rather than betray their comrades and pathetic mothers who wailed for their dead sons. A line from a fragment of a Wexford song that R.R. Madden claimed had been very popular among the people reminds us that United Irish tropes of women were not invariably pathetic and suffering: 'Erin's a sturdy old wench,/And so Master Bull you will find her'.[33]

The heroic figure of Erin depicted in William Drennan's famous poem 'Erin', the first song in the 1798 and 1803 *Paddy's Resource* songbooks and the first song published in the Dublin United Irish newspaper *The Press*, is maternal and human rather than a heavenly goddess. The poem's first line, 'When Erin first rose from the dark swelling flood,' evokes the ocean origins of the maiden harp rather than the sky goddess trope. Drennan portrays Erin in a heroic mode:

> With her back turn'd to Britain, her face to the West,
> ERIN stands proudly insular on her steep shore,
> And strikes her high Harp 'midst the Ocean's deep roar.

A mother figure, Erin declares, 'Let my sons like the leaves of their shamrock unite' and states:

> And the triumph of Erin her DAUGHTERS shall share,
> With their full swelling chests and their fair flowing hair,
> Their bosoms heave sighs for the worthy and brave;
> But no coward shall rest on that soft swelling wave.[34]

Other female images in the *Paddy's Resource* were even more human. Editors' prefaces in all four songbooks declared the editors had not 'toil'd in vain' if 'from the Virgin's heart one sigh/Be breathed to Heav'n for Liberty' and urged 'blooming' maids to 'inspire the Patriot Youth to arms' and 'bless him only' with her 'lovely charms'. A song entitled 'St Patrick's Delight' in the 1796 and 1803 songbooks declared 'The Ladies do so much adore' the words 'Erin Go Brah!' on 'Green

32 *Paddy's Resource: Being a Select Collection of Original Patriotic Songs, for the Use of the People of Ireland* (Belfast, 1796), pp 79–80, 46-7.   33 'Another Fragment of One of the Most Popular of the Rebel Songs of the Men of Wexford', in Madden, *Literary Remains*, p. 53.   34 'Erin', in *Paddy's Resource, or the Harp of Erin, Attuned to Freedom; Being a Collection of Patriotic Songs; Selected for Paddy's Amusement* (Dublin, 1803), pp 1-3.

Ribbons,' and concluded with this stanza which italicised references to female images of Ireland as indicated:

> You Ladies, true friends to *Hibernia*,
> The rights of old *Ierne* maintain;
> Futurity's history will mention
> Your actions of honour and fame;
> The Genius of *Ireland* defend you,
> May FREEDOM soon brighten the day,
> May her radience [*sic*] to LIBERTY guide you,
> And shield you from harm, I pray.[35]

Such images evidently influenced behavior and the perceptions of events. A contemporary described United Irishmen in 1798 wearing 'ornaments from females whose breasts beat as high in patriotic ardour as those of their husbands, their sweethearts, and their brothers'.[36] Volunteer and Masonic songs had also urged young women to reward only Volunteers and Masons.[37] Young women played a symbolic role in political celebrations in the late-eighteenth century Ireland. For example, in county Antrim on 20 June 1776, twenty thousand people celebrated the election of a candidate called 'the choice of the people' with a procession more than a mile and a half long that included music and colored banners embroidered with 'emblematical figures', 10,000 men in blue cockades, 1,000 horsemen, '400 free-masons, attired in their jewels,' and 500 young women called 'daughters of liberty' and 'patriot virgins' who were dressed in white with blue ribbons and carrying green boughs.[38]

The 1795 *Paddy's Resource* songbook was prefaced by an illustration, not of a goddess, but of a young woman standing serene and firm next to an oak tree, the traditional liberty tree, with a cottage and woods in the background. She is associated with the traditional emblems associated with the figure of the goddess Liberty in Volunteer verse and insignia: a pole or spear with a cap of liberty on the end, broken chains, and a maiden harp. An almost identical illustration appears on a Belfast broadside published about 1810 of the famous United Irish song 'The Exiled Irishman's Lamentation' which had appeared in the 1796, 1798, and 1803 *Paddy's Resource* songbooks and on numerous broadsides.[39] Despite its melancholy title, the Irish refrain in the first half of 'The

35 *Paddy's Resource* (1796), p. 23. 36 C. Dickson, *Revolt in the North: Antrim and Down in 1798* (Dublin, 1960), p. 228. 37 Masonic Song Number 10 in 'Appendix' of *Skylark*; 'The Female Volunteers', *The Irish Harper's Legacy* (Cork, 1814), pp 206-7. 38 Joy, *Historical Collections*, p. 135. 39 Broadside in the Linen Hall Library, Belfast.

Exiled Irishman's Lamentation', which translates 'Ireland, my darling! For ever adieu!', is replaced by a stirring refrain which translates 'Victory to you my darling! Ireland for ever' in the second half of the song which envisions a victorious Irish rebellion against tyranny with French help.[40] Thus the maiden in the illustration was evidently an inspiring icon rather than a pathetic victim. While the only human woman in the songs in the 1795 *Paddy's Resource* was the grey-haired mother frantically grieving for her son lost in Flanders, the 1796 song-book included the tropes of heroic and pathetic human maidens. In a song called 'Slumbering Ireland', the speaker described how 'Fair Susan, so charming, sat singing divinely' of Hibernia waking from her slumber and being blessed with 'Freedom'. By contrast, in the next song, 'Unity's School,' 'Poor Delia is now left to mourn/The loss of her darling sweet Boy' who has been hurled in a dark prison.[41]

By the end of the decade, a subtype of the suffering maiden appeared in the trope of a young female maniac, variously known as Ellen or Mary Le More, which became enormously popular. The earliest mention and record of the song that I have found occurred in 1799. A letter dated 1 January 1799 from an informer to the Home Office in London enclosed a printed ballad of 'Mary Le More' which recounted atrocities committed by British soldiers in Ireland and which was reportedly being circulated in Nottingham.[42] Exiled United Irishman John Daly Burk's 1799 account of the 1798 rebellion includes a description of how at Vinegar Hill, 'enthusiastic' United Irishmen 'disdaining the command to wait the attack, rushed upon their enemies singing the pathetic ballad of Ellen O'Moore'. The song opens with the words, 'Ah, soldiers of Britain, your merciless doings,/Long, long will the children of Erin deplore', and goes on to recount how soldiers stabbed Ellen's father Dermot, burned their home, and took Ellen to an 'outhouse' where 'by force they deflower'd sweet Ellen O'Moore' who now is 'a wild maniac' who roams 'the wild common' and 'sings of her father in strains more than human' and 'warns every woman against the soldiers of Britain'. The song concludes by exhorting the 'daughters of Erin, your country's salvation' to 'remember the wrongs of poor Ellen O'Moore' and 'with hearts hard as steel, or with spirits all fire,/Your husbands, your brothers, your lovers inspire'.[43]

40 *Paddy's Resource* (1803), pp 5-7. 41 *Paddy's Resource* (1796), pp 74-5. 42 C. Emsley, 'The Home Office and Its Sources of Information and Investigation 1791-1801', *English Historical Review*, vol. lxxxxiv (July 1979), p. 541. 43 J.D. Burk, *History of the Late War in Ireland* (Philadelphia, 1799), pp 107-8; a similar version, minus the rape motif, is printed as an untitled song beginning 'Oh, soldiers of Britain' in Madden, *Literary Remains*, pp 29-30.

The United Irishmen printed this similar song about 'Mary Le More' entitled 'The Maniac' as the second song in the 1803 *Paddy's Resource*, immediately following Drennan's heroic song 'Erin':

As I stray'd o'er the Common on Cork's rugged border,
While the dew drops of morn, the sweet primrose arrayed,
I saw a poor female whose mental disorder,
Her quick glancing eye and wild aspect betrayed.
On the ground she reclined, by the green fern surrounded,
At her side speckl'd daisies and shamrocks abounded
To its inmost recesses her heart had been wounded
Her sighs were unceasing – Twas Mary Le More.

Her charms by the keen blast of sorrow were faded
Yet the soft tinge of beauty still play'd on her cheek;
Her tresses, a wreath of fresh primroses braided,
And sprigs of fresh daisies hung loose on her neck;
While with pity I gaz'd, she exclaimed, Oh, my Mother!
See the blood on that lash – 'tis the blood of my Brother –
They have torn his poor flesh, and they now strip another,
'Tis Connor, the friend of poor Mary Le More.

Tho' his locks were as white as the foam on the ocean,
Those wretches shall find that my father is brave.
My Father, she cried, with the wildest emotion-
Ah, no, my poor Father now sleeps in his grave!
[They were friends of his son and of freedom who bore him,]
They have toll'd his death-bell – they've laid the turf o'er him;
He is gone, he is gone, and the good will deplore him,
When the blue wave of Erin, hides Mary Le More.

A lark from the gold-blossom'd furze that grew near her,
Now rose, and with energy caroll'd his lay;
Hush, hush, she continued, the trumpet sounds clearer,
The horsemen approach, Erin's daughters away;
Ah, soldiers, 'twas foul, while the cabin was burning,
An o'er her pale Father, a wretch had been mourning;
Go hide with the seamen [sea mew], ye maids, and take warning,
Those wretches have ruin'd poor Mary Le More.

Away, bring the ointment – oh God – see those gashes,
Alas, my poor Brother, come dry the big tear;

Anon, we'll have vengeance for those dreadful lashes,
Already the screech-owl and raven appear.
By day the green grave that lies under willow,
With wild flowers I'll strew, and at night make my pillow,
Till the ooze and dark sea-weed, beneath the cold billow,
Shall furnish a death-bed for Mary Le More.

Thus rav'd the poor Maniac, in tones more heartrending
Than Sanity's voice ever pour'd in my ear;
When lo! On the waste, and their march towards her bending,
A troop of fierce cavalry chanced to appear.
Oh, the fiends! She exclaimed, and with wild horror started,
Then through the tall fern, loudly screaming, she darted,
With an overcharged bosom, I slowly departed,
And sigh'd for the wrongs of poor Mary Le More.

  This song, entitled 'The Maniac' – 'Mary Le More' is fittingly the
first song in Madden's *Literary Remains of the United Irishmen of 1798*.
The wording of Madden's version, although he claims it is from the
Paddy's Resource songbook published in 1803, varies in several places;
the most notable differences are indicated above in brackets – the missing line in the third stanza and the words 'sea mew' instead of 'sea
men'.[44] Madden credits the song to the Liverpool bookseller, Edward
Rushton, while Charles Gavan Duffy, who included it in the enormously popular *The Ballad Poetry of Ireland* (1845), claims it was written by
George Nugent Reynolds, whom many claimed had written 'The Exiled
Irishman's Lamentation'. In Duffy's version the bracketed line in stanza three reads 'His white locks were bloody! No aid could restore him'.[45]
Such variant wordings indicate the song's popularity and the existence
of a vigorous oral tradition.
  Numerous printed versions of 'Mary Le More' survive in garlands
and songbooks in the National Library of Ireland and in the Dix Collection in the Royal Irish Academy. Versions very similar to the United
Irish song also appeared in the following collections of Irish songs: *The
Irish Harper's Legacy, Being a Choice Collection of Popular new Songs,
now singing with unbounded applause at the different places of Public Amusement* (Cork, 1814), which also included 'The Exiled Irishman's Lamentation' and other United Irish songs and tunes; and the *Little Warbler*
songbook (Belfast and Edinburgh, *c.*1820). The first edition of Michael

---

44 Madden, *Literary Remains*, pp 1-7. 45 C.G. Duffy, *The Ballad Poetry of Ireland*
(reprint of 40th Dublin edition of 1869; New York, 1973), pp 106-8.

J. Barry's *Songs of Ireland* (Dublin, 1845) contained a similar song called 'Ellen O'More,' while the second edition contained an anonymous 'Song of Moina the Maniac'. The maniac motif also appeared in other songs by and about United Irishmen, particularly Robert Emmet. In the song 'My Emmet's No More', an early-nineteenth century Irish broadside in the Royal Irish Academy, a distraught, evidently mad young women, a 'wild-eyed daughter of Erin' with 'despair in her wild eye,' wanders on sea cliffs in a storm as she laments the death of Robert Emmet with her 'wild harp'.[46] In United Irishman John Daly Burk's song, 'The Brown Thorn', a maniac with streaming hair amidst a storm flees a bloody battlefield with her baby after seeing the baby's father killed.[47]

In March 1808 Watty Cox's *The Irish Magazine and Monthly Asylum* published 'Mary, A Doggrel Poem' in which a county Meath maniac mourns only her father who is named 'Connor' (the name of Mary Le More's 'friend' in other versions) on the banks of the Boyne where she dies of grief: 'For sorrow she scarcely drew breath,/She hung down her beautiful face,/Then sunk in the arms of death'. The speaker buries her and vows vengeance:

> I press'd her cold frame to my breast,
> My heart it was ready to break,
> I cry'd when I put her to rest,
> *'Thy cause I shall never forsake'*.[48]

Cox's version is incomplete, ending abruptly with the first line of a new stanza, 'then Erin remember the day'.

The songs about Mary Le More also inspired post-1798 poems about the United Irishmen that incorporated the maniac trope. In 1810 James McHenry, whose fiction about the 1790s in Ulster provides an invaluable portrait of the times, published a poem entitled *Patrick: A Poetical Tale of 1798* in which Patrick's beloved Mary is raped by British soldiers after they kill her father and brother and she becomes 'a maniac sad thro' woods and wilds to stray' singing wild songs until Patrick rescues her.[49] In 1830 in the first volume of his *Ulster Monthly Magazine*, former United Irishman Charles Hamilton Teeling published a poem entitled 'The Rebel's Grave' which he claimed had been pub-

46 G. Zimmermann, *Songs of Irish Rebellion: Political Street Ballads and Rebel Songs, 1780-1900* (Dublin, 1967), p. 25. 47 McCreey, *Ancient Music of Ireland*, pp 47-8. 48 *The Irish Magazine and Monthly Asylum for Neglected Biography*, vol. i (March 1808), p. 140. 49 J. McHenry, *Patrick: A Poetical Tale* (Glasgow, 1810), p. 23.

lished ten years earlier in a Belfast newspaper. The poem describes how 'a maniac [named Mary] rushed – a wild flower wreath around her twined,/Her bosom bare – her garments torn' and flung herself on the grave of the United Irishman to whom she was betrothed and who had been hung and beheaded before his mother's house whereupon she immediately died of grief and Mary became 'a maniac wild'.[50]

Like so many other United Irish images of women, the trope of the maniac had multiple origins. While lurid reports of soldiers raping Irish women published in the *Press* and elsewhere beginning in the fall of 1797 no doubt formed the basis of the songs about maniacs, the trope was also grounded in traditional and literary models. Native Irish tradition contained ancient motifs about 'wild men', who wandered frantically in the wilderness speaking in the same incoherent, breathless style later used in the maniac songs, and 'wailing women' who, barefoot with their hair in disarray, wandered the countryside mourning the dead. Irish translations of medieval religious works conflated the wailing women of Irish tradition with the sorrowing Virgin Mary.[51] The famous poem describing Ellen O'Leary lamenting her husband Arthur O'Leary includes the trope of her going out of her mind with grief after his death.

Literature in English also provided models. Shakespeare's Ophelia's grief over her father's death deepens to madness as, singing old tunes and weaving garlands of wild flowers, she drowns. Thomas Percy's landmark study of traditional English songs, *Reliques of Ancient English Poetry* (1765), includes two eighteenth-century songs about the insane grief of young women, one called 'a mad song' about 'a frantic lady', the other in regard to the execution of a Manchester rebel in 1746.[52] Intense emotion and grief, almost to the point of madness, were also hallmarks of James Macpherson's enormously popular Ossianic poems, especially Malvina's laments for Oscar. The final issue of the *Northern Star* on 8 May 1797 contained an anonymous 'extract' from a 'poem in imitation of Ossian', a florid lament in the Ossianic style, that was written by Thomas Moore. Songs about young women maniacs were very popular in the British Isles and America in the late eighteenth century. 'The

---

50 C.H. Teeling (ed.), *The Ulster Monthly Magazine*, vol. i (Belfast, 1830). 51 A. Partridge, 'Wild Men and Wailing Women', *Eigse: A Journal of Irish Studies*, vol. xviii (1980), pp 25-37. 52 T. Percy, Reliques of Ancient English Poetry, vol. ii (New York, 1876), pp 42, 48-50. Percy brought his extensive knowledge of traditional songs to Ireland where he was bishop of Dromore in county Down from 1782 to 1811 and the friend and neighbor of United Irishman Thomas Stott, who wrote several United Irish songs in the early 1790s, and the countess of Moira who was noted for her antiquarian and literary interests and the friend of many prominent United Irishmen.

Maid of Bedlam' is locked up, singing 'sweet songs' and weaving garlands of flowers, after cruel parents sent her lover to sea.[53] Other songs
described maniacs named 'Ellen', who wanders at night over the wilds
and weeps at her lover's grave until she dies of grief, and 'Wandering
Mary' and her baby, who have been deserted by Henry or Harry, a
common name in the maniac songs.[54] The most popular such maniac
song was 'Crazy Jane', for which numerous texts and references survive.
In a narrative frame similar to that of 'Mary Le More', an observer
meets a mad young woman whose lover Henry abandoned her and who
is now 'a wandering wretched creature' whose 'frenzied looks' and mad
songs terrify observers.[55]

The United Irishman's use of the trope of the maniac epitomised the
disintegration of their earlier heroic and pathetic images of maids and
mothers because the maniac was neither maid nor mother. While the
maniac embodied the horror and despair felt by the people after 1798
and the songs of Mary Le More remained popular up through the mid
nineteenth century, other more idealistic, mundane, middle class and
respectable images of Irish women became the icons of later generations
of nationalists. Liberty, Hibernia, Mary Le More, and the 'genius of
Ireland' were eventually replaced by the sweet colleen so often seen
kneeling to O'Connell, Parnell and other nationalist leaders in nineteenth-century flags, banners, and illustrations. Similarly, the maiden
harp was replaced by an unadorned harp in the British royal arms in
1837, although it remained on the Lord Lieutenant's flag and some
nationalist flags. In 1914 Patrick Pearse ordered the maiden harp
replaced on nationalist flags and insignia and today the unadorned harp
is the official insignia of Ireland. The authority and power of the
unadorned harp and of the maiden or mother symbol of Ireland's suffering originated in the rich United Irish tradition of more heroic and
complex tropes of goddesses, mothers, maidens and maniacs who,
whether heroic or pathetic, were neither sectarian nor xenophobic. The
United Irish iconography of women embodied and synthesised images
from many traditions and thus was a paradigm of the pluralistic Irish
society envisioned by the United Irishmen.

53 *American Songster: Being A Select Collection of the Most Celebrated American, English,
Scottish, and Irish Songs* (New York, 1788), pp 20-1. 54 Untitled song in *American
Songster; or Federal Museum* (1799), p. 229; 'Wandering Mary' in *Irish Harper's Legacy*
(1814), p. 181. 55 *Crazy Jane. A Favorite Song* (Boston, 1800). W.B. Yeats used the
name Crazy Jane in his poems about an elderly county Galway woman known locally as
'Cracked Mary'.

Matilda Tone and virtuous republican femininity

Nancy J. Curtin

Perhaps second only to the fallen patriot in republican esteem was the widow left behind him. Honoured not only for her sacrifice of happy domesticity to the public cause, for giving up her husband to the nation, the widow remained as the living reminder that the unquiet graves of the patriot dead placed an obligation on successive generations. One of the most honoured widows of the United Irishmen was Matilda Tone, wife of one of the founders of early Irish republicanism, Theobald Wolfe Tone, architect of the United Irish alliance with France, who was sentenced to death for his service in the cause of the nation. Matilda exemplified all the virtues of republican womanhood, a woman who sacrificed a 'normal' domesticity and her husband to the patriotic cause. But it was to honour her fallen husband that the United Irishmen singled out Matilda Tone for distinction, and she herself would have had it no other way. On a visit to America in 1807 Matilda received a delegation from the Hibernian Provident Society of New York, which included such exiled associates of her husband as William James MacNeven and Thomas Addis Emmet. They came, they said, to express their 'very profound respect for the character and memory of your late illustrious husband, General Theobald Wolfe Tone, and their affectionate attachment to his widow and son'. To which Matilda replied, 'the sweetest consolation my heart can feel, I receive in the proof you now give me, that my husband still lives in your affections and esteem'.[1]

The reply suggests a woman content to live in the shadow of an illustrious husband. Indeed, if one is in quest of women who served as active agents in the quest for an Irish republic in the 1790s, the self-effacing Matilda Tone hardly promises to be one of the most illuminating figures. And yet if one is to understand fully the moral and political transformation the United Irishmen sought to effect in their benighted

---

1 William Sampson, *Memoirs of William Sampson an Irish exile*, written by himself (London, 1832), appendix, pp 392-3.

land, a closer look at the republican partnership that was the marriage between Matilda and Theobald Wolfe Tone is essential.

I

The radical departure of the United Irishmen, like that of the revolutionaries in America and France, was to sever citizenship from the rights and privileges of property and to expand the definition of the political nation to include everyone (although degrees of civic competence might still be mediated according to wealth and gender). Thus the universality of citizenship implicit in the United Irish project was the prerequisite for the assertion of Ireland and its people as a sovereign nation. Here then was a nationalism based not on history, language, religion, or ethnicity, but one firmly grounded in the principles of an emerging eighteenth-century liberalism, and in stark contrast to the romantic nationalism of the nineteenth and twentieth centuries. 'The basic characteristic of the modern nation and everything connected with it is its modernity', Eric Hobsbawm has written, dismissing the opposite assumption that national identification is somehow so natural, primary, and permanent as to precede history.[2] The notion that national identity is constructed in conjunction with or in reaction to emerging modernity forms the point of departure for such diverse treatments of the subject by scholars such as Ernest Gellner, Benedict Anderson, and Liah Greenfeld.[3] This consensus in the theoretical approaches to nationalism, however, is ignored by some Irish historians who, like anti-revisionist Brendan Bradshaw, seem to accept as immutable and unproblematic the notion of both a continuous national identity and a central nationalist dynamic in Irish history.[4] Approaches to Irish nationalism, then, tend to be more descriptively teleological than analytic, assuming a continuous development to which each generation builds upon the contribution of a previous one. Thus, the bedrock of modern Irish nationalism remains Theobald Wolfe Tone's assertion that 'Ireland would never be free, prosperous, or happy ... *whilst* the connection with England existed'.[5] If

2 E.J. Hobsbawm, *Nations and Nationalism Since 1780: Programme. Myth and Reality* (Cambridge, 1992), 14.   3 Ernest Geliner, *Nations and Nationalism* (Oxford, 1983); Benedict Anderson, *Imagined Communities: Reflections on the Origin and Spread of Nationalism* (London, 1983); Liah Greenfeld, *Nationalism: Five Roads to Modernity* (Cambridge, Mass., 1992).   4 See Nancy J. Curtin, ' "The Varieties of Irishness": Historical Revisionism, Irish Style', *Journal of British Studies* 35, no. 2 (April 1996).   5 William Theobald Wolfe Tone (ed.), *Life of Theobald Wolfe Tone* (2 vols, Washington, 1926) i, p. 32.

the United Irishmen made the political case for nationalism, successive generations added the cultural, romantic, and visionary elements.

But if we examine Irish nationalism and national identity as shaped within a particular vortex of circumstances and opportunities, with a field of vision lateral rather than forward, the exceptionalism, or parochialism as some might put it, of Irish nationalist history begins to break down, and the ubiquitous phenomenon of nationalism itself is illuminated. Confining our vision to the late eighteenth century, then, the primary definition of the nation was political and liberal, as Hobsbawm has argued, 'equating the "people" and the state in the manner of the American and French revolutions'.[6] The collective sovereignty of the people required political expression in a state in which mass participation and citizenship were integral to its legitimacy. Or as Liah Greenfeld has put it, 'the national principle that emerged was individualistic; sovereignty of the people was the implication of the actual sovereignty of individuals; it was because these individuals (of the people) actually exercised sovereignty that they were members of the nation'.[7] Membership in the nation was thus defined in civic rather than ethnic terms.

The universality implicit in liberalism and the Enlightenment project which informed this nationalism was perfectly capable of accommodating gender equality. John Locke approached such a position when he attacked the patriarchicalism of Filmer, but retreated quickly into a reassertion of household paternalism.[8] Indeed the liberal moment, to which the United Irishmen quite rightly belong along with republicans in France and America, offered the possibility of female inclusion in all the rights and responsibilities of citizenship. Mary Ann McCracken took the radicals' notion of the rights of man and the citizen to its logical inclusion – the extension of those rights to women. As she wrote to her incarcerated brother, Henry Joy McCracken, in March 1797, 'if we suppose woman was created for a companion for man, she must of course be his equal in understanding, as without equality of mind, there can be no friendship, and without friendship, there can be no happiness in society'. Certainly women, as rational creatures, were entitled to realise their full abilities and contribute to the public good under the enlightened government proposed by the United Irishmen. She asked her brother,

6 Hobsbawm, *Nations and Nationalism*, p. 18. 7 Greenfeld, *Nationalism*, p. 11. 8 See Melissa A. Butler, 'Early Liberal Roots of Feminism: John Locke and the Attack on Patriarchy' in Mary Lyndon Shanley and Carole Pateman (eds), *Feminist interpretations and Political Theory* (Pennsylvania, 1991), pp 74-95.

Is it not almost time for the clouds of error and prejudice to disperse and that the female part of the Creation as well as the male
should throw off the fetters with which they have been so long
mentally bound? ... There can be no argument produced in
favour of the slavery of women that has not been used in favour
of general slavery ... I therefore hope that it is reserved for the
Irish nation to strike out something new and to shew an example
of candour, generosity, and justice superior to any that have gone
before them.[9]

But like so many republicans in France and America, the United
Irishmen chose to ignore the sexually egalitarian implications for their
favoured political stance.[10] While employing a rhetoric of universal citizenship and fundamental human rights derived from liberal principles,
the United Irishmen refused to entertain the notion that women should
be active members of the civic polity. Eclectic amateur political theo-
rists, they grafted their liberalism onto the thriving plant of an ubiquitous classical republicanism which infused the rhetoric of all political
formations in eighteenth-century Britain and Ireland. As I have argued
elsewhere, the United Irishmen may have been liberals, but the vocabulary to articulate that liberalism was as yet half-formed, requiring
them to infuse new meanings into the readily accessible language of
civic humanism.[11] Classical republicanism was also a highly gendered
political language as well, allowing the United Irishmen to shed their
universal egalitarianism at the door of more reassuring patriarchal
assumptions regarding the sexual division of labour both in public and
in private.

Indeed, the ideology of the United Irishmen was the product of two
discourses, one dominant in the eighteenth century, republicanism, and
the other, liberalism, only emerging. Classical republicanism, or civic
humanism, provided a vocabulary to analyse corrupt and tyrannical government.[12] Privileging private interests over the public good created the

9 Mary Ann McCracken to Henry Joy McCracken, 16 Mar. 1797 (P.R.O.N.I., McCrack-
en papers, T.1210/7). 10 See, e.g., Linda K. Kerber, *Women of the Republic: Intellect
and Ideology in Revolutionary America* (Chapel Hill, 1980); Joan B. Landes, *Women and
the Public Sphere in the Age of the French Revolution* (Cornell, 1988). 11 Nancy J. Curtin,
The United Irishmen: Popular Politics in Ulster and Dublin. 1791-1798 (Oxford, 1994). 12
The fullest treatment of this tradition is still J.G.A. Pocock, *The Machiavellian Moment:
Florentine Political Thought and the Atlantic Republican Tradition* (Princeton, 1975); for its
proliferation in the British Isles, see Caroline Robbins, *The Eighteenth-century
Commonwealthman: Studies in the Transmission. Development. and Circumstances of English
Liberal Thought from the Restoration of Charles II until the War with the Thirteen Colonies*
(New York, 1968).

conditions in which the state ceased to be the *res publica*. A highly
moralised discourse, classical republicanism envisioned a polity on the
lines of an organism, whose health depended on the promotion and
maintenance of virtue, defined as the subordination of private interests
to the public good. Inclusion in the polity depended on one's capacity
to act virtuously, a condition which permitted republicans of all stripes
to define the attributes of citizenship. Democratic republicans like the
United Irishmen could thus claim that the capacity to act virtuously and
in the interests of the common good was universal, an inherent attribute
of fundamental humanity. Other republicans, however, could insist that
confessional conformity or sufficient property requirements would distinguish those who had a true interest in the preservation of the good
state from those liable to corruption or treachery. They accepted the
Aristotelian formulation that the best government contained an equal
mixture of monarchical, aristocratic, and democratic elements. Here was
the pride of the British state, so lauded by Montesquieu and providing
a model of good, and at least morally republican government for so
many continental reformers and philosophes. And within that state,
republican discourse was at once ubiquitous and variable, elements of
which were to be found in the rhetoric of court Whigs as well as that of
their Tory and country opponents.[13]

Thus the United Irishmen were petite-bourgeois revolutionaries,
possessed of a ideology that reflected an evolving transition from republican to liberal discourse.[14] Central to this liberal discourse was the
notion that sovereignty rests with the people, and that sovereignty is
best expressed through active citizenship in the nation-state, a collectiv-
ity of individuals. The indivisible, organic representation of the nation
implicit in the civic humanist tradition, helped to veil temporarily the
increasing socio-economic differentiation of the people propelled by
liberal modernisation. The contradictions and ambiguities of liberal
republican nationalism in Ireland, resting on an uneasy blend of a
potentially classless and organic civic humanism and a class-based political and economic liberalism, became increasingly difficult to reconcile

13 See, e.g., Reed Browning, *Political and Constitutional Ideas of the Court Whigs* (Baton
Rouge, 1982); Linda Colley, 'Eighteenth-century English Radicalism before Wilkes',
Transactions of the Royal Historical Society, 5th ser., 31 (1981), pp 1-19; H.T. Dickinson,
Liberty and Property: Political Ideology in Eighteenth-century Britain (London, 1977);
J.A.W. Gunn, *Beyond Liberty and Property: The Process of Self-recognition in Eighteenth-
century Political Thought* (Kingston and Montreal, 1983). 14 For discussion of a similar
transition in radical political thought in America and England, see Joyce Appleby,
Capitalism and a New Order: The Republican Vision of the 1790s (New York, 1984); Isaac
Kramnick, 'Republican Revisionism Revisited', *American Historical Review*, 87 (June
1982), pp 629-64.

as the liberal discourse, and the relations of production which supported it, emerged dominant in the nineteenth century.

The formulation of United Irish republicanism was thus based on a
series of choices from the buffet of existing and emerging political ide-
ologies. Civic republicanism offered the radicals the moral high
ground, as disinterested virtue and active intervention to counter the
cancerous growth of political corruption became the tests of civic inclusion. With its emphasis on the citizen-soldier and manly virtue, classical republicanism easily supported the homosocial paramilitary
organisation developed by the United Irishmen with so much acuity in
the 1790s, a notion deeply rooted in the Volunteer tradition. As the
expression of civic virtue as well as a model for their own organisation,
the Volunteers exerted a powerful pull on the republican imagination
of the 1790s. Then the French revolution contributed to the militarisation of Europe, which was mirrored by the militarisation within
Ireland, explaining as much as any single explanation could the paramilitary character of politicisation in the country. The virtual exclusion
of a popular voice in the established political arena of parliament,
mediated only through a tepid and elitist Whiggism, required a wider
arena for popular political engagement. Thus it was that the United
Irishmen emerged as an armed body of citizens, claiming for themselves the virtue of the nation. Even if the spell of the Volunteers had
been weaker on the United Irishmen, there were few alternative or
practical models for their mobilisation. This militarised politicisation
also meant that the soldier's ultimate test, patriotic self-immolation on
the altar of the nation, would emerge as one of the defining characteristics of Irish republican masculinity. It also meant that women,
excluded from such paramilitary homosociability, would be denied this
ultimate test of civic virtue.

This did not mean that women had no contribution to make to the
republican campaign. Indeed, they served as activists within the United
Irish organisation and as symbols of an oppressed nation.[15] But women's
and men's participation was limited by a gender-based division of
labour exemplified by Matilda and Theobald Wolfe Tone, and which
was implicit in the republican tradition. The United Irishmen appealed
to men and women to conduct themselves with classical republican probity. For both sexes this required subordinating private to public interest. In the male case, this meant active participation in liberating an

15 See Nancy J. Curtin, 'Women and Eighteenth-century Irish Republicanism', in
Margaret MacCurtain and Mary O'Dowd (eds), *Women in Early Modern Ireland* (Edinburgh, 1991), pp 133-44.

abused and feminised nation from dishonour. For women exercising citizenship involved republican motherhood – sacrificing husbands, brothers, and sons to the national struggle.

Men like Theobald Wolfe Tone, of course, filled the ranks, assumed the leadership, articulated the aims of the movement, and risked arrest, exile, and death for the cause. Women were most visible in the United Irish movement, invited in a sense into the public space of politics, as symbols prodding men to perform their national and republican duty. The feminised, maternal nation, Hibernia, Granu, Erin, the Shan van Vocht, by turns a graceful, dignified matron and an old woman summoning her sons to protect and defend her homestead, called upon 'the gen'rous sons of Erin, in manly virtue bold' to avenge her wrongs.[16] Widely circulated ballads and songs had the mother-nation directly enjoining her sons to action. Indeed, the liberation of Erin was the test of her sons' manhood. As the most famous poet of the United Irishmen, Dr William Drennan put it, 'and where Britain made brutes, now let Erin make men'.[17] Armed filial devotion to the mother-nation presented a rite of passage to full adulthood as well as a distinguishing characteristic of Irish masculinity. Indeed, United Irish claims to full civic competence contingent on gender drew on a range of masculine ideals, providing some over determination of the chivalric manly impulse, as well as appealing to all elements within the cross-class alliance that characterised the movement'.[18] Classical republicanism adapted the aristocratic ideal of manhood as rooted in military service by identifying citizenship with the bearing of arms, allowing paramilitary bodies like the Volunteers and the United Irishmen to claim for themselves masculine virtue.[19] Middle-class men asserted patriarchal claims to represent familial and economic dependants in the public sphere.[20] And Tom Paine and other plebeian democrats appealed to artisanal and working-class pride in productivity and skill in widening the scope of civic competence.[21] Thus militarised and disinterested patriotism, emerging separate spheres ideology, and the possession of productive skills contributed in part to a redefinition of masculinity undertaken by the politically excluded classes of the eighteenth and early nineteenth centuries. Add to this the destabilising context of the era of the French revolution,

16 R.R. Madden, *Literary remains of the United Irishmen of 1798 and selections from other popular lyrics of their times, with an essay on the authorship of 'The exile of Erin'* (Dublin, 1887), p. 86. 17 R.R. Madden, *Literary remains*, p. 41. 18 For United Irish social composition, see Curtin, *United Irishmen*, chapter 5. 19 Pocock, *Machiavellian Moment*, pp 183-218, 401-22. 20 Lenore Davidoff, *Worlds Between: Historical Perspectives on Class and Gender* (London and New York, 1995), chapter 8. 21 Anna Clark, *The Struggle for the Breeches: Gender and the Making of the British Working Class* (Berkeley, 1995), chapter 8.

the beginning of that Victorian prelude when elite British males cut their hair, donned trousers, found religion, and generally acquired more respectable bourgeois values to reinvent themselves in opposition to effeminate Frenchmen. And British women retreated into the private sphere to distinguish themselves from both polymorphously perverse Gallic court ladies and Parisian viragos.[22] If the United Irishmen adapted and transformed the dominant civic humanist discourse of Georgian England into a liberal, democratic ideology, so too they adapted prevailing and emerging notions of masculinity by appropriating male virtue to themselves, grounding their claims to political inclusion on reason, justice, and nature.

II

Republicanism, then, was a manly calling. Hibernia's bold defenders were called upon to protect her honour, to assert themselves in a just and righteous cause, to render filial devotion and husbandly care to their country. But women like Matilda Tone could also exert themselves as heroines exemplifying republican virtue, reflecting as well a redefinition of femininity that complemented new ideals of masculinity. The role of woman as patriot had a long heritage in the Roman tradition which inspired much of late eighteenth-century republicanism not just in Ireland but in America and France as well. Since the fundamental core of republicanism was the subordination of private interest to the public good, Roman women were expected to display their civic virtue by freely giving up their men to the affairs of state and the defence of the country, to ease the choice which men must often make between happy domesticity and public duty. This proscribed role for women in the state was echoed by Montesquieu as well as Rousseau, who were both concerned that women could seduce men from their civic obligations.[23] The United Irishmen wished to confer active citizenship on all adult males, but the women of the republic also had their own duties to perform as passive citizens – to favour republican heroes and to raise republican sons, to be the patriot mother or wife who would permit and encourage her menfolk to meet their civic obligations:

> You ladies, true friends to Hibernia,
> The rights of old Erin maintain;

22 Linda Colley, *Britons: Forging the Nation. 1707-1837* (New Haven, 1992), chapter 4, 6; G.J. Barker-Benfield, *The Culture of Sensibility: Sex and Society in Eighteenth-century Britain* (Chicago, 1992), chapter 7.   23 See, e.g., Susan Moller Okin, *Women in Western Political Thought* (Princeton, 1979), pp 106-66.

Futurity, history will mention,
Your actions of honour and fame,
The Genius of Ireland defend you.[24]

Mother Erin and her real-life daughters thus were to inspire men to self-sacrifice in the cause of the aggrieved nation. The feminised nation thus called upon its daughters to serve as models of domestic republican probity, consigning them to the private sphere where they would inculcate their menfolk with civic virtue and prepare them for the mother nation's service. The theme is one of heroic subordination. For men, though, the theme was active intervention in the public sphere and the sacrifice of domestic pleasures. Men gave their lives, but 'Ah,' said Drennan, 'what can woman give but tears'.[25]

This is certainly one way to describe the gendered division of sacrifice that characterised the partnership of Matilda and Theobald Wolfe Tone. Yet at the same time that Matilda Tone fulfilled her role in the private sphere to the height of republican expectations, circumstances and character impelled her to expand its boundaries a bit, perhaps contributing in her own, albeit unintentional, way to the opening of public space for women. If the possession of virtue entitled men like Tone to throw himself into radical political activity, it also legitimised Matilda's incursions in public to protect her children and safeguard the reputation of their patriot father.

We call her Matilda but her real name was Martha. With the sensibilities of latter age we might well be shocked to discover that Tone, in fact, rechristened his youthful bride, naming her after a heroine in sentimental literature, an astonishing exercise of male privilege. In 1785 the twenty-one year-old Trinity undergraduate, Theobald Wolfe Tone, spied through a window on Grafton Street the young woman he was to claim as his wife. 'She was,' he recalled, 'not sixteen years of age and as beautiful as an angel.' Tone discovered she was the daughter of William Witherington, a woollen draper, the granddaughter of a Church of Ireland minister, and she had a brother named Edward whom Tone contrived to meet. Invited into the family circle for cosy musical evenings, the attraction grew stronger and was well reciprocated. Knowing that his youth and circumstances hardly recommended him to the family as a welcome suitor to young Martha, Tone proposed elopement, and Martha 'accepted the proposal as frankly as I made it'.[26] The newlyweds hid out in Maynooth while their parents' anger abated.

24 Madden, *Literary Remains*, p. 89.   25 Madden, *Literary Remains*, p. 46.   26 Tone, *Life*, I, 21.

Tone was an elopement waiting to happen, and this imprudent marriage (for as Jane Austen might say, it wanted fortune on either side)
reveals much about his impetuous romanticism. He was on the rebound
from a chaste but passionate attachment to Eliza Martin, a married
women with whom he participated in amateur theatricals. Indeed, in
one such play, John Home's historical tragedy, *Douglas*, Eliza Martin
played the ideal of feminine gentility after whom Tone rechristened his
bride. In the play the heroine, Matilda, is the beautiful and virtuous
widow of a valiant fallen hero. She remarries, but her current husband
knows her heart is in the grave and she can offer him nothing more
than companionship and respect.[27] In that respect the play eerily previ-
sions Matilda Tone's own second marriage to the elusive, at least to the
historian, Thomas Wilson.

But if the elopement reveals Tone as the impetuous romantic, rather
insensitively renaming his bride after his last passionate attachment,
what does it tell us about the young Martha Witherington whom we
know as Matilda Tone? We can only speculate. Marriage at the tender
age of sixteen, while not uncommon, was nevertheless regarded by contemporaries as a tad too young. Matilda's lack of hesitation in agreeing
to the elopement suggests her own romantic impetuosity. These were
two children, in many respects, and Tone certainly acted somewhat
irresponsibly, not only in deceiving Matilda's family, but also in plight-
ing his troth with so little of the wherewithal to support it, especially
when the union was blessed with a daughter, Maria, nearly a year later.

One wonders if Matilda ever came to regret her impetuosity. Her
love for Tone never abated, and yet the life he provided for her was a
hard one. With Maria less than a year old Tone left his little family to
the care of his parents and went to the Inns of Court to pursue his chosen career as a barrister, but not before a frightful incident revealed his
bride to be a woman of great courage and character. In October 1786
the Tones were residing at Tone's father's home in Bodenstown, county Kildare. Six armed robbers seized Tone in the courtyard, bound and
gagged him, and then proceeded to break into the house. There they
secured the rest of the family and proceeded to wreak havoc in the
house in pursuit of loot. After they left the family inside the house
managed to untie themselves and vacated it in fear. During their panicked exodus, however, they realised Theobald was not among them,
and despite the others attempts to stop her, Matilda returned alone, not
knowing what horrors might have awaited her, to rescue her bound hus-

---

27 Marianne Elliott, *Wolfe Tone: Prophet of Irish Independence* (New Haven and London,
1989), pp 26-7, 38.

husband. 'I can imagine no greater effort of courage', Tone later recalled, 'but of what is not a woman capable for him she truly loves?'[28]

Matilda proved herself over and over again to be capable of a great deal. Her family never seemed to have reconciled itself to this marriage with an impecunious undergraduate, and the tepid rapprochement achieved shortly after the elopement gave way to decided hostility by 1789. Again, one can only speculate how this separation affected the young wife and mother. That it was still a painful episode to ponder in the 1820s is suggested by Matilda having excised all references to it from her husband's journals.[29] For emotional and material support she was thrown entirely on the Tones, and her husband was often absent from the family hearth. And to add to her difficulties, in 1789 Peter Tone went bankrupt.

She was married to a dreamer, and she came to share his dreams. Given her youth and inexperience at her marriage, her consequent estrangement from her own family, and her total dependence on Tone and his friends and family, Matilda could have done little else. Not quite sixteen when she met Tone, estranged from her own family, Matilda must have thrilled at Tone's own confessions about his ambitions for greatness. It would not be surprising that Matilda herself became strongly invested in her husband's ambitions and self-image. Certainly, their fortunes were precarious, and the realisation of her husband's ambitions would bring relief and comfort to his growing family. Sharing the dream, she more than shared the sacrifices that supported it. And what was that dream? That Theobald Wolfe Tone would make a mark for himself in the world.

III

Wolfe Tone's career took many early twists and turns. A clever and personable young man, he was generally liked wherever he went. His early inclinations for a military career were thwarted by his father. Then there was the possibility of becoming a Fellow at Trinity College, but his marriage closed that avenue of advancement. A married man with responsibilities, Tone more or less settled on the law. In the meantime he co-wrote a parody of a sentimental novel and unsuccessfully pursued a project of establishing a military colony in the Sandwich Islands, a base for bucanneering against the Spaniards. The project took little account of his wife's comfort or ease, and presumably she would be

28 Tone, *Life*, I, 22-4. 29 Elliott, *Tone*, pp 73-4.

waiting at home while Tone pursued the military glory he always craved.

Called to the Irish bar in 1789, Tone was restless in the career upon which he had grudgingly settled. The law frankly bored him, but 1789 was a year that was anything but boring. The French revolution burst on the scene, becoming as Tone later recalled, 'the test of every man's political creed'.[30] The siren call of politics fell on Tone's receptive ears, muting the murmurs of domestic responsibilities once again. Tone reshaped his dream, transferring his own quest for distinction to that of his nation – to bring Catholic and Protestant, native and settler together under the common name of Irishman, to use the moral weight of this united and inclusive nation to establish the independence of Ireland from Britain. Tone's thinking on the national question evolved, and as his son notes in the introductory preface to his father's *Life* in 1826:

> I believe that, in reading these memoirs, many people will be sur-
> prised at (and some perhaps will blame) the moderation of his
> views. The persecutions of government drove him much further
> than he proposed at first. But, from their fair and impartial
> perusal, none can possibly rise, without being convinced of his
> purity and patriotism, whatever they may deem his wisdom and
> foresight. No man who ever engaged so deeply and so earnestly
> in so great a cause, was so little influenced by any motives of per-
> sonal ambition, or so disinterestedly devoted to what he thought
> the interest of his country.[31]

We can assume that Matilda, as the uncredited collaborator in this edition of Tone's memoirs, fully endorsed and probably shaped her son's characterisation of his father's vision. She must have been equally as ardent in the pursuit of Tone's mission to bring just, liberal, and rational government to his country.

That Tone found his political life exciting and fulfilling should not detract from the great sacrifices he made, and Matilda shared them all the way. In easing Tone's mind about his family obligations she freed him, like a good republican matron, to bustle in the world. Any semblance to a normal domestic life was a rarity in her life with Tone. A brief interlude in 1790, before he ascended the stage of politics, stands out in Tone's own memory as the epitome of domestic bliss. 'I recall with transport the happy days we spent together during' a holiday in

---

30 Tone, *Life*, I, p. 43. 31 Tone, *Life*, I, preface, p. 5.

Irishtown, with visits from Tone's closest friend, Thomas Russell and members of the Tone clan:

> The delicious dinners, in the preparation of which my wife, Russell, and myself were all engaged, the afternoon walks, the discussions we have had, as we lay stretched on the grass ... My wife was the centre and soul of all. I scarcely know which of us loved her best; her courteous manners, her goodness of heart, her incomparable humour, her never failing cheerfulness, her affection for me and our children, rendered her the object of our common admiration and delight.[32]

Matilda may well have considered the sacrifice of such domestic pleasures as necessary to promote her husband's cause, now her cause, but she seems to have painfully felt the loss nonetheless. Recalling the birth of her son William in 1791, Matilda wrote:

> I see, feel, and hear all that was around me 36 years ago, my little room and everything in it, my bed, my babe in arms, and above all he that came every instant with a heart glowing with love and joy and tenderness to look if we were well, to caress and bless us, and my little Maria then 5 years old standing at the bedside ... how I was loved and cherished then![33]

But opportunities to feel her husband's glowing affection became few and far between as Tone became a leading figure in the Society of United Irishmen and the Catholic Committee. And Matilda, competent, understanding, and capable of a high level of self-sacrifice as she was, had her limits. In 1792 while Tone was engaged as secretary to the Catholic Committee, Matilda felt particularly neglected. Remember she was then the mother of two and a mere twenty-one herself. She preferred a quiet life in the country, with a small intimate circle of friends and family. But Tone's visits there were infrequent and brief, and Matilda deftly chided him for his neglect. She spent some time with him in Dublin, but disliked the social whirl in which he thrived.[34]

In 1794 Tone was implicated in the mission of a French agent, the Revd William Jackson, who arrived in Ireland to assess the potential revolutionary situation there. Thanks to friends in high places, Tone escaped the courts but agreed to exile himself voluntarily from Ireland.

---

32 Tone, *Life*, I, pp 35-6. 33 Matilda Tone to Eliza Fletcher, 29 April 1827 (quoted in Elliott, *Tone*, p. 164). 34 Elliott, *Tone*, pp 192-3.

Prior to his departure for America in June 1795, however, Tone had secretly engaged with republicans in Dublin and Belfast to undertake a mission to effect an alliance between the United Irishmen and republican France.

Discouraged at the cool reception he received from the French consul in Philadelphia, Tone resolved to spend the rest of his life as a gentleman farmer near Princeton, New Jersey. But although the family was united again, this was no happy time for Matilda and her husband. Tone developed 'a most unqualified dislike' for the Americans, 'a selfish, churlish race, totally absorbed in making money'. Both he and Matilda were especially worried about raising their children 'in the boorish ignorance of the peasants about us'.[35] Matilda later excised most of these extremely unfavourable references to America for the published edition of Tone's *Life* in the 1820s, when she herself was an American resident again. Yet in a rare letter (she found letter-writing an idle occupation to be engaged in only when strictly necessary) to Thomas Russell, she confessed her own great unhappiness, her ill-health, and the lack of comforts in her new home, as well as her gratitude for the financial support offered by her husband's friends in Belfast.[36] But Matilda's life with Tone had been schooled in hardship.

Exile had certainly heightened Tone's passionately romantic attachment to his homeland, and when the opportunity arose, he once again committed himself wholeheartedly to the Irish cause. Six months after his arrival in America, Tone assumed his promised mission to France. In this decision he had Matilda's full encouragement and support, even to the point where she withheld from him until after his departure the news that she was pregnant.[37] Perhaps no other incident better reveals Matilda's great commitment to the republican partnership that characterised the marriage. Quite deliberately she once again sacrificed any semblance of a regular domestic life, assuming once again the full burden of taking care of the family, and so permitting Tone to pursue his patriotic career.

Yet the sacrifice could also be seen as something of an investment, an indication that the pragmatic Matilda was nevertheless infected with her husband's boundless optimism. Life in America provided no promise of a happy future. Life in a liberated Ireland, honoured by a grateful nation, did. And if that particular dream failed, Tone, could look to France for a hospitable exile. In a letter to Matilda on the eve of his departure with the ill-fated Bantry Bay expedition in December

35 Quoted in Elliott, *Tone*, pp 266-7. 36 Matilda Tone to Thomas Russell, 11 Sept. 1796 (N.A.I., Rebellion Papers, 620/25/136). 37 Tone, *Life*, I, pp 135-6.

1796, Tone explored the possible consequences of his venture. If the mission should succeed, but he should die, he was confident that Ireland would provide for his widow and their children. If the mission should fail, and he should die, Matilda could count on the French government to support her in gratitude for Tone's efforts in their cause. And if the invasion should fail, and Tone should survive, 'I will then buy or hire a small farm, within a few miles of Paris, and devote the remainder of my life to making you happy and educating our children'.[38]

Tone survived briefly. The Bantry Bay expedition failed, as did several other attempts made by the French to launch an invasion and assist the United Irishmen. In the meantime, Tone became an Adjutant General in the French army, and sent for Matilda and their three surviving children in 1797. Then in October 1798, when the embers of the United Irish rebellion were dying out, Tone was captured in the last French invasion attempt at Lough Swilly. Dublin Castle, refusing to honour the uniform of a French soldier Tone wore, tried him at court martial for treason. To cheat an ignominious death by hanging, Tone took his own life, an eventuality he had discussed with Matilda and that seemed to have had her approval.[39] His last days were spent writing to everyone from the French government to Matilda's family attempting to secure her future. To Matilda he wrote:

> As no words can express what I feel for you and our children, I shall not attempt it; complaint, of any kind, would be beneath your courage and mine; be assured I will die as I have lived, and that you will have no cause to blush for me ... Above all things, remember that you are now the only parent of our dearest children and that the best proof you can give of your affection for me, will be to preserve yourself for their education.[40]

That Tone left the responsibility for his sons' education to Matilda, generally the task of a close male friend or relative, shows his great confidence in her judgement and abilities, as well he should, for Matilda had consistently shown herself the most capable of women. His brother William wrote to the widow, 'I have the consolation to feel that they [the children] can be no where under so proper an instructor'. William hoped to provide the money, but he trusted Matilda's 'own sense and observation will point out everything ... I am satisfied that nothing will

38 Theobald Wolfe Tone to Matilda Tone, 30 Nov. 1796 (*Life*, II, pp 329-36).   39 Elliott, *Tone*, p. 385.   40 Theobald Wolfe Tone to Matilda Tone, 10 Nov. 1798 (Tone, *Life*, II, pp 537-8).

be neglected on your part'.[41] Her career as a republican wife was over when Tone died, but the republican partnership continued as she devoted the rest of her long life to two goals. The first was to raise her son William (the other two children having died of consumption within a few years of Tone's own death) in his father's image, and, second, to guard and shape the memory of Tone himself. Indeed, the two were connected, for William was raised to be a living memorial to his father.

IV

Matilda lived a retired wife in France throughout the Napoleonic regime, invading the public space only when her obligations to Tone's memory demanded it. She secured the powerful good-will and support of Lucien Bonaparte in forcing the French to honour the pension owed her as a fallen general's widow. 'If the services of Tone were not sufficient to rouse your feelings', he implored the French legislature:

> I might mention the independent spirit and firmness of that noble woman, who, on the tomb of her husband … mingles with her sighs, aspirations for the deliverance of Ireland. I would attempt to give you an idea of that Irish spirit which is blended in her countenance, with the expression of grief. Such were those women of Sparta, who, on the return of their countrymen from battle, when, with anxious looks, they ran over the ranks and missed amongst them their sons, their husbands, and their brothers, exclaimed, He died for his country; he died for the Republic.[42]

In 1812, adhering to her son's own wishes and, as she said, 'certain that the army would have been his father's choice for him', Matilda enrolled William in the Cavalry School of St Germain, the best route to a distinguished military career.[43] She herself sought an interview with Napoleon to secure William's place and his subsequent naturalisation as a French citizen. Such careful tending was almost unearthed by United Irish exiles in Paris, who attempted to place William in the historic Irish Brigade. Matilda objected first on the grounds of William's health, which would have been tested too severely in an infantry brigade, and secondly, because such placement would thwart William's career. She dismissed the Irish brigade as a 'little corps of foreigners' and expressed

41 William Henry Tone to Matilda Tone, 2 January 1800 (*Life*, II, pp 560-62). 42 Tone, *Life*, II, pp 554-5. 43 Tone, *Life*, II, p. 570.

her own wish that her son should be a Frenchman. Matilda won.
Writing to William Sampson of her victory, she complained of this ill-
treatment by 'his father's friends', deeply wounded at the accompanying
charges that:

> I kept him [William] tied to my apron strings … Oh how ungen-
> erous they have been to me. Good God, how did the Irish ever
> get the character of a generous nation … Do the Irish think that
> because Tone volunteered in their service and shed his best
> blood in their cause and left his family destitute in a foreign
> country that his posterity are to be their slaves?[44]

Thus Matilda set the limits to her sacrificing. But in doing so, she
strongly felt she had Tone's approval. When William was subsequently
commissioned a lieutenant in Napoleon's army, Matilda looked on with
considerable satisfaction.

> Hitherto I had not allowed myself even to feel that my William
> was my own and my only child. I considered only that Tone's
> son was confided to me; but, in that moment, nature resumed
> her rights … But then I though my task was finished; my busi-
> ness in life was over … All I had ever suffered seemed before and
> around me at that moment, and I wished so intensely to close my
> eyes forever.

But then a lark hovered over her, singing a 'cheering, and, as it sound-
ed to me, approving note, that it roused me. I felt on my heart as if
Tone had sent it to me. I returned to my solitary home.'[45]

It was not to be solitary for long. With William making the best of
the opportunities she had provided him, living a retired life in Paris,
Matilda may have started to live once again for herself. She was only
twenty-eight when Tone died, forty-three when William left her home,
and three years later she married again. Little is known about the
Scotsman Thomas Wilson. He had accompanied Matilda on the journey
from America to France to rejoin Tone in 1797. That her husband knew
him and thought well of him can be attested by Tone's last letter to her
in which he adds the postscript, 'I think you have friend in Wilson, who
will not desert you'.[46] 'He was to my mother', William wrote about
Wilson, 'a brother, a protector, and an adviser during the whole period

---

44 Matilda Tone to William Sampson, 5 Nov. 1807 (quoted in Elliott, *Tone*, p. 406). 45
Tone, *Life*, II, p. 587. 46 Theobald Wolfe Tone to Matilda Tone, 10 Nov. 1798 (Tone,
Life, II, p. 538).

of our distress'.[47] When the fall of Napoleon put a stop to the career of the Bonapartist William Theobald Wolfe, Wilson immediately offered his services to relocate the family in a more hospitable environment. He and Matilda were married at the British Embassy in Paris in July 1816, where, as Matilda herself recalled, 'I accepted the protection of, and united my fate with that most pure and virtuous of human beings. Tone, in heaven, and his son, on earth, were approving witnesses'.[48]

Matilda wanted to return to Ireland, but Dublin Castle would not allow Tone's widow and son to become a focus for remnant Irish disaffection, and even successfully objected to their residence in England. So Wilson transported them back to America, settling in Georgetown. Her second sojourn in the United States seemed to have suited Matilda much more than the first. William studied law with United Irish exile William Sampson and married Sampson's daughter Catherine. Like his father, he soon abandoned the law books for a military career, securing a commission in the United States Army in 1819.[49] Wilson died in 1824. 'He is now, also, gone,' Matilda wrote, 'to tell Tone how faithfully he fulfilled the trust reposed in him.'[50]

V

It was then that Matilda and William joined in the project which installed Tone permanently in the pantheon of republican heroes – the publication of his memoirs, journals, and pamphlets in two volumes which appeared in 1826. The timing of the publication is interesting. Certainly Wilson's demise permitted Matilda to resume more tactfully her role as the republican widow of the fallen hero. She seems to have been provoked, however, by an article with appeared in the *New Monthly Magazine* in London, a purported account of the dazzling social life of Tone's widow in Paris.[51] Matilda felt that such false allusions to her frivolity demeaned not only herself but tarnished the reputation of Tone as well, and was jolted out of her usual silence.[52] A third reason for bringing out the *Life* of Tone in the 1820s may have been the re-emergence of Catholic emancipation, a cause to which Tone devoted his public career in Ireland, as Daniel O'Connell emerged as the colossus bestriding the stage of Irish popular politics. O'Connell chose to

47 Tone, *Life*, II, p. 538. 48 Tone, *Life*, II, p. 592. 49 For William Theobald Wolfe Tone's American career, see J.J. St Mark, 'Matilda and William Tone in New York and Washington After 1798', *Éire-Ireland*, vol. 22, no. 4 (Winter 1987), pp 4-10. 50 Tone, *Life*, II, p. 592. 51 *New Monthly Magazine*, xi (1824), pp 1-11, 336-47, 417-23, 537-48 and xiii (1825), pp 267-72.

distinguish his moral-force political campaign by denigrating the ultimate physical force nationalism of the United Irishmen. Tone's reputation was once again at stake, and so Matilda and William placed on the public record a true and accurate account of his career and the evolution of his political thinking, reminding the O'Connellites that Theobald Wolfe Tone was an early and eloquent champion in the cause of Catholic Ireland.

Here was probably Matilda's last and most significant contribution to the republican partnership she was engaged in with Tone. The *Life* proved to be a profound influence on Thomas Davis with its advocacy of an inclusive Irish nationalism. Patrick Pearse and subsequent twentieth-century republicans who gather annually at Tone's grave in Bodenstown, have taken for their bedrock his conviction 'that the influence of England was the radical vice of our government, and that Ireland would never be free, prosperous, or happy until she was independent, and that independence was unattainable whilst the connection with England existed'.[53] Included in the *Life* were Tone's extensive personal journals, musings and observations which were never meant for publication, but rather for the perusal of his close friend Russell and Matilda alone. Because it is personal and spontaneous, Tone's account of his own career and thought is open to many and contradictory interpretations. But what is consistently manifest is Tone's absolute charm, his disinterested pursuit of some degree of Irish independence, his boundless affection for family and close friends, and his obsession to act in all things honourably, as a gentleman. In editing the diaries with William, Matilda thus shaped and guarded Tone's posthumous reputation, presenting him at all times as a selfless patriot and willing martyr to his country, elevating him to the first rank of United Irish leaders. The convolutions and inconsistencies in Tone's public career are left to stand for posterity's perusal. What Matilda left out were unhappy references to Tone's breach with her own family, the Witheringtons, Tone's flirtations with other women, his highly critical observations of late eighteenth-century American society, and any incidents which could however remotely suggest that Tone was ever less than honourable in all his dealings.[54]

Matilda Tone lived a long and full life, but one constantly blighted by loss. She buried two husbands and survived all her children, William having died in 1837. A few months before she herself died in 1849, Young Irelander Charles Hart visited her in Georgetown:

---

52 Tone, *Life*, II, p. 567. 53 Tone, *Life*, II, p. 32. 54 For such excisions, see Elliott, *Tone*, pp 74, 267-8, 341.

She chatted very gaily [he recalled] spoke with great feeling and affection about Ireland ... I said she had a strong Irish feeling 'Ah, it was Tone gave it all to me ... here I am for 30 years in this country and I have never had an easy hour – longing after my native land'. She spoke approvingly of the men involved in the 1848 rising as 'very virtuous'.[55]

Virtue, as it was understood in the late eighteenth century, was the cement that sealed the republican partnership that was the marriage of Matilda and Theobald Wolfe Tone. Tone gave himself manfully to the cause of virtue in government. Matilda's virtue was exercised to the full in permitting him to do so. Their respective roles were determined by their gender. Later generations have, happily, contested those strictly defined roles which Tone and Matilda played out in such exemplary fashion. But in this the United Irishmen played a role, for their very radical republican commitment to full civic inclusion of all adult men in Ireland could not long withstand the logic that women must also be included in the polity as part of their basic humanity.

Matilda was honoured in the nineteenth century as the widow of a great Irish patriot whose reputation and place in the United Irish pantheon she helped to assure. As a patriot widow and mother she acquired authority to venture as far as she did in the public sphere, to protect and safeguard her husband's reputation and his son's future. She was no Abigail Adams who would remind Tone to remember to do something for the ladies when he fashioned his great democratic republic. Rather, Matilda fully accepted and approved of the division of republican labour imposed on her. She believed in it.

There were many other wives and sisters who also met their obligations as republican women by easing the transition of republican men into public life, women who collaborated in this reformulation of masculinity and femininity implicit in republican rhetoric and mobilisation. If republicanism did not offer a fully liberationist vision to these women, it did offer them, along with their men, honour and a certain moral ascendancy. Tone could never have done what he did without Matilda's republican virtue – her encouragement, and more important, her ability to manage their affairs so skilfully as to leave him free to bustle in the world. Her contribution to his career, masked by the tendency of historians to separate public from private, shows the interpenetration and symbiotic nature of these so-called separate spheres.[56] Male-domi-

55 C.J. Woods, 'Charles Hart's Account of a Meeting with Matilda Tone in March 1849', *Etudes Irlandaises* (forthcoming). I would like to thank Dr Woods for the typescript of this article. 56 See Davidoff, *Worlds Between*, chapter 8; also for this interpen-

nated popular movements depend on those wives and mothers and sisters. But like so many ellipses, the silences of these women dot the annals of history. Our understanding of the past, however, is only partial unless we take care to fill those omissions and amplify those whispers. Matilda may not have lifted a pike, nor did she ever publish a political tract or even a poem, and it was rare that she even put her thoughts on paper, but her republicanism was no less active than Tone's. Virtuous republican masculinity, the realisation of which drove the men of '98 like Tone, was both defined and complemented, by the construction of virtuous republican femininity, in which there was perhaps no more notable collaborator and exemplar than Matilda Tone.

etration of the public and private, see Dorothy O Helly and Susan M. Reverby (eds), *Gendered Domains: Rethinking Public and Private in Women's History* (Cornell, 1992).

Mary Anne McCracken: Belfast revolutionary and pioneer of feminism

John Gray

Mary Anne McCracken is usually remembered as the sister of Henry Joy McCracken, executed in 1798 for his role as the United Irish general at the Battle of Antrim, and as the unrequited lover of Thomas Russell, executed for his role as the northern general in Robert Emmet's rebellion of 1803. Thus she has been killed off as a person in her own right, and as a woman, in the cause of a pious male martyrology. Just as she sought to revive her brother, Henry Joy, when he was taken down from the scaffold, this paper will now attempt to revive her.

A revival has been tried before, but not in a way calculated to reveal fully her role. Perhaps the first author who sought to illuminate the role of women in the '98 rebellion was Helena Concannon, whose *Women of 'Ninety-Eight* was published in 1919.[1] Her pioneering role has more recently been picked out as 'exceptional and ... worthy of reconsideration in this regard' by today's generation of women historians.[2] In truth, however, Concannon was writing a very old form of women's history, reflected in her chapter headings – 'The Mothers of 98' is followed by 'The Wives of 98', while the chapter devoted to Mary Anne is titled simply 'The Sister of Henry Joy McCracken'.[3] The subject isn't even named, but at least she is given precedence over the next chapter which lumps together 'Some other Sisters of 98'. We are hardly talking here about 'sisters' in the parlance of today's women's movement – all Concannon's women appear only because of their relationships with men.

1 In addition to *Women of 'Ninety-Eight* (Dublin, 1919), Concannon also wrote *Daughters of Banba* (Dublin, 1922). 2 Margaret MacCurtain and Mary O'Dowd (eds), *Women in early Modern Ireland* (Edinburgh, 1991), p. 1. It is a cleverly double-edged tribute – one could more honestly say that all that was 'exceptional' about Concannon was that she addressed the role of women at all. 3 Anna McCleery, Henry Joy McCracken's grand-daughter, and first biographer of Mary Anne, at least gave her precedence in the title of her 'Life of Mary Anne McCracken, Sister of Henry Joy McCracken', in Robert M. Young (ed.), *Historical Notices of Old Belfast* (Belfast, 1896), pp 175-97.

This was romantic fiction for the new Irish nation. Concannon also wrote Catholic devotional literature, and her new Ireland of faith and fatherland, in so far as it required political heroines at all, required ones who acted out of devotion to male leaders. The following extract provides a flavour of her devotional text:

> [Mary Anne] had just completed her teens when Thomas Russell made his appearance in her native city ... and won forever her faithful heart. Alas! that he never suspected the treasure that was his ... Mary McCracken was for him a sister infinitely dear, a comrade infinitely staunch and true in the great cause. But she was nothing more; and with an unconscious cruelty which only the blindness caused by his absorption in his hopeless passion for another can excuse, he made her the *confidante* of his love for Miss Simms.[4]

But what if the story was quite another one, the reverse of Mrs Concannon's? What if Thomas Russell was 'nothing more' for Mary Anne McCracken than 'a comrade infinitely staunch'? Cast it in that light and Mary Anne McCracken begins to emerge in her own right.

This process, however, has been further delayed by the appearance of Mary McNeill's much more thorough biography, first published in 1960 complete with the imprimatur of a preface by R.B. McDowell, and since republished twice, most recently in 1997.[5] This was certainly a pioneering enterprise for the Ulster of the 1960, when liberal voices, willing to look again at the United Irishmen, were almost non-existent. In the context of that faint-hearted era, it was much easier to see Mary Anne McCracken as at heart a doer of good works, which indeed she was, rather than as a wholehearted revolutionary.

How was it that this sea-captain's daughter, member of a wider and prosperous Belfast Presbyterian merchant family came to play any role in a revolutionary cause. She shared the broader experience of her community – a tradition of Presbyterian dissent, and of republican governance within the Church, sharpened by surrounding oligarchic reality and the grievance of exclusion from the town's body politic and by family memory of an ancestor who had served as Sovereign of the town, before the ejectment of Presbyterians from such office.[6] The right of

---

4 Concannon, *Women of 'Ninety-Eight*, pp 224-5. 5 Mary McNeill, *The Life and Times of Mary Anne McCracken 1770-1866* (Dublin, 1960 and Belfast, 1988, 1997). 6 According to Mary Anne this was her great-grandfather, George Martin, serving at the time of the landing of William of Orange in 1690. In fact the only George Martin who served as Sovereign did so in 1649, however the sense of exclusion was more important than actu-

appointing the twelve burgesses who in turn chose the two Belfast M.P.'s in the unreformed Irish Parliament remained the gift of Lord Donegall in the 1780s and 1790s. Such political disabilities caused ever greater resentment against the background of growing economic success. Belfast's merchant Presbyterians traded with the world, and were particularly open to ideas and developments elsewhere which might assist them in their local predicament.

They generally sympathised with the American revolution, indeed many of those caught up in the great wave of emigration in the early 1770s had played an active part in its success. At home, Belfast provided the leading centre of the Volunteer movement, formed ostensibly to defend an Ireland denuded of regular troops from invasion, but almost simultaneously to assert the rights of the Irish parliament against English dominance, particularly in the field of trade. Henry Joy junior, Mary Anne McCracken's uncle, and editor of the Belfast *News Letter*, served as secretary of the Volunteers and was a radical within their ranks.[7]

Characteristically, the McCracken children were not educated at Lord Donegall's conventional school, but at an experimental school run by David Manson which was notable for being co-educational, the absence of physical punishment and the system by which pupils might advance to become 'prince' or 'princess' on a basis of merit alone.[8] These were meritocratic republicans.

And yet the great wave of enthusiasm of the early 1780s broke on the walls of what itself was an unreformed Irish parliament. Presbyterians alone could not reform it and yet many hesitated to enlist alongside that greater disenfranchised Irish majority, the Roman Catholics, in the cause of reform. It is indeed as well to remember that throughout this period most Presbyterians continued to subscribe to the Westminster Confession with its strictures against Popery. It was only with the French Revolution of 1789, a democratic revolution in a Roman Catholic country, that further impetus was given to the arguments of the more radical Presbyterians, leading to the formation of the Society of United Irishmen by prominent merchants of the town in October 1791.

al memory of it. For this see Anna McCleery, 'Life of Mary Anne McCracken', pp 175-6. 7 *The Manuscripts and Correspondence of James, First Earl of Charlemont* (London; HMSO, 1891), 1, '1745-83', p. 113 (Historical Manuscripts Commission. Twelfth Report, Appendix. Part X. C – 6338 – II). For a brief biographical note on Joy see Isaac W. Ward, 'Henry Joy (1754-1835)', in *Belfast Literary Society 1801-1901* (Belfast, 1902), pp 43-4. 8 J.J. Campbell, 'The Play School of David Manson (1726-1792) of Belfast', in *Capuchin Annual* (1956-7), pp 159-69.

Eventually Mary Anne McCracken, her sister, Margaret, and her brothers, Henry Joy (Harry) and William were to become fully committed to the cause. One brother, John, was far less sympathetic, and elsewhere in the family, Mary Anne's uncle, Henry Joy junior, the erstwhile radical of the early 1780s, was to prove one of the most influential opponents of the United Irishmen. We can say no more than that such divisions between radicals and moderates who later became conservatives was characteristic of many Belfast families in the years to come.

Initially, at least, supporters of the United Irishmen were hardly committed to social revolution. In July 1792, while Belfast was celebrating the anniversary of the fall of the Bastille, and pressing forward with demands for political reform embracing all religions, the revived Volunteer movement, very much their militia force, was engaged in helping to suppress strikes and serious unrest amongst more plebian cotton weavers. Indeed the only military action the Volunteers ever undertook, and in a futile attempt to prove their willingness to work with lawful authority, was to use their cannon to assist in the eviction of a tenant on the earl of Hertford's estate.[9]

How did this early social conservatism of the United Irishmen during their constitutional phase affect their attitudes to the rights of women? In Paris women led the march on Versailles, presaging the downfall of the King, and were demanding political rights in any new revolutionary settlement.[10] Yet, in Ireland, as Curtin sees it, the United Irish *Northern Star* appeared 'close to ridiculing women's active participation in politics'. The paper indeed noted that in Ireland rich and landed widows actually had the right to nominate representatives to the Irish Parliament and that, 'so far does the actual absurdity of our practice soar beyond the wildest dreams of French visionaries'.[11]

Yet this Irish practice was an absurdity for any reformer, and there is convincing evidence that Belfast radicals were taking women's rights more seriously. Mary Wollstonecraft published her pioneering *A Vindication of the Rights of Women* in 1792, containing an angry denunciation of the 'baneful lurking gangrene' of 'the tyranny of man over woman'.[12] This soon attracted the interest of Belfast publisher, William Magee, also a proprietor of the *Northern Star*, and in October he adver-

9 See 'The Memorial of the Volunteers of Belfast' [March 1793], republished in [Henry Joy and William Bruce] (eds), *Belfast Politics* (Belfast: Henry Joy, 1794), pp 131–5. 10 See Rosalind Miles, *The Women's History of the World* (London, 1989), pp 179–80. 11 *Northern Star*, 13 June 1792. Quoted in Nancy Curtin, 'Women and Eighteenth Century Irish Republicanism', in MacCurtain and O'Dowd, p. 142. 12 *A Vindication of the Rights of Women* (London, J. Johnston, 1792), pp 21–3.

tised his own edition of Wollstonecraft's work in the *Star* giving it precedence over a list of other titles, albeit attaching its attractions to the contrary title of Thomas Paine's best-seller – 'of this able and spirited performance we shall say no more than that it was with Mrs Wollstonecroft [that] the title of Mr Paine's two works on The Rights of Man originated'.[13]

The *Star* went on to review Wollstonecraft's 'justly celebrated' book in glowing terms:

> The work abounds with ingenious observations, which do equal honour to the head and heart of the writer; it affords [a] variety of judicious instruction for the early management of the female mind, and frequently, and pertinently, corrects the assumptions of the *tyrant man*, with a boldness and justice which demand admiration and conviction.[14]

By 1793 the Belfast Society for Promoting Knowledge (later the Linen Hall Library) had acquired a copy, and indeed from 1792 onwards admitted women to membership.[15] Even in this brief period of democratic debate, the question of women's rights did not play a prominent part, and in so far as it did, it was the opponents of radical reform who decried them, thus the Revd William Bruce, the main speaker on the losing side at the great town meeting on 28 January 1792, argued that:

> If we follow, without restriction, the *theory* of human rights, where will it lead us? In its principle it requires the admission of *women*, of persons under age, and of paupers, to suffrage at elections; to places of office and trust, and as members of both Houses of Parliament.[16]

This meeting, and others in 1792, were principally concerned with the admission of Roman Catholics to the body politic, and no direct radical response was made to Bruce's attack on women. But he was right that the radical majority at these meetings took their stand on absolute prin-

---

13 *Northern Star*, 27 October 1792. No extant copy of this purported Belfast edition has been located but J. Stockdale printed a Dublin edition in 1793. 14 *Northern Star*, 22 December 1792. 15 John Killen, *A History of the Linen Hall Library 1788-1988* (Belfast, 1990), p. 20. See in particular *Rules of the Belfast Society for Promoting Knowledge, with a Catalogue of the Books* (Belfast, 1793) *and Catalogue of the Books Belonging to the Belfast Society for Promoting Knowledge, with their Rules, and a List of the Members* (Belfast, 1795). 16 *Belfast Politics*, p. 19.

ciple, one that embraced Roman Catholics at home, slaves abroad, and one that might reasonably be presumed to include women.[17]

It was a presumption that could never be fully put to the test in Belfast where the era of democratic debate and politics was short-lived. The Volunteers were suppressed in March 1793, war with France followed soon after, and the United Irishmen henceforth increasingly operated underground. Flourish they might, but they could never assume responsibility for public policy in the way that their French exemplars did. Nor, one should add, did they have the opportunity for betrayal on the French scale, where most of the women leaders of the revolution went to the scaffold in Robespierre's terror.[18]

In the painful period of United Irish reconstruction which followed the severe reverses of 1793, the radicals principally responsible for the revival of the movement defined a new social radicalism. Thus Thomas Russell now advocated reliance on the men of no property, but at the same time noted in his journal that, 'women in public offices [were] as clever as men. Queens, poetesses, etc., etc. In merchants houses keep the accoun[t]s as well as men.'[19] Russell's interest in the subject suggests that it was one of more general debate, perhaps carried on in the McCracken household. Nevertheless, there is no mention of either Henry Joy or Mary Anne McCracken amongst the plethora of others referred to in Russell's *Journals*, which, although incomplete, cover principally the period March 1793 to the end of 1794.

The McCrackens and Russell came together in May 1795, on the occasion of Wolfe Tone's arrival in Belfast, en route to America. Yet, this celebrated gathering followed a traditionally segregated fashion. Tone, Russell, Henry Joy McCracken and other men climbed to McArts Fort on the summit of Cave Hill and swore, 'never to desist in our efforts, until we had subverted the authority of England over our country, and asserted her independence'. Meanwhile, the families, including no doubt Mary Anne and her sister Margaret, assembled below at the Deer Park for a delicious picnic.[20]

When, in September 1796, a new government clampdown against the resurgent United Irishmen commenced with the arrest of Thomas

17 Although the connection was not made clear at the time, the link between the anti-slavery movement and the womens' movement became explicit by the mid-nineteenth century. For this see Miles, p. 242, 'Of all the causes that fuelled the fight for the rights of women, most important was the parallel struggle against the slavery of the southern states of America.' 18 Miles, *The Women's History*, pp 179-86. 19 C.J. Woods (ed.), *Journals and Memoirs of Thomas Russell* (Dublin, 1991), entry for 11 July 1793, pp 86-7. 20 W.T.W. Tone (ed.), *The Life of Theobald Wolfe Tone* (Washington, 1826), vol. 1, p. 128.

Russell, Samuel Neilson and others, Mary Anne's response was hardly one of direct involvement. Her earliest extant letter, to her sister-in-law, does not suggest immediate personal concern for the victims; 'as yet we have met with no misfortune, tho' numbers of people have been taken up here this family has escaped'.[21] However, any such complacency was soon dispelled by the arrest of her brother, Henry Joy or Harry, on 10 October, followed by their oldest brother, William, in April 1797.[22] A main source for our knowledge of Mary Ann's views and actions is to be found in her correspondence with the prisoners at Kilmainham, and although no doubt constrained by the knowledge that all such letters were likely to fall into the hands of the authorities, it is explicit enough.

By March 1797 her full commitment to the revolutionary cause is evident:

> Let us not be terrified or dismayed, but repose with unlimited confidence where we can never be deceived. If the complete Union of Ireland should demand the blood of some of her best Patriots to cement, if they will not sink [from] their duty, but meet their fate equally unappalled, whether it be on the scaffold or in the field convinced that in the end the cause of Union and of truth must prevail.[23]

Thus she foreshadowed the blood sacrifice of her own brother, and in doing so enlisted a religious imperative 'as all things are under the direction of a Being infinitely wise & powerful who can bring good out of evil & who orders all things for the best'.

What then was a woman's role to be in such affairs? Again in March 1797 Mary Anne wrote of her intention to visit 'some female societies in this town' and indeed a society of United Irish Women had been in existence since at least October 1796.[24] Mary Anne did not altogether approve of the idea of separate women societies, but for entirely liberated reasons. She would have preferred the admission of women to the main societies, 'as there can be no other reason for having them separate but keeping the women in the dark and certainly it is equally ungenerous and uncandid to make tools of them without confiding in them'. However, as far as these women were concerned, she wanted 'to know if they have any rational ideas of liberty and equality for themselves or

21 Trinity College Dublin. MS 873, Madden Papers, Mary Anne McCracken to John McCracken's wife, September 1796 (quoted in McNeill, pp 109-10). 22 McNeill, *Life and Times*, pp 111, 117 and 119. 23 Madden Papers, 150, Mary Anne to Harry [Henry Joy McCracken], 26 March 1797 (McNeill, p. 138). 24 See *Northern Star*, 17 October 1796 for a letter from Lucy Sterling, secretary of the Society.

whether they are contented with their present abject and dependent situation, degraded by custom and education beneath the rank in society
in which they were originally placed'.

She now asked of Harry, 'is it not almost time for the clouds of error
and prejudice to disperse and that the female part of the Creation as
well as the male should throw off the fetters with which they have so
long been mentally bound ...?' She went on to express the hope that, 'it
is reserved for the Irish nation to strike out something new and to shew
an example of candour, generosity, and justice superior to any that have
gone before them'. In this she had some confidence in her brother as,
'one whom I suppose to be capable of forming an opinion from his own
experience without consulting the stupid multitude of common
thinkers'.

True there is no other evidence of Mary Anne's involvement with
the 'women's societies', but it is too much to presume, as Mary McNeill
does, that 'one is strongly inclined to assume that she did not' join them.
In any case, as male leaders were arrested women increasingly had to fill
the gaps, and not least in the concealment of arms. Mary Anne was able
to assure Henry Joy that, 'a certain article which was the only cause of
uneasiness to you at the time you were taken up, was concealed in the
house until the late strict search ... and not daring to keep it any longer,
we gave it in charge to a man in whom we had confidence, who buried
it in the Country'.[25] Her sole reservation in such matters was a principled opposition to political assassination, arguing that:

> it is a great pity the people did not always keep in mind that they
> should never do evil that good may come of it and that what is
> morally wrong can never be politically right. Have you not
> observed that since the assassinations began the cause of the peo-
> ple (which before had been rapidly gaining ground) has gradual-
> ly declined.[26]

She also intervened decisively in a debilitating dispute amongst the
prisoners in Kilmainham where Samuel Neilson and others, often under
pressure from their families, sought individual terms for early release to
the fury of the McCrackens. Harry wrote to Mary Anne, 'you will say
we see the worst side of man in Jail; true, but I did not think he had so
bad a side'.[27]

25 Madden Papers, 151, Mary Anne to Harry, 16 March 1797 (McNeill, *Life and Times*,
pp 125-8). 26 Madden Papers, 122, Mary Anne to Harry, 2 June 1797 (McNeill, *Life
and Times*, pp 141-2). 27 Madden Papers, 132, Harry to Mary Anne, August 1797
(McNeill, *Life and Times*, p. 153).

In October 1797 Mary Anne and her sister Margaret paid a second visit to the prisoners, and the resolution of this dispute was an important priority. She now chided Harry; 'ought men of superior sense and probity, who have long enjoyed mutual esteem and confidence, and who never for an instant suspected each other's integrity, to suffer themselves to be disunited by the misrepresentations of fools or knaves'. It was a matter for the movement as a whole – 'is it not injurious to the cause of Union when two men, who from the first went hand in hand in endeavouring to promote it, are thus at variance', and only then a cause of additional woe to their families – 'ought you needlessly to add to their unhappiness'. She concluded, 'I therefore entreat you will seriously reflect on the subject, and remember that an entire reconciliation between you is not only the earnest wish of all your friends, but must be that also of every friend to your cause'. Long after Mary Anne annotated this letter with the words, 'The reconciliation afterwards took place'.[28]

The notable feature of this letter to her imprisoned brother and of her correspondence generally, is the sense of authority wielded by Mary Anne, and her apparent leadership in their relationship. Harry was certainly a man of action, but of all the McCrackens, he was hardly a man of business.[29] He was, indeed, by confession a poor correspondent, but his sister had urged him to read. She sent Mrs Wollstoncraft's travels through Norway and Sweden, William Godwin's latest novel and on other occasions she encouraged him to learn French – and not we may presume just for simple edification.[30]

The two McCracken brothers were released on bail in December 1797, and although some of Harry's correspondence has survived from the intervening months before the rebellion, we know nothing of Mary Anne's immediate response to those difficult months leading up to her brother's last minute assumption of the command of the rebels in Antrim.[31]

---

28 Madden Papers, 136, Mary Anne to Harry, October 1797 (McNeill, *Life and Times*, pp 159-60). 29 His first venture, beyond the anxious tutelage of his family, a partnership in the calico business was short-lived and failed in 1796. See R.R. Madden, *The United Irishmen, their Lives and Times*, Second Series, vol. II, pp 394-5. 30 McNeill's verdict that Henry Joy was 'no great letter writer' (p. 117) seems fair; Mary Wollstonecraft, *Letters Written During a Short Residence in Norway and Sweden* (London: J. Johnston, 1796). William Godwin's latest novel was probably, *Things as they are: or the Adventures of Caleb Williams*, first published in London in 1794, but with a Dublin edition published by John Rice appearing in 1795; Madden Papers, 150 and 151. Mary Anne to Harry, 16 and 26 March 1797. In the latter she wrote, 'Do not forget the French dictionary. syntax and grammar, all which are very necessary at present as almost everybody in Belfast are learning French' (McNeill, *Life and Times*, pp 128 and 138-9). 31 Madden Papers, 143, Will-

There is one view of the actual rebellion in the North – that in the face of the arrests of many leaders, the faint heart of others, news of Wexford 'massacres', disillusion with French imperial designs and so on, that accordingly those who participated merely acted out of a sort of hopeless sense of duty to the cause. This begs the question as to how a significant rebellion could actually have been mounted on such a basis, and recent historians as various as Nancy Curtin and A.T.Q. Stewart, despite taking on board the apparent constraints on action, have, nonetheless, tended to emphasise the extent of the endeavour.[32] No doubt a desperate one, but hardly hopeless for those marching out onto 'the field convinced that in the end the cause of Union and of truth must prevail' as Mary Anne had put it to her brother a year earlier.[33]

In the immediate aftermath of the defeat at the Battle of Antrim, it was Mary Anne who took the heroic initiative. She had influential contacts which lead her to Henry Joy and the 'Spartan band' of fugitives hiding in the Belfast hills. Certainly she advised them that, for the moment, the cause was lost. She was instrumental, too, in making arrangements for Henry Joy's unsuccessful escape via Carrickfergus. Likewise, she was at the centre of efforts to save him from the scaffold, and then to revive him when he was taken down from it. Only in failure did she come close to fainting.[34]

At that moment it becomes impossible to separate Mary Anne's commitment to the rebellion from her affection for her brother, yet it is mistaken to assume that it was the latter alone which had fuelled her enthusiasm. To argue thus is to ignore the extent to which she had stiffened his resolve in the preceding years. If, however, she was a victim of the hopeless loyalty syndrome, and the more reprehensible female variant of it, by which women might be expected to support the folly of their men folk willy-nilly, her duty surely ended with the death of Henry Joy. In the event far from it.

In January 1799 when debates on the Act of Union were rising to a crescendo, we find Mary Anne in correspondence with her cousin,

iam McCracken to Mr and Mrs McCracken (senior), 9 December 1797 (McNeill, *Life and Times*, pp 163-4). 32 Nancy Curtin, *The United Irishmen: Popular Politics in Ulster and Dublin, 1791-1798* (Oxford, 1994); A.T.Q. Stewart, *The Summer Soldiers: The 1798 Rebellion in Antrim and Down* (Belfast, 1996). For the factors militating against rebellion see Curtin pp 260-4, and Stewart pp 60-2, yet most of the available opinions are from government or pro-government sources. Curtin is most explicit on the actual turnout: 'The remarkable thing, however, was that, under such adverse circumstances, at least 27,000 men in Antrim, Down, and east Derry actually took part in one or more engagements with government forces' (p. 277). 33 Madden Papers, 150, Mary Anne to Harry, 26 March 1797 (McNeill, *Life and Times*, pp 138-9). 34 Madden, *The United Irishmen*, second series, vol. II, pp 479-91.

Grisel or 'Grizzey', sister and housekeeper to another cousin, the Dublin-based Counsellor Henry Joy, who had looked after the legal interests of Harry and William while they were in prison in 1796 and 1797, while rigorously disapproving of their principles. The political dimension of this correspondence opens with Grisel's account of Counsellor Joy's new found enthusiasm for politics, and his vehement and published opposition to the proposed Act of Union.[35] Grisel is caught up in the spirit of her brother's campaign and goes on to express her disappointment at the lack of support from Belfast – 'I have no patience with Belfast'.

Mary Anne's contempt for Counsellor Joy's late conversion was scathing. Her 'extreme pleasure' at Counsellor Joy's 'unexpected change' is bitterly cynical, and more so than in the milder extracts quoted by Mary McNeill:

> As the dumb have been made to speak and the blind to hear, I should think myself totally deficient in their Christian charity, was I not to rejoice that so many of my countrymen, and countrywomen, have recovered the right use of their senses. However disagreeable those truths may be, that can only be forced on our observation by painful experience, yet ... as the feelings of the majority of mankind are so torpid, as only to be aroused by the idea of individual sufferings, I consider any event as fortunate, which obliges people, at last, to open their eyes ... in regard to the situation of Ireland.[36]

Thus Harry's blood sacrifice had not been in vain – it had served to convert Counsellor Joy who was one of 'those who for so long preached up non-resistance and passive obedience to all existing governments, and who excoriated those as monsters who even wished for a revolution because a [reform] could not be effected without bloodshed'. Now, apparently, Joy was speaking of 'opposing force to force', but it was a luxury he could afford because he had chosen a time when the people, 'are left without the means of resistance, if they had the inclination or temerity to have recourse to it'. It was all very well for Joy to engage in Dublin bombast, but if people in Belfast adopted the same course they, 'would run a great risque [*sic*] of having their houses demolished, besides being committed to the military prison'.

35 Madden Papers, 98 and 99, Grisel Joy to Mary Anne, 12 November 1798 and January 1799 (McNeill, *Life and Times*, pp 201-2). Counsellor Joy's address 'To the Electors of Ulster' appeared in the *Anti-Union* of 19 January 1799. 36 Madden Papers, 100, Mary Anne to Grisel Joy [*c*.January 1799] (McNeill, *Life and Times*, pp 202-4).

Mary Anne was also suspicious of Joy's arguments – 'is there no other argument against this union, than "that it will lessen the property of the rich"? The question I ask myself is, can it increase the sufferings of the poor?', that is those who 'were finally driven to their late unhappy insurrection; – I say unhappy because unsuccessful'. For the moment they 'must patiently submit to the new wrong that is now in meditation for them'.

Cynical though Mary Anne may have been about the motives of some, such as Counsellor Joy, who now opposed the Act of Union, her view of the Union, as revealed in another letter which McNeill fails to quote, was one of emphatic opposition expressed by a telling metaphor:

> What a wonderful clamour is now raised at the name of Union, when in reality there has always been such an union between England and this country, as there is between husband and wife by which the former has the power to oppress the latter.[37]

On the basis of her correspondence, one can hardly doubt that in 1799 Mary Anne was entirely unrepentant about the rebellion of the preceding summer, except in so far as it had failed. It did not require romantic interest to enlist her sympathies with those willing to foment Emmet's rebellion of 1803, notable amongst them, Thomas Russell, the 'Northern General' in the enterprise. According to McNeill this was a wholly different endeavour to the '98 rebellion:

> Close though it was in point of time to '98, and often considered as its delayed conclusion, in point of fact it was the opening of a new era, for in ideology the two risings were worlds apart. The rebellion of 1798 had been fundamentally a great struggle for social justice ... With Emmet's rising, on the other hand, modern Irish nationalism was born.[38]

Mary Ann's sympathies with the latter can then only be explained in romantic terms, and her presumed love for Thomas Russell. The positive evidence for such feeling is non-existent. Indeed, McNeill concedes that 'it is impossible to say how closely Mary Ann had kept in touch with Russell since the day in October 1796 when he was arrested'. Yet, by 1803 McNeill finds her ready to 'lavish adoration' as 'the strongly emotional side of her nature hungered for the beauty, the idealism, the

37 Madden Papers, 101, Mary Anne to Grisel Joy [c.January 1799]. 38 McNeill, *Life and Times*, pp 215-16.

gaiety of Thomas Russell ... this was the man that Mary loved'.[39] McNeill does 'not know ... whether or not she had longed for marriage', but we know from her 1799 correspondence with Grisel that she took a pretty jaundiced view of that station in life.[40]

Why not consider Mary Ann's own testimony on the subject? Writing many years later to Madden she made it clear that she was aware of at least some of the difficulties of Russell's love life:

> His admiration for Miss [Eliza] Goddard was so apparent, and her seeming pleasure at his attentions that it was generally supposed that the attachment was mutual, but she having been attached from childhood whence [   ] she knew she could never hope for her father's consent, she was forced to conceal it ... Her father was a harsh man and she had no choice.[41]

As late as 1857 Mary Ann had reservations about revealing these details for fear that some of these ladies connections might still be alive. No such complication would have affected any muted suggestion of an attraction on her part, but she did not give it. Her recollections are in fact fully borne out by Russell's *Journals* and in Mrs McTier's correspondence with William Drennan.[42]

Perhaps then Mary Ann McCracken was far more consistent than McNeill suggests. She fully supported the revolutionaries of 1798, regretting only their failure, and was in no mood to compromise with the post-rebellion order of things. The objectives of the revolutionaries of 1803 would have seemed little different to her than those of the earlier United Irishmen: contrary to McNeill's assertion, they had clearly determined on revolution and separation rather than reform.

The distinction in 1803 was rather one of means – the preference for the conspiratorial approach, rather than the open movement. Secrecy certainly preserved the new enterprise from the easy betrayal which had so damaged the United Irishmen, but it lessened contact with the ordinary people on whom any new rising would eventually depend. In the end the fatal difference, at least in the North, lay in the lack of will both amongst surviving leaders and the people to rise again. Even this, however, can be read two ways – one interpretation suggests that Ulster had already come to terms with the Act of Union and the new order. A sec-

39 McNeill, *Life and Times*, p. 211. 40 McNeill, *Life and Times*, p. 222. 41 Madden Papers, 70, Mary Anne McCracken to Madden, 13 November 1857. 42 *Journals*, see 15 references in index; D.A. Chart (ed.), *The Drennan Letters* (Belfast, 1931), p. 332. According to Mrs McTier writing to William Drennan on 4 November 1803, Russell was still dreaming of Eliza Goddard while in Downpatrick Jail.

ond reading, closer to the truth and to Mary Anne's perspective, suggests that while deep discontent remained, it was the crushing of the United Irishmen and the post rebellion repression which had destroyed any immediate opportunity for another rising. This, however, did not undermine the validity of re-organisation.

In this context the willingness of Mary Anne and her sister Margaret to find lodgings for Thomas Russell with one of their weavers in the Castlereagh Hills, in July 1803, in spite of the risks, becomes far more rational.[43] The advice Russell received from surviving Northern leaders was equally rational – that no immediate rising was possible. The premature outbreak of the rising in Dublin on 23 July, before Russell could return there, prevented any exploration of more cautious options. Russell made his futile attempt to rally support in county Down and failed. The McCracken sisters were sufficiently committed to him to arrange and finance his escape to Dublin where he was arrested. Then even greater risks were taken in seeking to bribe his jailers to secure his escape, without success, and at a cost of at least £300. As Mary Anne later told Madden, 'it ruined both my brother and my sister and myself'.[44]

Russell was brought north to Downpatrick for trial. Mary Anne was instrumental in arranging and paying for his defence but did not go to the trial herself. Her family's fears of government retribution, and her own fears in this regard, prevented her from doing so.[45] It was a matter of anguish to her that she did not go, but nothing in the two letters she sent Russell at Downpatrick Jail suggest more than the solidarity of a sister in the cause, indeed the last of the two concludes, 'I am joined by my sister in every sentiment of attachment and veneration'.[46] Again, writing many years later to Madden, she said of these efforts:

> How was it possible to shrink back when told that human lives were at stake, which my exertion might be instrumental in saving, and that no other person dare make the attempt ... and, we having undertaken it, there was no question of drawing back for pecuniary risk.[47]

After 1803, Mary Anne McCracken had to come to terms with a dramatically changing world. She lived through final British victory in

---

43 McNeill, *Life and Times*, p. 212. 44 Madden Papers, 80, Mary Anne McCracken to Madden, 2 February 1859. 45 Madden Papers, 107, Mary Anne to Eliza Templeton, October 1803 (McNeill, *Life and Times*, p. 222). 46 Madden Papers, 644, Mary Anne to Thomas Russell, October 1803 (McNeill, *Life and Times*, pp 223-4). 47 Madden Papers, 80, Mary Anne to Madden, 2 February 1859 (McNeill, *Life and Times*, p. 218).

the Napoleonic Wars in 1815, the triumph of British capital and the rise of empire. Likewise, she witnessed Belfast's fitful industrial revolution, and its growth from small town to city. She lived long enough to be photographed shortly before her death in 1866.

We only know her views towards the end of this process, as none of her correspondence survives between 1803 and the late 1830s by which time she even had kind words to say of Queen Victoria:

> And now a better day has dawned. The old prophecy that these countries would never be well ruled until a virgin queen should come to the throne seems to be realised ... she is so truly amiable and feminine that she is universally beloved.[48]

This can be read as a new found enthusiasm for the Union. It is perhaps more an enthusiasm for all that appeared possible in the 1830s. After all Daniel O'Connell the architect of Catholic Emancipation, and the campaign for the repeal of the Union was sufficiently encouraged by Victoria's apparently liberal sympathies to call her 'the darling little queen'.[49] And what then of Mary Anne's views of O'Connell? She conceded that, 'O'Connell has often been most tyranically despotic and viciously abusive to those who differed from him in opinion', but had no doubts in her admiration for what he had achieved – 'the great moral regeneration which ... he has effected in the character of the Irish people cannot be too highly estimated, and entitles him to the lasting gratitude of all true philanthropists'. For her O'Connell had the capacity to ensure that Ireland 'would be the finest nation in the world'.[50]

Inhabiting as she did the northern arena in which 'many sincere and ardent liberals who were violently opposed to the union before it took place, are now as much opposed to repeal', she was bound to find the issue problematical. One had to ask 'whether the people of this country might not have their liberty and happiness better excercised in being an integral part of a great and powerful nation'? Yet to adopt such a position one had to 'lay aside the natural feelings of national pride and love of independence which is not easily done'. In part her resistance to the ever more powerful allure of the Union remained based on an emotional Irish nationalism, even if now led by O'Connell; it was, however, also based on the precedent of 'former history' and of 'how little was gained for centuries before' by the English connection, and then again on her

48 McNeill, *Life and Times*, p. 248. 49 Charles Chevenix Trench, *The Great Dan* (London, 1984), p. 245. 50 Madden Papers, 156, Mary Anne to Madden, 15 October 1844.

assessment of present conditions in the context of which she asked; 'how is it possible for people to be contented who are in a state of starvation in the midst of plenty?' Perhaps neither Repeal nor Union offered the open road to the levelling policies, far beyond mere philanthropy, which she still advocated. She favoured the abolition of all indirect taxes and the introduction of 'income tax or property tax', although, ever realistic, she saw this as 'too just a principle to be approved in the present state of society by the very rich'.[51]

In her correspondence with Madden one can indeed find an increasingly jaundiced view of developments. In the 1830s the Whigs had gone far towards suppressing Orangeism. By 1851, and the aftermath of the Young Ireland revolt, it was a different matter as Mary Anne complained, 'I fear the labours of the United Irish are about to be overturned and the Orange system of religious discord will be re-established. It seems as if the world was going back in place of advancing'.[52] By 1858 she was deploring the 'disgraceful' conduct of Irish landlords, and condemning 'the horrid cruelties perpetrated in India under British rule'.

Nonetheless she still had hopes that 'the rising generation (if not myself) will see the millenium', one in which such ills would be done away with.[53] Unlike the hopes of '98 or even 1803, however, the reality of this was much less likely, because the body of support for radical reform no longer existed. The Presbyterian Church was now as much the church of 'Roaring' Hugh Hanna as of the reformers. Even in great old age she maintained the Belfast anti-slavery campaign but support had evaporated – 'Belfast, once so celebrated for its love of liberty, is now so sunk in the love of filthy lucre that there are but 16 or 17 female anti-slavery advocates'.[54] In this respect at least the principled anti-slavery stance of O'Connell was infinitely preferable to the backsliding of erstwhile liberals in Belfast.[55]

In other respects, too, hopes had faded. She noted how 'the sphere of woman's industry is so confined, and so few roads lie open to her, and those so thorny'. Mere economic transformation offered no guarantees to women. As Rosalind Miles has recently argued, 'each of the changes of the Industrial Revolution proved to have an adverse impact on women's lives; coming together, the result was devastating, in ways that could never have been foreseen'.[56] Mary and Margaret McCracken

51 Madden Papers, 155, pp 16-17, Mary Anne to Madden, 15 October 1844.   52 Madden Papers, 71, Mary Anne to Madden, 26 November 1851. 53 Madden Papers, 88, Mary Anne to Madden, 26 October 1858.   54 Madden Papers, 78, Mary Anne McCracken to Madden [n.d.] (McNeill, *Life and Times*, p. 295).   55 See Maurice O'Connell, *Daniel O'Connell the Man and his Politics* (Dublin, 1990), pp 121-31. O'Connell had a far better record on slavery than either the Ulster Liberals or the Young Irelanders.   56 Miles, p. 187.

had run their own muslin business, but had been forced to close many years earlier, mainly because of that old 1790s sense of duty to their weavers – in times of recession they kept them on.[57] No such compunction affected their brother John – a hard task master who did not even shrink from exploiting Jemmy Hope, the weaver veteran of '98.[58]

And if a woman was out of the increasingly male and factory-oriented world of work what was left for an unmarried woman from the merchant class. Yes she could undertake good works in a strictly confined sphere, and Mary Anne for many years played a leading role on the Ladies Committee of the Belfast Charitable Society which ran the Clifton Street Poor House, and caused much difficulty for the male managers on behalf of women and children.[59] When in very old age she was in straightened circumstances it was no doubt largely thanks to this role that a substantial collection was taken up in the town on her behalf. Even the Revd Arthur Chichester Macartney, Vicar of Belfast, and part of the old establishment against whom the United Irishmen had fought, contributed. Mary Anne chose to interpret the gift as 'a testimonial to my brother's memory'.[60]

How in the end did she look back to '98? In writing to Dr Madden sixty years later she appeared to regret that the rebellion had ever happened as she hoped that his work would be both, 'interesting and instructive shewing the certain evil, and uncertain good of attempting political changes by force of arms'.[61] In writing thus, however, she was merely echoing Madden's own objectives in producing his voluminous work on the United Irishmen. He wished to redeem the characters of the United Irishmen, while pointing to the disaster of the rebellion, and thus to enlist them for the cause of moderate Irish nationalism in the mid-nineteenth century.[62] She was bound to reflect constantly on the personal loss and yet as she also put it, 'I never once wished that my beloved brother had taken any other part than that which he did'.[63]

57 Madden Papers, 82, Mary Anne McCracken to Madden, 22 February 1859. 58 McNeill, *Life and Times*, pp 242-3. 59 McNeill, *Life and Times*, pp 257-87. 60 Madden Papers, 79, Mary Anne McCracken to Madden, 23 June 1859. McNeill saw this a little differently, as evidence of how, 'Old animosities were being forgotten' (p. 300). 61 Madden Papers, 77. Mary Anne McCracken to Madden, 3 September 1858. 62 R.R. Madden, *The United Irishmen, their Lives and Times*, 1st ser. (2 vols, London: J. Madden, 1842), I, pp 209-11. 63 McNeill, *Life and Times*, p. 192.

Bearing witness: Female evidences in courts martial convened to suppress the 1798 rebellion

Thomas Bartlett

The role of ordinary women in the 1798 rebellion has hitherto received scant attention from historians. Admittedly, loyalist historians such as Sir Richard Musgrave in his *Memoirs of the Irish Rebellion* (1801)[1] did print a large quantity of depositions by such women detailing what they had seen, heard and endured during the rebellion; and in the later nineteenth century a number of lengthier narratives of female loyalists were published: but such statements, while very useful to the historian, were essentially contributions to an Irish *genre* of atrocity literature designed to illustrate the 'unnatural' character of the rebellion and the 'unfeeling' nature of the rebels, rather than to highlight the behaviour, much less the role, of loyalist women.[2] In nationalist writings, ordinary women have received even less attention, for it was 'the Boys of Wexford' (and the priests) who contrived to dominate the historiography.[3] It is true that Helena Concannon published a strongly nationalist volume, *Women of 'Ninety-Eight*, but this book, written in 1919 at the height of the War of Independence was assuredly designed more as a boost to the national struggle than as a contribution to the history of the rebellion.[4] Her work was dedicated to the 'memory of all the dead women and in homage to all the living women who have given their dear ones to Ireland', and her main concern was to stress the lines of continuity between the women of her generation and those of 1798, many of whom, she noted in a revealing aside, undertook 'what we of today

1 Sir Richard Musgrave, *Memoirs of the Irish Rebellion of 1798* (reprint of 4th edition, Fort Wayne, Indiana, 1995). The addition of an enormous index has considerably enhanced the value of this indispensable work. 2 John Beatty has edited these for publication: *Narratives of Loyalist Women and the Irish Rebellion of 1798* (Indiana, forthcoming). 3 On the historiography of 1798 see Kevin Whelan, "'98 after '98: the Politics of Memory' in his *The Tree of Liberty: Radicalism, Catholicism and the Construction of Irish Identity* (Cork, 1996), pp 133-75. 4 Mrs Thomas Concannon, *Women of 'Ninety-Eight* (Dublin, 1919).

should call *Cumann na mBan* work'.[5] That said, Mrs Concannon's essays were a pioneering venture into hitherto unexplored territory. Certainly, her presentist remarks and her relentless hagiographical treatment of her subjects are jarring to the modern ear; but she did identify the topic, and while the whole of her work is devoted to the mothers, wives, sisters, and sweethearts of the State prisoners and rebel leaders – Tone, Fitzgerald, Emmet, and Neilson inter alia – she did find space, in her last, short, chapter for those whom she termed 'some obscure heroines of 'ninety-eight'.[6]

I

The reasons for this neglect of the experiences of women during the rebellion period are not hard to uncover. First, rebellion was perceived as men's work: it was a sort of reserved occupation which women, unfitted by their sex for action and decision, could never fittingly aspire to. Since women could never be generals, soldiers, judges, jurors, legislators or voters – how could they be rebels? And in those documented cases where women had acted a 'manly' role as rebels (or revolutionaries, as in France), the conviction was that they had acted under the influence of their menfolk, or that they had been led astray by their wilful nature, that they had in fact been 'unsexed' by designing men or by their innate weakness. In either case they were seen as abject objects of pity (or repulsion) rather than as fit subjects for judicial condemnation. Hence, although there was clear evidence that Lady Pamela Fitzgerald was acting as a messenger for her husband, Lord Edward, she was not arrested and put on trial, but was instead ordered out of the country.[7] Again, poor Anne Devlin who was tortured and imprisoned for her connection with Robert Emmet was not brought to trial, presumably because, whether found guilty or acquitted, 'justice' itself might stand condemned.

And if we leave Anne Devlin to one side (she was arrested in 1803),[8] it is a striking fact that the 1798 rebellion produced no female State prisoner;[9] no woman was sent to Fort George or included in the

5 Concannon, *Women of 'Ninety-Eight*, p. 320. 6 Concannon, *Women of 'Ninety-Eight*, pp 311-23. 7 Paul Weber, *The United Irishmen and Hamburg* (Dublin, 1997), p. 86; Stella Tillyard, *Citizen Lord: Edward Fitzgerald, 1763-98* (London, 1997), pp 214, 251, 264. 8 For Anne Devlin, see John Finnegan (ed.), *Anne Devlin, Patriot and Heroine* (Dublin, 1992). 9 One possible exception to this sweeping statement is Margaret Monro, Henry's sister. She had been active in hosting dinners for the United Irishmen of Lisburn. After the rebellion she was arrested and imprisoned for a time in Carrickfergus gaol. Charles Dickson, *Revolt in the North* (Dublin, 1960) p. 251.

Banishment Act;[10] no woman was sentenced to death by court martial – indeed I have found only two who were brought before one[11] – and certainly no woman appears to have been executed for rebellion and treason (though many were murdered and abused on and off the battlefield). Since there was clear evidence that women were involved at a number of levels both in the planning of the rebellion and in its execution; and since the ordinary courts of the time in England and Ireland had shown, and would continue to show, no compunction about sentencing women to execution or flogging or transportation,[12] the near total absence of rebel women in the lists of those tried by courts martial would appear to confirm the argument that rebellion was perceived as work for men only and that courts martial were only considered appropriate for the trial of male suspects.

Second, Irish women were ignored in nationalist historiography because in general nationalism in the nineteenth century had little time for women, at least in a public role: the United Irishmen, for all their talk of a more equal representation in parliament, had never envisaged women as voters or legislators (much to the disgust of Mary Ann McCracken, Henry Joy's sister), and their successors were no less exclusive.[13] The woman's sphere was held to be entirely within the home

10 Though, as noted above, Lady Pamela Fitzgerald was ordered out of Ireland by the Irish Privy Council; and the posthumous Act of Attainder against Lord Edward deprived her and their children of their inheritance. See George Campbell, *Edward and Pamela Fitzgerald* (London, 1904), pp 184-200. 11 At Clonmel, Catherine Kelly was brought before a court martial on 28 March 1799, charged with 'being concerned with divers other persons not yet taken in the murder of John Delahunty of Tullamore, Middlethird, county Tipperary. However no one appeared to prosecute her and she was acquitted with an order to enter into securities to give evidence in the affair: N.A. Rebellion Papers, 620/6/69/5. Musgrave claims that Catherine Whelan was convicted at a court martial in New Ross, county Wexford, on 11 August 1798 of urging the killing of Protestants. According to him, she was sentenced to transportation. I have not found the record of this court martial. Musgrave, *Memoirs*, p. 391. 12 For England see V.A.C. Gatrell, *The Hanging Tree: Execution and the English People, 1770-1868* (Oxford, 1994): Peter Linebaugh, *The London Hanged: Crime and Civil Society in the Eighteenth Century* (Cambridge, 1992): John Bohstedt, 'Women in English Riots, 1798-1810', *Past and Present*, no. 120 (Aug. 1988), pp 88-122. For Ireland, see Neal Garnham, *The Courts, Crime and the Criminal Law in Ireland, 1692-1760* (Dublin, 1996) and Brian Henry, *Dublin Hanged* (Dublin, 1994). James Kelly has written several important articles on violence against women in eighteenth-century Ireland: ' "A most inhuman and barbarous piece of villainy". An exploration of the crime of rape in eighteenth-century Ireland' in *Eighteenth-Century Ireland*, 10 (1995), pp 78-107; *idem*, 'Infanticide in eighteenth-century Ireland' in *Irish Economic and Social History*, xix (1992), pp 5-26; *idem*, 'The Abduction of women of fortune in eighteeth-century Ireland' in *Eighteenth-Century Ireland*, ix (1994), pp 7-42. 13 Nancy Curtin, 'Women and Eighteenth-century Irish republicanism' in Margaret MacCurtain and Mary O'Dowd (eds), *Women in Early Modern Ireland* (Dublin, 1991), pp

where it was desired of her that she would inculcate republican virtue in her sons and where it was expected that she herself would remain as a model of republican probity or womanly chastity. As Nancy Curtin points out, Matilda Tone was a particular exemplar in this respect.[14] Women could be symbol or model or victim but, by and large, the role of actor, activist or combatant – *in a political context* – was denied them. Hence while Anne Devlin's story had been taken down by the noted collector of 1798 memoirs, Br Luke Cullen, in the 1850s, it was not published until the 1960s;[15] and it was only in the 1890s that W.G. Lyttle wrote the melodramatic story of Betsy Gray, who had fought at Ballynahinch, county Down, and was murdered shortly afterwards.[16]

There were, then, sound socio-political reasons for the neglect of the women of '98, at least on the nationalist side. But alongside these must be placed the stark fact that there was also a perceived absence of evidence, at least where ordinary women were concerned. The dozen or so narratives of loyalist women which found their way into print during the nineteenth century had no counterpart in nationalist historiography; and while a number of the surviving leaders of the rebellion penned their memoirs, no woman involved on the rebel side appears to have done so. To that extent, even if there had been an interest – and there is no suggestion that there was – in reconstructing the experience of ordinary women in the 1798 rebellion, there would have been major evidential difficulties in the path of any such project.

It is the argument of this paper that the deficit in the evidence where women are concerned can be made good by a scrutiny of the surviving records of the courts martial convened after June 1798 to try rebels and repress the rebellion. All Ireland had been placed under martial law on 30 March 1798, and following the outbreak of rebellion on 23 May courts martial were speedily convened for the trial of rebels. There is no doubt that in the early weeks of the rebellion, such courts were little more than summary tribunals where the defendants received the most perfunctory of hearings and where sentences were promptly executed. However, as the months passed these courts martial became more elaborate, acquiring many of the trappings of Assize courts and with the defendants frequently employing civilian lawyers. Lord Camden's successor as Lord Lieutenant, Marquis Cornwallis, absolutely insisted on equitable hearings for the defendants – this made him most unpopular with loyalists – and equally he demanded that all sen-

133-44: for Mary Ann McCracken's protest see Mary McNeill, *The Life and Times of Mary Ann McCracken* (1988 reprint, Belfast), pp 128, 131. 14 See below, pp 26-47. 15 Finegan (ed.), *Devlin*, pp 9-10. 16 W.G. Lyttle, *Betsy Gray or Hearts of Down* (Newcastle, county Down, reprint 1968).

tences be reviewed by him personally before being carried out. From a documentary point of view, the result was dramatic: the hasty scrawls recording the fate of forgotten rebels in early June 1798 gave way to the lengthy reports in a clerk's hand that found their way on to Cornwallis's desk for his perusal.

For the authorities, courts martial offered speedy trials without the delays and formalities of civilian courts and without the necessity (or expense) of keeping prisoners in custody until Assizes were held. Until martial law fell into disuse in 1801, upwards of 800 trials at court martial, for which we have extant record, took place throughout Ireland. In law, only crimes in furtherance of rebellion were supposed to come before military tribunals but as will be seen, a wide range of 'ordinary', even domestic offences were frequently prosecuted at them. As noted above, the level of detail in the court martial records varied from place to place and from month to month, but for our purposes, what is striking is the large number of female evidences called upon both for the prosecution and for the defence. A rough estimate – and precision is impossible here given the incomplete nature of the evidence – would be that in upwards of twenty-five per cent of these courts martial there was a significant contribution by women: indeed on at least one occasion the *only* witnesses for and against the (male) defendant were women. In these military tribunals, we hear women having their say in their own words in a semi-public forum: women accusing and excusing, denouncing and defending, pleading – and lying.

In addition, very many of these trials gave rise to an appeal in the form of a petition to Cornwallis, seeking mercy or mitigation of sentence, and women were, customarily, heavily involved in pleading on behalf of their husbands, brothers and fathers, and sometimes acting as intermediaries. Taken together, these courts martial records and the State Prisoners' Petitions (including the separate but related Prisoners' Petitions) constitute the largest body of female testimony compiled in Ireland since the depositions collected after the Rising of 1641.[17] What does an examination of these court martial and petition records tell us about the role of women in the 1798 rebellion and about their position in the quasi-judicial process that repressed it?

17 For the Depositions, see Aidan Clarke, 'The 1641 Depositions' in P. Fox (ed.) *Treasures of the Library of Trinity College Dublin* (Dublin, 1986), pp 111-22. For their possible use see Nicholas Canny, 'The 1641 Depositioins as a source for the writing of social history: County Cork as a case study', in P. O'Flanagan and C. Buttimer (eds), *Cork: History and Society* (Dublin, 1993), pp 249-308.

II

As noted above, few (if any) women were tried by court martial: none the less a study of the surviving records indicates that women were involved in the rebellion. This is not at all a new point for we have known for some time that women played a role in the preparations for the rebellion, and in the fighting itself. Memoirs by former rebels such as Miles Byrne, Charles Teeling and Thomas Cloney contain information on such matters. Contemporary writers too, such as Samuel McSkimmin, noted the role of women. In his account of the rebellion in county Antrim, McSkimmin wrote of women wearing green to signal their sympathies with the insurgents, and he described how women baked oaten cakes for their men at 'the turn out'. More significantly, he recalled how it had been a woman who had resolved a stand-off in Randalstown between the insurgents and the local yeomanry, by setting fire to the market house in which the latter were sheltering.[18] Recently, Nancy Curtin has indentified women who 'served as activists within the United Irish organisation' carrying messages, gathering intelligence, suborning soldiers and even participating in the United *Irishwomen*. This oath-bound society 'attended to fund-raising and providing amenities for imprisoned United Irishmen and their families'.[19]

The incidental evidence of the courts martial confirms this picture of female involvement in the rebellion. For examples, at the trial of John Gunning at Coleraine in July 1798, Mary McHenry of Prospect defiantly told the court that she had joined the rebels 'of her own free will and accord', and that she had helped capture John Leech, detained by the rebels lest he give information about them.[20] In the same month in Belfast, at the trial by court martial of several men accused of breaking down the Flow Bridge at Killynure, county Down, Betty McCann admitted that she had been one of the party involved in that action which was designed to disrupt troop movements.[21] At a court martial at Glenarm, county Antrim, in July 1798, Jane McStravick was not afraid to admit that she had remonstrated with the two accused, who had apparently some authority among the rebels, for not acting quickly to seize the local castle. 'What the devil in hell commission have you', she reportedly asked, 'that you do not proceed and [capture the castle]?'[22]

18 See also Cloney's account of how Moll Doyle, the 'point of war', refused to leave captured cannon behind after the Battle of Ross. Thomas Cloney, *Personal Narrative* (Dublin, 1832), pp 41-2. 19 Curtin, 'Women', pp 133-4; Concannon, *Women of 'Ninety-Eight*, pp. x-xiv, 258; Samuel McSkimmin's, *Annals of Ulster, 1790-1798* ed. by E.J, McCrum (Belfast, 1906), p. 38 20 National Archives, Rebellion Papers 620/2/8/10. 21 N.A. Rebellion Papers, 620/2/9/29. 22 N.A. Rebellion Papers, 620/3/28/5.

And it will be remembered that the notorious informer, Bridget 'Biddy' Dolan, boasted of her exploits with the rebels in Wicklow, admitting among other things that she had 'set fire to baggage cars belonging to his majesty'.[23]

In addition, there is scattered evidence in the trial records of women being sworn and swearing others into the rebel conspiracy. Rachel Taggart told a court in Dungannon in July 1798 that 'about eighteen months ago [John Cooper, the accused] came to her house and asked evidence if she would be put up; that she consented and was sworn on a book to keep secret everything she should hear or see regarding the United Irishmen'.[24] At Cork, in October 1798, at the trial of John Griffith charged with attempting to seduce soldiers from their allegiance, evidence was given that he had sworn his wife into the United Irishmen;[25] at the Galway court martial of Michael Summerville in March 1799, there was testimony that the prisoner had sworn in Michael Geraghty, his mother and his sister. Geraghty's mother, however, denied she had been sworn, adding (convincingly), 'I was frightened sick' and William James MacNeven was reportedly sworn into the United Irishmen by Miss Moore, daughter of James Moore, Thomas St, Dublin, a friend of Lord Edward Fitzgerald.[26]

Such confirmation of female involvement in what was regarded as men's work – rebellion – is useful but the real value of the courts martial records (and the petitions) lies both in the direct way they detail the roles which women played in the trials themselves and in the light they shed on their position in late eighteenth-century Irish society.

III

As might be expected, many women were called before courts martial to tell what they had seen and suffered at the hands of the rebels. Musgrave in his *Memoirs* published a list of the names of upwards of 120 Protestant women from Wexford and the surrounding area who swore informations concerning, in the large majority of cases, the murder of family members, usually their husbands, by the rebels;[27] but the court martial records reveal that women prosecuted in all areas of

---

23 Examinations of Bridget Dolan, 3 Oct. 1799 and 7 Jan. 1800: N.A. Rebellion Papers, 620/17/35,36: *The Trial of Billy Byrne of Ballymanus* (new edition, Wicklow 1996), p. 9. 24 N.A. Rebellion Papers, 620/3/23/4. 25 N.A. Rebellion Papers, 620/2/14/2: Griffith was sentenced to death. 26 N.A. Rebellion Papers, 620/6/63/9: it may be significant evidence was produced that Geraghty and Summerville had had a dispute over a woman; R.R. Madden, *The United Irishmen, their lives and times*, 1st series, vol 2 (London, 1842), p. 399. 27 Musgrave, *Memoirs*, appendix no. xix, 9.

Ireland. Many cases were apparently open and shut, but even so, it is evident that women, frequently the sole or main evidence, were listened to with great attention. At a court martial held in Carlow town in April 1799, Margaret McEvers successfully prosecuted the notorious John Whelan, alias 'Black Top', for the murder of Hannah Manders (her aunt) and her two sisters;[28] in Dublin, in May 1799, Elizabeth Crawford was the main prosecution witness against James Magee accused of killing her husband and grand-daughter;[29] and in the same month, at Waterford, Margaret Deacon was the chief witness in the trial by court martial of John Lacy accused of treason and rebellion. Her evidence certainly carried conviction: 'I have known the prisoner [Lacy] many years since I went to school. He lived within two miles of my father's house and for that reason I could not be mistaken as to him'.[30] Again, a year later, in March 1800, in Wexford, Anne Cavenagh positively identified Patrick Bolger as 'aiding, assisting and abetting' in the murder of Thomas Cavenagh at Vinegar Hill;[31] in April 1800, also in Wexford, Mary Hall prosecuted Nicholas Walsh to conviction for the murder of her husband whom Walsh had dubbed 'that bloody Orangeman'.[32] All five accused were sentenced to death.

In less serious cases, too, the word of the woman was generally taken over that of the man. Ann McMeekin was the only prosecution witness against Hugh Alexander of Donaghadee, county Down, in August 1798 charged at Newtownards with exciting and encouraging rebellion in Ireland' by dint of being in possession of a pike. Alexander was convicted and given 200 lashes of which, the record laconically notes, he received 150.[33] At Killala, county Mayo, in September 1798, Robert Rogers was given 100 lashes for kicking Biddy Welsh and striking her over the head with a bayonet when she refused to 'get out' of his house;[34] and Mrs Anne Spencer, a clergyman's wife, successfully prosecuted at a court martial in Downpatrick in July 1798 two carmen, William Watson and William Creen, who had abused her on the journey to Downpatrick. Both drivers had demanded extra money for the fare, then bought drink with it, and Creen had got in beside Mrs Spencer, 'so close to my petticoats', she told the court martial, 'that I did not know

28 N.A. Rebellion Papers, 620/5/58/54: Eliza McDaniel swore that Whelan slept in her kitchen all and that he had never left the house that night. For the story of the killings of those at Mrs Mander's house, see Musgrave, *Memoirs*, p. 260.   29 N.A. Rebellion Papers, 620/5/61/18.   30 N.A. Rebellion Papers, 620/6/70/7: Margaret Deacon for the prosecution swore that one of those with the prisoner had said that they would burn the women and make 'a Protestant pie'.   31 N.A. Frazer MSS, iv, trial of Patrick Bolger, 10 March 1800.   32 N.A. Frazer MSS, iv: Mary Hall swore she later saw the prisoner 'dancing around the liberty tree'.   33 N.A. Rebellion Papers, 620/2/15/47.   34 N.A. Rebellion Papers, 620/3/21/1.

what he meant'. Happily, one MacMahon, a publican from Down-patrick, came to her rescue and the two drivers were sentenced to 50 lashes each by the affronted army officers who made up the court.[35]

Women who prosecuted ran no small risk in coming forward, for in addition to the social obloquy attendant on testifying in serious cases, in many parts of the country a smothered rebellion, consisting of arms raids, ambushes, nocturnal beatings, cattle-houghing and general intim-idation continued long after the rebel defeat at Vinegar Hill. Women like Jane Montgomery soon learned that informing was a high-risk activity. From her prison cell in 1799, she sent a petition to the Lord Lieutenant, claiming that because she had given evidence against the United Irishmen of county Down, they in their turn 'immediatedly bribed two women to swear against me'. She had been in prison with-out charge for fourteen months and sought permission to go to Amer-ica.[36] It was surely considerations of this sort that led Michael Gready's wife, Eilis, to denounce him when he turned approver and to swear that 'she would never live with him but that she and the children would quit him'. Gready was the prime witness at a court martial of three alleged houghers in Galway in March 1799: but his wife and daughter flatly contradicted his evidence and swore vehemently that he had not left the house that night, adding, 'not even to go out to do his little occasions'.[37]

By contrast, some women were fully prepared to resist threats and blandishments in order to press their case to the end. At the court mar-tial in Dublin in October of James Archbold, accused of having 'acted traiterously, rebelliously and hostilely', Jane Tompkins was undeterred by the fact that two other witnesses had vanished after speaking with the prisoner's brother and wife, nor by the evident intimidation she had faced from Archbald himself. She told the court that he had sworn 'he would as soon take my life as a rat's' and that after the rebellion he had come up to her and 'said in a scoffing manner to my tenant, William Barnes, "Ah my fellow, have you taken possession already?"' Archbold was convicted and sentenced to hang.[38] Again, at a court martial in Dungannon, county Tyrone, in June 1798, Nancy McKinley told how she had refused offers of money from the prisoner's father and brothers to stop her prosecution. In the event, John Breen was found guilty of 'using improper language and irregular conduct' toward McKinley, he having taken her child from her and 'damned her for a bitch, telling her that it would not be long before he would put a spear through her and her child's Orange soul'. He was sentenced to 50 lashes: but Nancy

35 N.A. Rebellion Papers, 620/2/15/64. 36 Petition of Jane Montgomery, *c.*1799: N.A. Rebellion Papers, 620/51/91. 37 N.A. Rebellion Papers, 620/6/63/4. 38 N.A. Rebellion Papers, 620/3/16/11.

McKinley would surely have to be careful thereafter.[39] As indeed would
Mary Powell, the sole witness at the court martial in Cavan of James
McIntyre, accused of having a pike 'about six feet long' and on his way
to join Humbert's army and his Irish allies. The prisoner's defence that
he was fleeing the French, not running to join them, was dismissed and
he was sentenced to 500 lashes and ordered to find sureties for his
future behaviour.[40] Perhaps Nancy Daly, was more fortunate than either
McKinley or Powell whose victims continued to reside in the area. In
August 1798, at a court martial in Armagh of John Sutton, accused of
treason and rebellion and of being 'a chief or head' of the United
Irishmen, Daly told how the prisoner (Sutton) offered to procure a
piece of land she and her husband then held 'at the old rent' if she
would swear against the main prosecution witness, 'which she refused to
do'. Luckily for her, Sutton was found guilty and given 200 lashes; but,
no doubt to her relief, he was also transported for life.[41]

Such trials were straightforward enough, but there was sometimes
more than the suggestion of pressure from *both sides* in a high-profile
case. For example, at a court martial in Wexford town in November
1798, Mary Connors swore that she had been offered £10 not to prosecute James d'Arcy ('a corn factor, in good circumstances'),[42] accused
inter alia of murdering her father. However, her defiant reply to the
offer – 'I would not sell my father's blood in that manner' – shed some
of its lustre when another witness, Catherine Ross, swore that Connors
had told her that 'she was forced to prosecute the prisoner and that she
told Archibald Jacob [a prominent magistrate] she did not wish to come
forward and that she was not sure of the man'. Jacob indignantly denied
that he had pressured her into giving evidence, but he was notorious for
his prosecuting zeal – the rebels had offered £50 for his head[43] – and
the suspicion of arm-twisting remained.[44]

An additional risk for the prosecutrix was that there was always a
chance that the defendant would be found not guilty and released back
into the community. Consider Anne Sparks' dilemma. In June 1800 she,
along with her mother, were the main witnesses at the court martial in
Wexford of Gregory Whelan accused of the murder of her husband,
Roger, killed on Vinegar Hill. Anne testified that she found his body
there; and her mother swore she saw Whelan with Roger, but that was
the extent of their evidence, and the court had little option but to
acquit, especially in view of Cornwallis's stern refusal to approve ver-

39 N.A. Rebellion Papers, 620/3/23/3. 40 N.A. Rebellion Papers, 620/2/12/12. 41
N.A. Rebellion Papers, 620/2/10/3. 42 Musgrave, *Memoirs*, p. 345. 43 Court martial
of Nicholas Walsh, Wexford, 24 April 1800: N.A., Frazer MSS, iv. 44 N.A. Rebellion
Papers, 620/3/26/14.

dicts reached in the face of (or absence of) the evidence.[45] In a similar instance, at a court martial at Newtownbarry, county Wexford, in November 1798, Rachel Murphy swore against John Doyle, accused of being 'a rebel and having arms concealed'. She testified that she knew Doyle and that he had told her that 'if the battle of New Ross and Newtownbarry were gained, there would not be a Protestant in the country left alive': but the court martial was unimpressed and Doyle walked free.[46] Judith Lynch must also have been in an awkward situation following the 'not guilty' verdict on Connor Trolowe [*recte* Turlowe?] at a court martial held in the Cork Council Chamber in April 1799. She had sworn that Trolowe was one of two men who broke into her house, shot her husband (he died of the wound) and then 'one of them put his hand on her bosom and kissed her'. The court, however, was not convinced and while Trolowe's co-defendant was convicted and sentenced to death, Trolowe himself was freed.[47] Finally, bearing witness must have caused Elizabeth Tyrell, a servant on Lord Harberton's estate in county Kildare, no little unease. At a court martial in Dublin in June 1799, she swore that John Bermingham and Andrew Kelly were the men who had murdered Mary and Hester Grattan, two dairymaids on the estate. Tyrell revealed that the accused had forced her to swear an oath of secrecy and that they had told her that 'they had drowned one and shot the other', for they were both Protestants and 'the women [the Grattans] often said that they would discover [i.e inform] if they dare'. Birmingham and Tyrell were duly convicted, but within days, the former, wearing women's clothes, had escaped from gaol and remained at large.[48]

On occasion, some women thought the better of it, and simply refused to proceed with their testimony. At a court martial held in July 1798 in Coleraine of Samuel Robertson, charged with 'being a rebel and displaying rebels colours [a green flag] on the Market House at Ballymena to excite rebellion and felony', Eleanor Hanna withdrew her earlier statement now claiming that 'she does not know what she swore before Mr Babington [a magistrate] nor what the colours were put on the steeple for; cannot form any opinion whether they were for the purposes of rebellion nor does she know that green is the colour worn and used in the rebellion'.[49] A similar attack of amnesia appears to have

45 N.A. Frazer MSS, iv: trial of Gregory Whelan, 28 June 1800.   46 N.A. Rebellion Papers, 620/3/26/13.   47 N.A. Rebellion Papers, 620/5/60/26.   48 In all four men were tried for the murder of the Grattans and all were sentenced to death: their trials from which these details have been drawn are in N.A. Rebellion Papers, 620/5/61/6, 13, 16: Sergeant Robert Cromley of the Invalids was tried for neglect of duty for allowing the esape of Birmingham. He was acquitted.   49 N.A. Rebellion Papers, 620/2/9/23.

overtaken Isabella Murphy, a publican's wife, who bluntly told a court martial, in Coleraine in April 1799 that, in effect, she could remember nothing: she could not recall seeing the defendant, William Caulfield, in her husband's public house, and she had no recollection of when the rebellion occurred.[50] The military courts took a dim view of such back-sliding or 'prevarication': when in March 1799, Honora Doolan refused 'being sworn or to give testimony against the prisoners' whom she had accused of raping and robbing her, a military court at Cork immediately ordered her into custody and freed the accused soldiers.[51] Similarly, a court martial in Waterford in May 1799, gaoled Anne Byrne for 'her gross and frequent prevarication' at the trial of Mogue Shaw, rebel balladeer.[52]

IV

Inevitably, female witnesses figured prominently for the defence where they were clearly considered vital in confirming stories, establishing alibis, giving 'characters' in favour of the accused and, hopefully, eliciting sympathy for the accused. In the tension between sense and sensibility lay the best hope of the accused. Many of the men charged with rebellion claimed that they had acted under duress, and their servant girls were often brought before the court martial (with, be it said, little effect) to confirm this. Thus Margaret Keenan and Isabella Cary, two servants of the noted United Irishman, Alexander Clandennon, swore at a court martial held in Newtownards, county Down, that armed men forced their master to join them; and Elizabeth Patterson told the court that the prisoner was forced to give up his arms. None the less, Clandennon was convicted and sentenced to transportation, though in keeping with the general policy adopted towards leading United Irishmen in Antrim and Down, he was permitted to remove himself to the United States.[53] Similarly, Catherine Sloan, servant to the Revd Adam Hill, charged at Carrickfergus, county Antrim, in August 1798 with having aided and abetted the rebels, told the court martial that her master had been forced to join the rebels; and at Coleraine, county Londonderry, in July of that year, Rose Taggart swore at the court martial of Samuel McCormack, accused of treason and rebellion and 'employing a blacksmith to make him pikes', that men had called to their house and told McCormack that 'if he did not consent to turn out,

---

50 N.A. Rebellion Papers, 620/6/67. 51 N.A. Rebellion Papers, 620/5/60. 52 N.A. Rebellion Papers, 620/6/70/22. 53 N.A. Rebellion Papers, 620/2/15/48.

they would run him through and destroy his house'. Neither Sloan's testimony nor that of Taggart had any effect on the court martial's deliberations and both men were convicted.[54]

So far as alibi evidence is concerned, it has to be said that the alibis lacked both conviction and, indeed, imagination. Jane Connor, in the face of strong evidence that her son had played an active role in the destruction of the barracks at Dunboyne, county Meath could only swear futilely that Thomas Connor had not left the house that night.[55] Again, Hans Weaver, accused of 'treason and seditious practices' at a court martial in Downpatrick, county Down in July 1798 could only produce in his defence his wife and daughter both of whom swore (to no avail) that he was at home at the times in question.[56] And Robert McKeague, charged at the same court martial with 'treason, forcing persons into rebellion and seditious practices', had similarly no success when his wife and daughter claimed that he too had been at home 'from sunrise to sunset'.[57] Perhaps it was the realisation that her brother's case was truely hopeless that led Mary Ann McCracken to spurn Mrs Harry Thompson who had offered to swear that Henry Joy McCracken was in Belfast at the time of the battle of Antrim.[58] Certainly, when Rose Ann McGladdery, Henry Joy's sister-in-law, gave the Revd Robert Gowdy, a noted United Irish leader, an alibi, it had no effect whatsoever, and he was sentenced to hang.[59]

Many women claimed that their menfolk could not have taken part in the crimes laid against them because they could not have left the house without their knowledge. For example, Bridget Walsh swore that her man could not have gone out on the night the Grattan women were murdered because 'she did not sleep at all that night the times were so troublesome, she slept very little during the rebellion'.[60] Others were more elaborate. There was, a cynic might claim, a minor epidemic of sick children at the times in question, which of course resulted in many women having to stay up all night. Thus at a court martial in Galway in March 1799, Bridget Malone swore that her husband could not have left the house to hough cattle without her knowledge because she had tended a sick child all that night and would have seen him go out;[61] Jane Dwyer, at the court martial of her brother, John, at Cashel, county

54 N.A. Rebellion Papers, 620/2/9/6 and 620/2/8/6: perhaps Sloan's testimony had an effect? Hill was merely sentenced to three months' imprisonment and a modest fine. 55 N.A. Rebellion Papers, 620/3/16/14. 56 N.A. Rebellion Papers, 620/2/1/5/9. 57 N.A. Rebellion Papers, 620/2/15/7. 58 Mary McNeil, *The Life and Times of Mary Ann McCracken, 1770-1866: A Belfast Panorama* (Belfast, reprint edn, 1988), p. 182. 59 N.A. Rebellion Papers, 620/2/15/38. 60 N.A. Rebellion Papers, 620/5/61/13. 61 N.A. Rebellion Papers, 620/6/63/6.

Tipperary, in April 1799 for robbery, swore that while getting milk for a sick child, she had seen her brother asleep in his bed;[62] at a court martial in Cork at which Daniel Mahony was charged with raiding a house for arms, Jane Williams swore that he could not have done so because, though she had lain with him, she had not slept, 'her child being uneasy';[63] and in September 1799, at a court martial in Carrick on Suir, county Tipperary, Jean Power swore that Michael Power could not have left the house to commit armed robbery because she had slept in his room (though in separate beds) and that she had been awake all night because 'I had a young child which was very cross'.[64] Alas! Such pleas to sensibility had little or no effect on the army officers who made up the courts martial, and all the above were convicted.

On a number of occasions the alibis offered were more elaborate and centred on the sleeping arrangements in the various households. At a court martial in Tipperary in March 1799, William Ryan, alias 'Ding', and Dennis Carroll, were charged with burning two houses in which five people perished. Mary Ryan offered as an alibi that she and her husband 'Ding', and his brother and their child had all slept in the same bed on the night in question and none could have left without everyone knowing; and it was claimed that on the same night Carroll and his wife and the next door neighbour all slept in the one bed together, thus giving each of them an alibi. Both Carroll and Ryan were sentenced to death.[65] Similarly, though Sarah Flanagan, servant to Michael Rochfort currently on trial for robbery and murder at Cork in September 1798, swore that she had slept in the same bed with Rochfort and his wife and could swear he had not left the house on the night stated, the court martial was unimpressed and he was sentenced to death.[66] Nor was a court martial held at Ennis, county Clare, in August 1798 convinced by the alibi offered on behalf of Timothy Duggan, accused of 'aiding and assisting in the rebellion'. His sister-in-law swore that for a whole week she had slept with her sister and her husband in the one bed and that he had never gone out at night.[67] And Bridget Whelan, a servant girl, was ignored at a court martial in Carrick-on-Suir in September 1799 when she swore that she had slept with her master, John Fanning, and his wife on the night when he was accused of committing armed robbery.[68]

At the trial in Wexford of Michael Breen and Owen Doyle for the gang-rape of Anne Oliver, servant in Richard King's house, both of the common alibi defences were deployed. Oliver told the court three men

62 N.A. Rebellion Papers, 620/6/69/23. 63 N.A. Rebellion Papers, 620/5/60/15. 64 N.A. Rebellion Papers, 620/6/69/26. 65 N.A. Rebellion Papers, 620/6/69/3. 66 N.A. Rebellion Papers, 620/5/60/10. 67 N.A. Rebellion Papers, 620/2/13. 68 N.A. Rebellion Papers, 620/6/69/27.

broke into her master's house, that one Forristal, still at large, 'went into the bed for her and used her ill; that Michael Breen next came into the bed and done what he pleased to her and that then Owen Doyle came into the bed to her and also done what he pleased to her; that she screamed out and they swore they would shoot her if she spoke'. In the prisoner's defence, Mary Doyle, his wife, swore that Owen had never left their room on the night in question: she knew this because she had been up and down with a 'sick child'. And Simon Doyle, Owen's brother, told the court that he had slept in his brother's bed, along with Owen's wife, their servant and their three children. For Breen, the alibi was even more elaborate. Bridget Breen, his sister, testified that for a full two weeks, Michael had slept in her bed along with her mother and sister and that he had never gone out after dark. Unfortunately for Breen and Doyle, there were discrepancies in their respective alibis – the witnesses contradicted each other as to their precise position in the beds – and the two men were convicted.[69]

It would, however, be a mistake to believe that no alibi evidence was ever successful. At a court martial in Dublin in July 1798, Judith Hayes swore that Peter Broe, a deserter from the Clane Yeomanry, had been involved in the massacre of Captain Swayne and the City of Cork Militia on 23 May in Prosperous, county Kildare, and further that he, in fact, had ridden his horse over the corpses of the soldiers. However, various members of his family swore that Broe had slept in the one room with his mother, father, sister, a young boy and a servant on the fateful night. Broe was acquitted but the court committed him to gaol on the grounds that he was simply too dangerous to be set at liberty.[70] Again, Nelly Reilly's alibi for Philip Hickey, charged with 'acting, aiding, and assisting in the rebellion' and tried at a court martial in Cashel, county Tipperary, was accepted. She claimed that after he had come in on the evening in question, 'she bolted the door of the house and being up before him next morning, she again unbolted it when the prisoner was within'.[71] Similarly, Mary Bell, a servant girl, swore at a court martial in Galway in February 1799 that Laurence Egan, charged with cattle-houghing, tendering oaths, and attending United Irish meetings, could not have left the house without her knowledge as 'her bed was next the door'. Her statement was accepted and Egan was acquitted.[72] Even the 'sick child' gambit was successful on occasion. Bridget Murphy, another servant girl, swore that Patrick Cole could not have murdered the informer William Cole of Moneybeg, county Carlow,

69 N.A. Frazer MSS, iv, trial of Owen Doyle and Michael Breen, 27 March 1799. 70 N.A. Rebellion Papers, 620/3/16/16. 71 N.A. Rebellion Papers, 620/3/22/1. 72 N.A. Rebellion Papers, 620/6/63/3.

because he had slept in the same bed as his tenant, James Mooney (who, the court was told, paid him 27*s.* a year in rent) on the night of the crime. She could swear that no one could have left the house without her knowledge as she had been looking after a sick child all night. The court martial at Carlow barracks accepted her testimony and Patrick Cole was acquitted; in fairness, the evidence placing him at the scene of the crime appeared quite nebulous.[73]

At this distance, it is quite impossible to explain why the testimony of some witnesses was accepted and that of others rejected. The weight of the evidence was clearly important but so too was the witness's bearing, character and social standing; and no doubt the temper of the times and the political temperature in the locality also played a part. At a court martial in Cork in June 1799, nine men were charged with robbing the house of the Revd William Stopford in March 1798. Margaret Croneen swore that one of the nine, Dennis Donoghue, had not left his house all night, but unlike the other defence witnesses she had furnished herself with a 'character' from the local parish priest who testified to her honesty. Donoghue was freed but the others were found guilty.[74] Similarly, when William Curtain and Thomas Ward were accused of being United Irish captains, and of conspiracy to murder, the testimony of Mrs Peard, Curtain's employer, was crucial. She told the court martial in Cork in September 1799 that she, a widow, had offered Curtain employment on very strong recommendations, that he had lived in her house, that he was honest and sober, that he had bought and sold cattle on her behalf and that he could have fled but had not. In the face of such weighty testimony, the evidence of the informer was discredited and both men were acquitted.[75] Something similar seems to have happened at the court martial in Clonmel of James Gibbons, alias Fitzgibbon, 'charged with being an emissary to the rebels'. Elinor Weldon, the leading witness for the prosecution found herself denounced in no uncertain terms by Honor Mahony for the defence. Mahony told the court that 'the parish priest at Killenaule [had] excommunicated her [Weldon] and banished her out of the place ... because she was a common woman, a whore'. Notwithstanding this testimony, Gibbons was in fact found guilty and sentenced to death, but a clearly uneasy Cornwallis reviewed the case and mitigated his sentence to transportation for life.[76]

In general, attempts by female evidences to discredit the prosecution witnesses had little success. When Jonathan Finn and Patrick Hart were charged in Galway with 'levying war' on the King, Elizabeth Conniff

73 N.A. Rebellion Papers, 620/5/58/11. 74 N.A. Rebellion Papers, 620/5/60/20. 75 N.A. Rebellion Papers, 620/5/60/12. 76 N.A. Rebellion Papers, 620/6/69.

did her best to cast doubts on the trustworthiness of the main witness. Conniff stated that in the course of her work as a rent-collector on behalf of one, Daly, she frequently had dealings with the prime informer, Peter Galvin, because he was constantly in arrears. Drawing on her experience of him, she swore that she would not believe a word he said. To no avail, for both men were convicted and sentenced to serve abroad for life.[77] Again, at the trial of Revd Thomas Ledlie Birch at Lisburn, county Antrim, an attack on the main witness, Francis Gordon (he swore that Birch's sermons 'made me detest the present government') came to nothing. In an extraordinary development, Francis Gordon was denounced by his own mother. 'From his youth up I never could depend on what he said', Jane Gordon told the court martial, adding: 'He never yet told me a perfectly true story'. None the less, Birch was convicted: he was, however, permitted to exile himself to America.[78] Again in the north, at a court martial at Downpatrick in July 1798, John Kelly was charged with 'treason, having a command in the rebel army and seditious practices'. Two women, Jane Garvin and Agnes Kearns, pronounced Jeremiah McKibbin, the chief prosecution witness, and a former employee of theirs, to be entirely untrustworthy, he being both a thief and a liar. Garvin told the court that she had left out some money which he had promptly stolen, but she added, 'when he confessed with a smile ... I thought a pity of him' and she had kept him on. As for Kearns, she told the court martial that 'to the best of my knowledge, I never knew him [McKibbin] to tell the truth unless I knew it before'. The evidence of both women was disregarded, the verdict was guilty, and the death sentence was swiftly carried out.[79]

V

So far, we have looked at the role of female evidences in trials that, ostensibly, appear straightforward: but even a casual glance through the courts martial records reveals a zeal for the prosecution of former rebels which in a number of instances quickly developed into a lust for persecution. In this latter endeavour, women were heavily involved. Elsewhere in this volume, Ruan O'Donnell has detailed the activities of Bridget ('Biddy') Dolan or Doolan who was a prime witness against many Wicklow United Irishmen.[80] But there were a number of Biddy Dolans throughout the country, and there can be little doubt that they were

77 N.A. Rebellion Papers, 620/6/63/25. 78 N.A. Rebellion Papers, 620/2/9/56. 79 N.A. Rebellion Papers, 620/2/15/12: unusually, the court martial note states that the sentence was carried out. 80 See below, pp 87-112.

groomed by loyalist magistrates to testify at courts martial in order to destroy those local United Irish leaders who looked as if they might escape punishment for their alleged crimes. In the 'White Terror' that unfolded in parts of the south-east after Vinegar Hill, female approvers like Biddy Dolan were often the preferred instrument of loyalist retribution.

One clear example of this occurred in Cork in November 1799, at the court martial of John Devereux of Shilbeggan, county Wexford. He was accused of high treason and of complicity in the burning of Protestants at the barn in Scullobogue: but in reality he was on trial because he was wealthy, socially prominent and had been very active among the United Irishmen during the rebellion in Wexford. The principal witness against him was Elizabeth Jacob. She told the court martial that when she was at Taghmon, county Wexford, Devereux had ordered a man to be shot and she swore that she had heard him give the order to burn the barn at Scullabogue. She also revealed that she saw Nancy Lett approach Devereux and 'offer to turn to mass and to marry him', if he would spare her, but instead he had spurned her and had thrust her back into the barn. Furthermore, she heard the prisoner order the burning of a school in which a husband, his wife and their child perished.

It was Devereux's good fortune that the trial took place in November 1799 because by that date the furies ignited by the rebellion had to an extent abated; and Cornwallis's close scrutiny of courts martials kept sharp practice within limits. Moreover, a certain amount of case law from courts martial had been produced and this was to his advantage. In addition, Devereux, a wealthy middleman, was determined to have the best advice available and he had, following recent practice, fee'd a civilian lawyer to defend him at the court martial. Under relentless cross-examination, Jacob's story crumbled. It was soon shown that she had only the vaguest idea of when the various incidents she described had taken place – for example, she thought that the battle of Vinegar Hill had taken place on Easter Monday 'or some such day'. Devereux's lawyer elicited the damaging admission from her that she could neither read nor write (what price now her information?) and he successfully raised doubts as to whether Nancy Lett was in fact dead or whether a school-house with people inside had really been burned.[81]

In his defence, Devereux produced a 'character' from none other than General Sir William Fawcett, commanding at Wexford, and several witnesses came forward to deny that he had been at Vinegar Hill. In

---

81 Musgrave failed to record the 'deaths' of a 'Nancy Lett' or of those in the school-house: this silence is surely significant.

a damaging development for the prosecution, Devereux showed that Elizabeth Jacob had, in effect, a 'history'. She was known under various names – Jacob, O'Connor and Roberts – and there was a strong inference that she was a common garrison prostitute hired to prosecute at courts martial. Henry Sheppard, a member of the Royal Irish Artillery, swore that Jacob had come into the camp at Duncannon shortly before the rising and that some of the women there had 'grumbled at her being in the barracks' because she was or appeared to be unmarried. Jacob's evidence was fatally undermined. None the less, Devereux was found guilty, but because the court martial acknowledged that 'there are so many contradictions in the evidence', he was only sentenced to seven years' transportation. In post-rebellion Cork, this was tantamount to an acquittal, and the piquancy of the sentence was not lost on observers, for all were well aware that John's brother, Walter, had been convicted and hanged on the same evidence a year earlier.[82]

There was a similar debacle in November 1798 at the trial by court martial of William Barker, 'a brewer and merchant of Enniscorthy and a rebel general'. On the face of it, an impressive array of (mostly female) evidences produced enough damning evidence to convict him twice over. In particular, Elizabeth Stacey told the court that she had known the prisoner socially before the rebellion – she kept a public house and a ball-alley – but that in the rebellion she had seen Barker pike her husband. Elizabeth Plumber swore that the rebels regarded Barker as a general among them; and Mrs Valentine Gill claimed that the rebels called him variously general, colonel or captain. Barker's defence, however, was formidable. He produced a number of character witnesses who testified that in the rebellion he had helped loyalists; for instance, Mrs Anne Patton, 'a Protestant and of a Protestant family in this country' told how Barker had protected between twenty and thirty Protestants and she hotly denied she had seen him dance around a tree of liberty 'to the music of Miss Carty'. Crucially, Brigadier General Francis Grose, military commander in Wexford from July to September 1798, told the court that in all that time Mrs Stacey had made no accusations about the murder of her husband. Moreover, under cross-examining, Mrs Stacey admitted that she had no licence for liquour at her premises; but she denied that she had been forced 'by threats of being deprived of the means of subsistence [her beer licence] in case of refusal' to give false testimony against Barker. The case was thrown out and Barker acquitted. In a memorial to Cornwallis, Barker claimed that Archibald Jacob

82 N.A. Rebellion Papers, 620/5/60/22: Musgrave noted with disgust that when Walter Devereux was taken he had protections from five general officers on him. *Memoirs*, p. 500.

(whom we have already met) was behind the trumped-up charges, and that the magistrate had been moved by 'active malice' to haul him before a court martial.[83] Barker's case, and that of Devereux (and some others), were clearly of a piece with those involving Biddy Dolan in Wicklow.

In other instances, it would appear that family and local rivalries and hatreds found a forum in the courts martial. At the trial in Tipperary town in March 1799 of Timothy Fahy, charged with attempting to swear a soldier into the United Irishmen, the chief prosecution witness was Denis Dwyer. The defence maintained that a quarrell between the two men over Peg O'Donnell lay behind the accusation. A witness told the court that Dwyer had sworn in a public house that he would marry O'Donnell 'if Tim Fahy would clear her but by God if he does not clear her I will be up with him'.[84] Again, at a court martial in Maguiresbridge, county Fermanagh, of Robert Lyttle and a number of other men charged with being 'unlawfully assembled for seditious purposes' (in fact they had been at a wake), it emerged that the main prosecution witness had fought with Lyttle over a girl. The case was thrown out.[85] So too was that against Denis Brian, tried at Wexford in July 1799 for 'aiding, assisting and abetting in the murder of one Prior, a guager … during the rebellion'. Brian successfully claimed that the main prosecution witness, his own brother-in-law, hated him. Brian told the court: 'The prosecutor swears against me because I married his wife's sister. He hoped as there was no son to get the farm to himself. He has often threatened my life'. Fortunately for Brian, Eleanor Dempsey, a witness to the Prior murder, failed to identify him as being among those present, and he was acquitted.[86] Not so fortunate was John Concannon, charged with being a United Irishman and tried by court martial at Galway in June 1799. Three members of the Johnston family, Lucy, the mother and Susan and Mary, her daughters, told the court that Concannon had been overjoyed at news of the French landing in Mayo, that he had 'leaped and jumped about [saying] that there was as many French come into Tuam [county Galway] as would cover a mile … [and that] he would have a longer pike made than he ever had'. Susan Johnston added that Concannon had told her that she would get back the lands 'that my father was before possessed of'. Lucy Johnston was questioned by the court: 'Have your family any grudge against the prisoner?' To which she made a revealing answer: 'He did endeavour to

83 Musgrave, *Memoirs*, p. 346: Barker's trial is at N.A. Frazer MSS, iv, and his letter to Cornwallis on 12 November 1798 is Frazer MSS, i, no. 39. 84 N.A. Rebellion Papers, 620/6/69/2. 85 N.A. Rebellion Papers, 620/6/62. 86 N.A. Frazer MSS, iv, 20 July 1799.

scandalise our family'. Other evidence was given that Concannon had
contradicted Lucy Johnston at an earlier court martial, and that she had
sworn to have revenge on him. One witness claimed that Johnston had
said, 'If truth would hang him, he would never return from gaol';
another that she had vowed 'She would hang the prisoner if she could'.
Despite such apparently weighty testimony, Concannon was convicted
and sentenced to death, though this sentence was later mitigated to military service abroad for life.[87]

VI

The final role for women in the courts martial of the rebels lay in their
involvement in the petitions which were sent up to Lord Cornwallis
seeking mercy or a reduction in the sentence. Those historians interested in crime and criminals in the past have long recognised that such
petitions were an integral part of the judicial process and a vital legit-
imising element in the state's administration of justice. As V.A.C.
Gatrell points out, in the English context 'the felon who sought mercy
from the King exalted the King by repaying him with gratitude and
deference'.[88] Petitions to the lord lieutenant of Ireland fulfilled a similar
function and were closely scrutinised by the authorities for that reason.

Some women – and it was mostly women who petitioned – sought
the intercession or mediation of well-born or aristocratic ladies,
undoubtedly calculating that such pleas carried greater weight than
their own. Thus Lady Sarah Napier wrote on behalf of one Hampson,
conveying at the request of his wife 'some circumstances that may possibly be of service to save her husband';[89] and Lady Louisa Conolly[90]
and Lady Cecilia La Touche also became involved in deserving cases.
The latter wrote on behalf of one Murphy seeking his release from
Arklow gaol where he had been languishing for months. A note at the
bottom of the page illustrates the effect that such high-level intervention could have: 'This is the case Lady Cecilia La Touche mentioned to
Lord Castlereagh. Lord Castlereagh desires this may be done if there
should be no particular objection to it'.[91] However, powerful friends,

87 N.A. Rebellion Papers, 620/6/63/19. 88 Gatrell, *Hanging Tree*, p. 200. 89 N.A.
Frazer MSS, ii, no. 101. 90 N.A. Prisoners' Petitions, no. 427, June 1800: Lady Louisa
wrote on behalf of Robert and Rowland Goodman; and see her efforts on behalf of Lady
Pamela (Campbell, *Edward and Pamela*, pp 185-6; Thomas Moore, *Lord Edward
Fitzgerald* (Glasgow edn, N.D.), p. 274). 91 N.A., Rebellion Papers, 620/51/72: the La
Touches had a reputation for benevolence. See the affecting letter addressed to 'Mrs
Peter Lettuce' [i.e. La Touche] by the insurgent leader Joseph Holt. The letter is pub-

real or imagined, could not always or even often soften the hearts of the authorities. When the sisters of William Byrne of Ballymanus, sentenced to death, appealed for mercy and cited the Marchioness of Buckingham as 'our only relative of consequence sufficient to give any weight to our application', their pleas were given short shrift, and Byrne was duly hanged. It was noteworthy, however, that the person who scrutinised the sisters' petition took pains to point out that the Byrnes had no connection whatsoever with the Marchioness.[92]

For those who had no influential contacts, there was still a chance of a mitigated sentence or even a release. James Doyle's wife in her petition pointed out that her husband had been whipped twice and had been eighteen months in gaol. Major Swan, a leading Dublin magistrate, to whom the petition was referred, approved Doyle's release, but he noted that Doyle had given information and 'on that account only' should be shown clemency.[93]

Most petitions, however, appear to have had little effect.[94] Grace Sampson's deferential address to Cornwallis seeking his intervention to free her husband, William, the noted United Irish lawyer, banished from Ireland and now incarcerated in a Portuguese gaol, fell on deaf ears. She wrote, 'If there be any apparent presumption or infringement against the rules of decorum in this address from a distressed woman, I beg your excellency will attribute all such appearances to my ignorance of the properest forms and to the urgency of my suit'. Cornwallis, however, did not intervene and it was to be some years before Sampson was able to make her way to the United States.[95] And of course, there was always the hard luck story. A petition from the wife of the United Irishman, John Temple of Rasharkin, county Antrim, seeking to have his sentence of transportation reduced, and supported by his local rector, was abruptly halted by the news that the prison ship had already sailed for New South Wales.[96]

VII

In his study of the prisoners' petitions generated by the English judicial system, Gatrell writes that 'a phantasmagoric array of characters weaves

lished in Thomas Bartlett, ' "Masters of the Mountains"; the insurgents careers of Michael Dwyer and Joseph Holt, 1798-1803' in Ken Hannigan (ed.), *Wicklow: History and Society* (Dublin, 1994), pp 379-410. 92 *The Trial of Billy Byrne of Ballymanus* (new edition of 1799 work, Wicklow, 1996), pp 67-9. 93 N.A. Prisoners' Petitions, no. 354. 94 This is a subject which requires a good deal more research. 95 N.A., Rebellion Papers, 620/47/10. 96 N.A. Prisoners' Petitions, no. 783.

its way through this vast archive … In these papers we hear the voices of the common people'.[97] The Irish historian, too, trolling through the neglected records of the courts martial and State Prisoners' Petitions cannot but arrive at a similar conclusion.[98] The voices of those facing execution, flogging, transportation or forced military service (and hoping for acquittal) – and of their loved ones – ring through with an immediacy and urgency that the more measured notes of the political record – the pamphlet, the debate, the letter – can rarely achieve. There is in the court martial records a merciful absence of windy rhetoric, and this is particularly evident in the testimony of female witnesses. Everywhere in Ireland, and not just in the traditional zones of the rebellion, whether accusing, defending, or pleading, 'the women of 'ninety Eight', in bearing witness had their say.[99]

97 Gatrell, *Hanging Tree*, p. 199. 98 I hope to complete a full study of the courts martial used to suppress the Rebellion. 99 My thanks to Kevin Whelan, Richard Alymer, Tim O'Neill and Dáire Keogh for their comments on this essay.

Bridget 'Croppy Biddy' Dolan: Wicklow's anti-heroine of 1798

Ruan O'Donnell

The 'women' were the diametric opposite to the 'men of '98', an unmistakably inclusive term now inseparable from the image of an idealized pikeman as presented by Oliver Sheppard in his fine commemorative memorials. That the men represented the human face of the rebellion is appropriate insofar as the military history of that year is concerned but if the recent progressive trend of social, cultural and political re-evaluation of 1798 is to advance other aspects of the experience must be addressed. A comprehensive treatment of women who found themselves within the rebel camps and behind their lines is beyond the scope of this chapter but an assessment of the experiences of Bridget Dolan may be instructive.

I

Dolan's reputation, although that of an acknowledged member of the United Irish forces, sits uneasily in the company of the martyred Betsy Gray, Dublin's Molly Weston and Wexford's Mary Doyle.[1] Her name is equally incongruous when listed alongside the other more celebrated Wicklow women of 1798; Anne Devlin of Cronebeg, 'Mary of the Mountains' Dwyer of Knockandarragh, the anonymous 'Moving Magazine' and other lesser figures.[2] While a very minor character in the

1 Thomas Cloney, *A personal narrative ... 1798* (Dublin, 1832), pp 41-3; Thomas Pakenham, *The year of liberty, the story of the great Irish Rebellion of 1798* (London, 1969), pp 231-6; Daniel Gahan, *The People's Rising, Wexford 1798* (Dublin, 1995), p. 132 and *Songs and ballads of '98* (Wexford, 1938), pp 30-1. 2 Richard Robert Madden, *The United Irishmen, their lives and Times* (Dublin, 1842-6), 4 vols, III, pp 404-18; Joseph Holt, *Memoirs of Joseph Holt, General of the Irish rebels in 1798* (ed.) Thomas Crofton Croker, 2 vols (London, 1838), I, pp 50-3; Joseph H. Fowler, *Chapters in '98 History* (London, 1938), 'Leaflet no. 11, The Women of '98'; Luke Cullen Papers, National Library of Ireland, MS 8339, p. 118 and 'They [*sic*] life and times of Joseph Holt', Mitchel Library, Sydney, MS A2024, p. 25.

grand scheme of rebellion history Dolan was notorious to her contemporaries and must, therefore, have been far better known than either Devlin or Dwyer. Devlin's fame was largely posthumous recognition which sprang from decades of near complete obscurity, at least beyond the borders of Wicklow and Dublin. It came too late to rescue her from the poverty into which she had descended in later life and stirred the consciences of nationalists all the more as a result.[3]

Dolan, by contrast, achieved the dubious distinction of incurring the opprobrium of Lord Lieutenant Cornwallis in 1799 while being simultaneously reviled in nationalist quarters for her role in the prosecution of the prominent Wicklow rebel leader William Byrne of Ballymanus. Byrne's execution in September 1799 was felt with much greater keenness than that of several other senior Wicklow United Irish leaders and it could be argued that the subsequent reverence in which he was held was due in no small part to Dolan's input. Certainly, the notion that he had been unjustly sentenced rested largely upon the contention that he had fallen victim to her perjury. Moreover, those seeking to highlight this infamous role had access to her testimony as early as 1800 when a transcript of the proceedings and other relevant documents were published in Dublin. The trial text apparently inspired the author of the popular ballad 'Billy Byrne of Ballymanus' in which Dolan's name appeared and the song was probably instrumental in fixing it in south Leinster folk memory.[4]

Dolan was established as an important 'woman of '98' by 1800 in Wicklow, Wexford and Dublin, if not further afield. nationalist commentators accorded her no such status but she merits consideration in that her involvement in the rebellion was wholly voluntary and proactive notwithstanding her perceived treachery in its aftermath. That much of this experience is documented is significant as it spawned a series of valuable depositions between 1798 and 1801. The items attributed to Dolan are problematic but they throw much light on the dynamics of the insurgent armies of Wicklow and north Wexford when not engaged in combat and the varied experiences of the women who

3 See 'The life, imprisonment, sufferings and death of Anne Devlin ... by a Milesian [Luke Cullen]', N.L.I., MS 9761 published in part by John Finegan as *Anne Devlin, Patriot and Heroine* (Dublin, 1968); Madden, *United Irishmen*, III, pp 407, 416-17 and *Weekly Celt*, November 1857. 4 Miles Byrne, *Memoirs of Miles Byrne* (Shannon, 1972), 2 vols, I, pp 158-9, 195, 323-4 and *The tryal of William Byrne of Ballymanus County of Wicklow, Esq* ... (Dublin, 1800), p. 51. See also Conor O'Brien, 'The Byrnes of Ballymanus' in Ken Hannigan and William Nolan (eds), *Wicklow, History and Society* (Dublin, 1994), pp 305-39 and Georges-Denis Zimmerman, *Songs of Irish Rebellion, political street ballads and rebel songs, 1780-1900* (Dublin, 1967), p. 149.

shared their lot. It also permits some insight into the process through which Dolan defected from the republican to the loyalist cause in September 1798. This was a comparatively rare occurrence for a woman but her active role in the post-rebellion 'white terror' visited on Wicklow by vengeful loyalists was perhaps unique. 'Lady Betty', the alleged Kerry murderess turned Roscommon hangwoman of Whiteboys and rebels, is probably her closest equivalent.[5]

The first comprehensive published account of 'Croppy Biddy's' life and times appeared in 1872 as an appendix to W.J. Fitzpatrick's popular sixth edition of *The Sham Squire; and the informers of 1798*. This inauspicious forum signalled the tenor of the piece which was based around a long extract from Luke Cullen's 'Clondalkin Manuscript', which the then deceased Carmellite monk had kept at the Mount Saint Joseph's monastery where he had lived and worked until January 1858.[6] While this remains the single most informative source for her biography the naked prejudices of the compiler permeate the narrative and detract from its usefulness. Cullen's somewhat hysterical account as propagated by Fitzpatrick obscures the fact that Dolan was one of the most important of two dozen or so agents employed by the administrators of Wicklow's court-martial program to bring United Irishmen to justice. The most effective state's witnesses tended to be former insurgents motivated by either conviction or, more generally, in hope of eliciting mitigation in their own cases. Such testimony, when coupled with that advanced by loyalists who had been prisoners of the rebels in 1798, was extremely difficult to refute and resulted in the passing of at least eighty-seven death sentences by Wicklow court martials in 1799.[7]

Dolan was an ideal witness as she had been acquainted with many of the leading personalities of the south Wicklow United Irish cells from their inception in the late spring of 1797 and was prepared to incrimi-

---

5 O'Ceirin (eds), *Women of Ireland*, pp 20-1. 6 William James Fitzpatrick, *The Sham Squire and the informers of 1798* (Dublin, 1866), p. 327. Cullen, from Bray, county Wicklow, devoted much energy to collecting first hand accounts of the rebellion and its aftermath from south Leinster veterans in the early 1800s. While it is clear that George Kearns, James Doyle and Laurence O'Keefe had known, or at least observed, Dolan in 1798 many more of those he interviewed were only familiar with her reputation. Luke Cullen, *Insurgent Wicklow, 1798, the story as written by Rev. Bro. Luke Cullen, O.D.C. (1793-1859) with material from other MSS* (Dublin, 1948) (ed.) Myles V. Ronan, pp 71, 73. See also R.R. Madden, *The life and times of Robert Emmet* (Glasgow, n.d.), p. 124; Charles Dickson, *The life of Michael Dwyer with some account of his companions* (Dublin, 1944), pp 411-12 and *Irish Book Lover*, May-June 1929, pp 56-7. 7 See Ruan O'Donnell, 'Marked for Botany Bay'; The Wicklow United Irishmen and the development of political transportation from Ireland, 1791-1806' (PhD thesis, Australian National University, 1996), chapter five.

nate them to magistrates. She named Johnny Toole as a 'head rebel' and implicated him in the election of an officer. Elsewhere Dolan described Tom Cooke of Carnew as 'a secretary among the United Men and great Numbers were sworn by him'.[8] She had attended several of the pivotal outdoor 'night meetings' which had been contrived by United Irish agitators during the winter of 1797-8. These nocturnal gatherings presaged a brutal campaign of counter-insurgency and had heralded the conspicuously early spread of martial law to Wicklow. Dolan's precise position in the organization, however, has hitherto been misrepresented whenever addressed and the opportunity to closely examine the activities and status of women has been squandered.[9]

She was born in the south Wicklow village of Carnew in 1777 to an impoverished thatcher whose profession necessitated frequent absences. Her mother was reputedly an inattentive and remote woman who neglected the education of what was probably her only daughter as well as other fundamental aspects of her upbringing; she was probably illiterate and signed a rebellion era deposition 'X'. The extent of this deprivation is unknown but it was cited by Cullen's sources as an explanation for Bridget's rapid drift from infancy to political apostasy in her late teens, which was presented in terms of an incremental process of moral degeneration.[10]

The 1780s were a time of national political upheaval in which constitutional and economic reforms were sought with increasing vociferousness in the Irish Parliament. The Wicklow economy underwent massive growth in the decade as the linen, quarrying, mining and woollen goods industries boomed. As the 1790s progressed popular disenchantment with the handling of the reform question accelerated Wicklow's transformation from one of the most passive districts in Ireland to a hot bed of seditious intrigue. By January 1798 the county possessed the largest United Irish force in Leinster and a notably radical county leadership.[11]

It is impossible to say whether Dolan's flirtation with the United Irishmen from 1797 reflected sincere ideological commitment to republicanism but it proved shallow and ephemeral. It is probably unrealistic

8 Trial of William Byrne, p. 9 and 14 November 1799, National Archives, 620/17/30/42. 9 Trial of William Byrne, p. 9; Fitzpatrick, Sham Squire, p. 328 and Camden to Portland, 15 November 1797, P.R.O., H.O. 100/66/60. 10 Information of Bridget Dolan, 3 October 1799, N.A., 620/17/3. See also Cullen quoted in Fitzpatrick, Sham Squire, pp 327-8. 11 Edward Wakefield, Account of Ireland, statistical and political (London, 1812), 2 vols, II, pp 306, 377, 409; The last county, the emergence of Wicklow as a county, 1606-1845 (Wicklow, 1993) and Arthur Young, A Tour in Ireland, 1777-1779 (London, 1780), new ed. (Shannon, 1970), 2 vols, I, pp 52, 283.

to assume that the young and illiterate Dolan possessed an in depth appreciation of prevailing political issues but her residency in the heart of Earl Fitzwilliam's bailiwick would have ensured exposure to the main controversies at a popular level. Questions of 'Protestant Ascendancy' and the concession of political rights to Catholics were not simply theoretical matters in the predominantly Protestant village of Carnew where it was alleged that no church was permitted for the use of its minority creed. Carnew's conservatives were irritated that the absentee Whig Fitzwilliam dominated the selection of county level representation and his recall from the Viceroyalty in 1795 unleashed considerable ferment.[12]

When, if ever, such controversies impinged on the life of Dolan is unknown but she probably remained oblivious in 1791 when the young teenager reputedly mixed with boys and rode asses which belonged to visiting 'tinkers'. She also apparently learned to master the horses which had been brought into Carnew's forge for shodding and developed her considerable flair for riding animals of all sizes. This was an uncommon skill for a poor girl and one which enabled her to associate with active rebel corps in June 1798 during their exhausting traverses of the Wicklow mountains. Yet what might easily have been mere childhood adventures yielded disquieting results as they were not balanced by parental attention. Cullen's sources implied that the attainment of Dolan's life skills had come at a heavy price, in figurative if not literal terms. He claimed: 'this pampered informer of the county Wicklow, at thirteen years of age, was an avowed and proclaimed harlot, steeped in every crime that her age would admit of; and her precocity to vice was singular'.[13]

The Dolans of Carnew, Coolatin and Croneyhorn were nominally Catholic in the 1790s but Bridget's personal ignorance of 'Christian truths' had marked her in Cullen's estimation as an 'infidel vieing [*sic*] with, and even outdoing, the vilest soldiers, in unheard of blasphemous language. Every sentence that she spoke was sacrilegiously sealed with some person of the Blessed Trinity'.[14] Such conduct condemned Dolan as an outcast from the spiritual as well as the temporal world and it moved the deeply religious Cullen to some of his most venomous language. She was described in unmistakably misogynistic terms as a 'female hyena', 'witch', a 'virago' and a 'libidinous wretch'.[15] The sing-

---

12 See L.M. Cullen, 'Politics and Rebellion: Wicklow in the 1790s' in Hannigan and Nolan (eds), *Wicklow: History and Society*, pp 411–502. 13 Cullen quoted in Fitzpatrick, *Sham Squire*, p. 328. 14 Ibid., pp 329–30. See Church of Ireland Parish Registers, Carnew and Catholic Baptismal Registers, Carnew (Tomacork). 15 Fitzpatrick, *Sham Squire*, pp 331, 334.

ling out of Dolan's physical traits, such the contention that she possessed a 'face of the most absolute impudence that ever a woman was heiressed to', points to a less than objective assessment of her experiences.[16] In Cullen's eyes the ambit of Dolan's betrayal was comprehensive and her corruption absolute: she had transgressed against her sex, her creed, her comrades, her ideology and even her humanity. This diatribe did not simply reflect the prejudices of a middle-aged monk, however, as it mirrored William Byrne's blistering condemnation of Dolan at his trial from which Cullen may have taken his cue. On 1 July 1799 the beleaguered Byrne described his accuser as a 'monster of immorality, whose heart is not only divested of all the softness of her sex, but of every sentiment of humanity'. He also captured something of her renowned levity when he claimed to have been chilled by 'that laugh which made one shudder to see the human nature so depraved'.[17]

Nevertheless, her bad reputation and her apparent work as a prostitute did not prevent Dolan from securing a position in Carnew as servant to William McCormick. It is unknown when this service commenced but it may be significant that it terminated in or just before January 1798. This coincided with the period when the United Irish movement consolidated its position in the half barony of Shillelagh where it then boasted 1,080 members. The agitation they fomented by arms raiding and proselytisation may well have compromised Dolan's job and she claimed to have attended an illegal meeting at the townland of Tombreen during that month.

December 1797-January 1798 was also the period in which informers provided the authorities in southern Wicklow with their first real insight into the nature of sedition in the district. One of those most likely to have been made privy to such disclosures was Dolan's employer McCormick who, from October 1796, was a member of Captain Thomas Swan's Carnew yeoman infantry. It is possible, therefore, that Dolan had withdrawn from his household owing to suspicions arising from her own politics or those of her associates. McCormick's duties entailed patrolling the neighbourhood to guard against the movement of republican emissaries and arms raiders but his personal zeal marked him as an extremist.[18]

Such tendencies came to light in early January 1798 when elements of the Carnew garrison, probably members of the North Cork Militia

16 Cullen, N.L.I., MS 8339, p. 118. 17 *Trial of William Byrne*, pp 51-2. 18 Ibid., pp 6, 9 and William Ridgeway, *Trial of William Michael Byrne* (Dublin, 1799), pp 94-5. See also Cullen, *Insurgent*, p. 20; Information of John Kavanagh, 4 January 1798, N.A., State of the Country Papers, 1017/612; Wainwright to Fitzwilliam, 10 December 1797, N.L.I., MIC 5641 and O'Donnell, 'Holt', pp 101-4.

who had been based in Shillelagh for over a month, arrested an inebriated Patrick Doyle for uttering 'improper words'. McCormick and another yeoman visited Doyle in the guardhouse and proceeded to interrogate him using the 'half hanging' technique of repeated partial strangulation. Dolan's employer, therefore, was an active participant, if not the prime instigator, of one of the first recorded bouts of torture practised in southern Leinster in the rebellion era. The incident was publicized nationally by the anti-government paper the radical *Press* and may have convinced the pragmatic Dolan that the time had come to move on.[19]

While clearly on the periphery of Carnew's United Irish underground prior to the rebellion, Dolan would not have been a *bone fide* member of the organisation's basic twelve 'man' cell or simple society. There is no reliable evidence that she or any Wicklow women was ever formally inducted and she would not, therefore, have sworn the 'military oath' which bound recruits to obey orders issued by their superiors and to turn out when called to aid their French allies. It is highly probable, however, that Dolan was administered the basic 'oath of secrecy' which might have gained her entry to the meetings where dues paying and voting conspirators congregated on a monthly basis. Lieutenant-Colonel Caldwell and his court-martial panel deemed it 'probable' that Dolan had taken the secrecy oath and may well have had stronger grounds to suspect this than they saw fit to indicate on the trial record. Dolan, moreover, disclaimed knowledge of the appointment of officers within the United Irish forces, a task which pre-occupied all full members at least once every three months prior to April–May 1798.[20] The secrecy oath could be given by any United Irishman and simply bound the taker not to disclose the business the organisation. While generally the first step taken to initiate new members it was primarily intended to discourage loose talk by those who had been or were likely to become privy to sensitive information. It also served the purpose of attuning the recipient to the concept of traitorous dealings and the likely consequences, a point underlined by the gruesome murder of suspected informer in Blessington in August 1797.[21]

The 'military oath', sometimes called the 'second oath', however, was a more pro-active undertaking which could only be given by men 'who had the authority' in south Wicklow.[22] When Dolan claimed to

19 *Press*, 20 January 1798. See also Major Joseph Hardy to Fitzwilliam, 24 December 1797, N.L.I., MIC 5641. 20 *Trial of William Byrne*, p. 8. 21 Information of John Tyson, 17 January 1798, N.A., S.O.C., 1017/62, Holt MS, p. 23, *Faulkner's Dublin Journal*, 10 August 1797 and *Hibernian Chronicle*, 18 August 1797. 22 Information of John Tyson, 17 January 1798, N.A., S.O.C., 1017/62. See also Information of Hugh Ollaghan [Woolaghan], 2 January 1798, ibid.

have attended a meeting of thirty persons at Tombreen in January 1798 at which 'women as well as men' were sworn she was almost certainly referring to the widely disseminated secrecy oath. William Byrne, a formally elected United Irish captain, detected an improbability in Dolan's account on this issue and queried in his cross-examination of her whether 'it was usual to swear United Irishmen in the presence of women'. A misprint or transcription error in the published trial account has Dolan declaring 'I was a Captain sworn at Tombreens [*sic*]' but the context of the passage clearly shows that this comment should have read 'It was a Captain'.[23] The prevalence of such oath giving practices evidently lay behind the declaration of north Wicklow magistrate William Colthurst that 'every woman from Tinahinch [*sic*] Bridge to Roundwood was a United Irish man'.[24]

II

The Carnew district where Dolan lived was the principal stronghold of Wicklow's ultra-loyalist elements in the late 1790s and fielded a considerable number of yeomanry corps after their inception in October 1796. The village was the commercial and political hub of south Wicklow's conservative interest stemming from the heavily planted Fitzwilliam and Carysfort estates and the excess pro-government manpower was channelled into supplementary units such as the sixty-strong Tinahely 'True Blues'. Wicklow's yeomanry corps were almost exclusively Protestant in membership and all the southern units were sympathetic towards the precepts of the Orange Order if not affiliated with the three official lodges which had been established in their midst by 1797. This powerful grass roots loyalist bloc was a volatile resource and was prone to extreme responses when provoked by United Irish arms raiding in the baronies of Shillelagh and Ballinacor South in the winter of 1797-8.[25]

The maltreatment of rebel suspects in Carnew gaol set in train grievances that led inexorably to the execution of dozens of loyalist prisoners after the rebellion commenced. This reaction had probably been anticipated and the outbreak of rebellion in west Wicklow on the morning of 24 May 1798 created a climate of great loyalist insecurity on the county's borders with Wexford and Carlow. Carnew's garrison under Captain Robert Rowan were determined to forestall rebel mobilization

23 *Trial of William Byrne*, p. 9. 24 Holt MS, p. 27. 25 24 May 1798, N.A., 620/37/139; Hereward Senior, *Orangeism in Ireland and Britain, 1795-1836*, pp 97-8 and *Press*, 7 October 1797.

in their sector and took a leading part in brutal pre-emptive attacks on suspected rebel groupings in north Wexford in the last days of May. These operations were characterized by murders and house burnings and culminated in two prison massacres in the village on 27 May and 1 June that claimed around fifty lives; eighteen Wicklow women lost their husbands. Activities of this type sealed the fate of many yeoman who later fell into rebel hands and it was in connection with these reprisals that Dolan's testimony was sought in 1799.[26]

Dolan claimed to have joined the rebel forces between the death of Colonel Walpole at Tuberneering (4 June 1798) and the battle of Arklow (9 June 1798) but was present in Gorey Hill camp from 8 June 1798 at latest when the Wicklow rebels arrived under William Byrne of Ballymanus. She apparently remained with the insurgents until late August but had stayed in their mountain base camps when the main force left for Meath on 7-8 July and at other times.[27] Some women did accompany the rebels to Meath, however, and after the chaotic retreat from Ryndville Hill, Joseph Holt, to his 'great surprise', fell in with the aged Catherine Kearns of Newtownmountkennedy who had become separated from her rebel husband. She may have been one of the 'vast crowd of women' he had earlier observed in a state of consternation on viewing the murderous conduct of the army.[28] Carnewmen, known and related to Dolan, were very well represented in the ranks of the 'Ballymanus Division', an almost 2,000-strong contingent of Wicklow rebels which attached itself to the north Wexford 'Gorey' army for much of the insurrection. The unit had been formed at Mount Pleasant Hill camp, south east of Tinahely, in the week preceding 8 June and incorporated elements which had already seen action in the Wexford theatre. Its commander was a member of Wicklow's leading Catholic family and the younger brother of the county's United Irish Adjutant-General elect, Garret Byrne, who did not join his men until the evening of 21 June 1798.[29]

Extant memoirs, news accounts, trial transcripts and Castle documents indicate that the position of women in the rebel army was not that of fighters even though some inevitably found themselves in the midst of battles and massacres. The wife of Hugh McClane for one was certainly killed by the military during the battle of Stratford-on-Slaney

26 See O'Donnell, 'Holt', pp 138-40; Hardy to Loftus, 28 May 1798, N.A., 620/37/190; Byrne, *Memoirs*, I, pp 127-8; Wainwright to Fitzwilliam, 6 February 1800, N.L.I., MIC 5641 and Edward Hay, *History of the Insurrection of Wexford* (Dublin, 1803), pp 106-8. 27 *Trial of William Byrne*, pp 5-7.   28 Holt MS, p. 49. See also ibid., pp 47-8.   29 O'Donnell, 'Holt', pp 141-3, Dickson, *Dwyer*, p. 57 and Hay, *History*, pp 215-17.

on 24 May 1798. Another woman who died as a direct result of the battle was Rachael Valentine of Manger who was put to death by James
Hughes' rebel faction in February 1799 in revenge for her betrayal of
the wounded Thomas Kavanagh on 24 May 1798. Many others suffered
personal ill-treatment at the hands of the military and hundreds of
Wicklow women would have been traumatised by having their dwellings
destroyed in punitive expeditions.[30]

For the most part the women who followed the insurgents probably
feared remaining at home when their rebel husbands and brothers were
absent. The prospect of being called to account for such absences was
clearly not to be welcomed, particularly in view of the fact that the
Ancient British Light Fencible Dragoons were known to have injured
women whom they suspected of disloyalty in north Wicklow on 11
April 1798. Individual United Irishmen may have insisted that their
female dependents accompany them to their hill top camps where they
would be relatively secure and could provide logistic support to the
insurgent effort. Women certainly conveyed messages, intelligence
reports and supplies to the rebels and often nursed the wounded.[31]
Movement to and from the camps was relatively easy for women from
non-loyalist families and became common in districts where the insurgents enjoyed ascendancy.

Dolan never claimed to have been fielded as a combatant in 1798 or
even issued with a weapon but explained that she had decided to
accompany the rebels when 'we thought we would have had the day'.
Gravitating towards the winning side was a consistent aspect of her life
and one which may have reflected her social insecurity and/or amorali-
ty. The evacuation of Carnew by its loyalist community in the first days
of June may have narrowed her options but the decision to enter the
rebel camps was probably a deliberate undertaking. It may well have
been made on 7 June when much of the village was fired by rebels raiding from Gorey Hill camp in the build up to the assault on Arklow
three days later.[32] Her day to day role with the insurgents, however,
never approached the prominence she was granted at the 1799 trial
appearances and it is unclear how she occupied herself. The sole seditious act that she was prepared to acknowledge was assisting in the
burning of several 'baggage cars belonging to his majesty' although

---

30 Madden, *United Irishmen*, I, pp 335-6; Cloney, *Narrative*, p. 82; Dickson, *Dwyer*, pp
31-3 and Petition of Hugh McClane, n.d. [1799?], N.A., 620/51/64. 31 Holt MS, pp
127, 151, 157; Cullen, *Insurgent*, pp 16-18 and Thomas Parsons to Sir Laurence Parsons,
17 April 1798, N.L.I., MS 13,840/3. 32 *Trial of William Byrne*, p. 6. See also Lake to
William Wickham, 7 June 1798, Public Record Office [England], Home Office
100/81/31 and G.A. Hayes-McCoy, *Irish Battles* (London, 1969), pp 288-9.

there is some evidence that she was more deeply engaged on occasion. Even then Dolan indicated a certain distance in asserting that '*the rebels* pulled the furze and I set fire to them'. The baggage car incident was an allusion to the ambush of a large military supply convoy at Kilballyowen near Aughrim on 7 August 1798, a raid which resulted in the piking of two drivers in cold blood.[33]

For a few women the rebellion was an opportunity to ply the trade of prostitution and to perhaps gain a measure of status that they could not have hoped to attain in more settled times. In terms of demand for services the rebellion probably offered the most lucrative opportunities since the short-lived Croghan gold rush of 1795. When called to account in June 1799 for her means of support during the rebellion, an unusual requirement from a state's witness and one which implied awareness of misdealings, Dolan gave no direct answer but admitted that 'the men' had given her provisions.[34] Cullen or his sources was unambiguous in declaring her to have acted the part of a 'public prostitute'.[35]

Hostile commentators also asserted that Dolan had taken a lugubrious interest in the execution of loyalists during the rebellion and, true to form, had behaved in a 'revolting' manner on the occasion of William Byrne's execution on 19 September 1799. Her ability to give detailed descriptions of such events in 1799-1800 indicates that she had indeed been present at pikings such as that of Isaac Langrell which had taken place some way from the base camp of Gorey Hill. Her many acts of perjury, furthermore, typically concerned the placing of specific individuals at the killings rather than the nature of the incidents and are imbued with a gritty authenticity.[36]

Although Carnew loyalist John James understood that Dolan had been 'a most active and violent rebel' during the insurrection his statement was based entirely on hearsay and was intended to boost her credibility as a trial witness. There is, in fact, no evidence that she had participated in any combative situation other than the firing of the military convoy at Kilballyowen. She had, however, been through the insurgent camps at Mount Pleasant Hill, Kilcavan Hill, Gorey Hill, Carrigrew Hill, Vinegar Hill, Aghavannagh, Ballymanus and Whelp Rock between early June and late August. Dolan had also apparently

33 *Trial of William Byrne*, p. 7, emphasis added. See also ibid., p. 51, 28 March 1799, N.A., 620/17/30/24; *Saunder's Newsletter*, 8 and 13 August 1798 and O'Donnell, 'Holt', p. 199. 34 *Trial of William Byrne*, p. 7. See also Dickson, *Dwyer*, p. 64. 35 Cullen, *Insurgent*, p. 71. 36 Cullen quoted in Fitzpatrick, *Sham Squire*, p. 335. Dolan allegedly 'took delight' in attending pikings. Ibid., p. 329. See also *Trial of William Byrne*, p. 51 and *The Wicklow Star*, 26 November 1898.

been present at or very close to the battles of Ballyellis and Carnew on
30 June and that of Ballyrahan Hill (Tinahely) on 2 July 1798. It may
well be significant that these engagements, as well as the Kilballyowen
attack, had all arisen at short notice when the rebel army was in transit.
Dolan further claimed in 1800 to have seen Shillelagh man John
Synnott pike the bodies of loyalist prisoners 'at Newbridge in the county of Carlow'. No such allegation was apparently made by her during
the 1798 and 1799 trials, however, and the balance of probability suggests that she had not witnessed the alleged event.[37]

Conversely, it is evident that Dolan had not witnessed any major
confrontation in which the rebels had set out from their high ground
camps with the specific aim of doing battle with the crown forces. She
was no pikewoman and did not attend the battles at Tuberneering,
Arklow and Hacketstown even though the fighting elements of the rebel
forces she accompanied had been committed. Her trial observations are
limited to what had occurred in the Carnew district prior to the rebellion, the events which had taken place inside the camps and their immediate environs in June-July 1798 and to several controversial episodes
which had arisen during the shifts between camps. A rare exception was
her presence in Carnew in mid-June with a party of up to twenty rebels
who had taken yeomen John Hope and John Brady prisoner, both of
whom were later executed. This might have been explained by her
desire to visit her home village and it had evidently occurred when the
'Gorey' army was briefly divided between Kilcavan and Mount Pleasant
camps on 17-18 June 1798.[38]

While Dolan obtained a commandeered horse the colourful story
that she had ridden with the mounted element of the rebel army is
inherently unlikely. Rebel officers were often mounted during battles
but the insurgents lacked the training and equipment to deploy cavalry
units in large-scale combat and never did so. In general, the horses
seized from loyalist farmers were employed to help transport wounded
men, civilian dependents and goods. They were also occasionally used
for reconnaissance, small-scale raiding and foraging and it may be that a
rider as expert as Dolan could have held her own in such roles. She
would have been among those who could have vouched for her skill and
ex-rebel George Kearns recalled seeing her 'riding behind' Holt. Dolan

---

37 Information of Bridget Dolan, 7 January 1800, N.A., 620/17/36. See also 14
November 1799, N.A., 620/17/30/41-2 and 29 April 1800, N.A., 620/17/30/28. A
young loyalist captured at Kilballyowen mentioned seeing 'a furious looking hag of a
woman who had one half of a pair of tailor's shears tied upon the end of a pole' but there
is no evidence that any Wicklow woman sported a pike in battle. Quoted in Holt,
Memoirs, I, p. 199. 38 14 November 1799, N.A., 620/17/30/41.

admitted having ridden Jack Flynn's horse on Kilcavan Hill on the morning of 21 June 1798.[39]

That she remained with the rump forces under Holt was significant given that the vast majority of active rebels and their non-combatant followers had seized the opportunity offered by the Amnesty Act to return home by mid-July 1798. Relatively few insurgents remained under arms when the French incursion of August 1798 had occurred and the brief augmentation which ensued never rivalled the strength of the pre-Amnesty force. The fighting had become more sporadic and small scale with frequent shifting of camps. Many women visited the rebels whenever they arrived in their neighbourhoods but Dolan was evidently one of those few who braved the privations of life in the mountains. Her presence in the camps, however, had become a bone of contention by late August 1798 when tensions had arisen from leadership and doubts surrounding the commitment of the ailing Holt to the effort.[40]

Many of Cullen's informants of the early 1800s had belonged to the Talbotstown faction headed by Michael Dwyer which had distanced itself from Holt's main force in the late summer of 1798. Some asserted that the immorality of Holt's 'public intercourse with one of the greatest and most sham[e]less vagabonds that ever disgraced the female character, the notorious Bid Dolan' had lessened their respect for the Roundwood man. If there was more substance to this grievance than retrospective scorn intended to castigate Dolan for her subsequent misdeeds and to embarrass the somewhat unpopular Holt it would appear that the Carnew woman had played a part in the disintegration of the last sizable armed rebel force in Ireland. That Dolan might have coveted the company of the charismatic Holt was entirely in keeping with her gregarious personality and a sexual dimension to their association cannot be ruled out. This would presumably have been complicated by the fact that two of Holt's rebel brothers William and Jonathan, his sister Mary and more importantly, his wife Hester, were frequently at his side. Indeed it seems that Hester's arrival in the camp was one of the principal factors which obliged Dolan to remove herself from the company.[41]

39 Cullen, N.L.I., MS 8339, p. 118. See also 14 November 1799, N.A., 620/17/30/41; Cullen cited in Fitzpatrick, *Sham Squire*, p. 328 and Major-General Sir Francis Needham to Lake, 9 June 1798, P.R.O., H.O. 100/77/122.   40 O'Donnell, 'Holt', pp 200-20; Byrne, *Memoirs*, I, pp 221-7; Major-General John Moore to Cornwallis, 20 August 1798, N.A., S.O.C., 1017/64 and SNL, 13 July 1798.   41 Cullen, N.L.I., MS 8339, p. 118. Cullen's monkish sensitivity on this point is signalled by his assertion that the morals of Irish Catholics were 'the purest of any people on Earth.' Ibid., p. 119.

Holt apparently alluded to Dolan only once in his memoirs when he mentioned 'a young woman a friend of mine' who had assisted in searching the home of a suspected spy in Athdown for concealed food caches.[42] The nature of their relationship is not explicitly defined by him or in the traditional accounts although Cullen's assertion that 'his and her imprudence in dashing into farmers houses in the presence of virtuous women and their daughters' implied that it was not merely platonic. Moreover, Laurence O'Keefe description of Dolan as 'Holt's miss' is compelling and is supported by other witnesses.[43] Yet Cullen's is a consistently negative record on matters pertaining to Holt and elsewhere he specified that 'the only one that enjoyed this wretched gallantry was Francois [Joseph] the Hessian [*sic*]', a Frenchmen who was obliged to quit the rebels on shooting one James Byrne of Imaal.[44]

An account written by a young Wexfordman who had spent several weeks with the rebels after being captured during the Kilballyowen ambush provides a more neutral perspective on Dolan's profile in the camp, albeit that of someone who was about twelve when the events occurred. As an adult he recalled that Holt had:

> at one time' been 'constantly attended by a very handsome young woman dressed in a green habit, a kind of uniform with epaulets, her name was ____, she was the daughter of a farmer, and was called 'the general's lady'. She was a determined rebel, and appeared highly gratified with her distinction. This lasted some weeks, but at length Mrs Holt joined the army, and from that time the heroine in the green uniform disappeared, and we saw no more of her.[45]

Men with prices on their heads had strong reasons to resent the flirtations of someone of Dolan's background with their commander and his apparent obliviousness to their concerns could only have weakened his authority. The outrage detected by Cullen was more likely to have derived from such pragmatic concerns than from moral qualms. In October 1798 the re-appearance of Hester Holt in Glenmalure elicited an extremely forthright protest from his followers who distrusted her well known negotiations with government to secure terms of capitulation for her husband. In 1799 Mary Dwyer, a woman of unimpeachable

42 Holt MS, p. 80. 43 Cullen, N.L.I., MS 9762, p. 215. 44 Cullen, N.L.I., MS 8339, p. 119. See also Information of Francis Joseph, 5 July 1799, N.A., 620/56/110. 45 Quoted in Holt, *Memoirs*, I, p. 202. See also Holt MS, pp 109-11 and 28 March 1799, N.A., 620/17/30/24, Ruan O'Donnell, 'General Joseph Holt' in Bob Reece (ed.), *Exiles from Erin, convict lives in Ireland and Australia* (Dublin, 1991), pp 48-9.

nationalist credentials and the wife of the Imaal leader since 16 October 1798, was ejected from his faction's billets and forbidden to return. Mrs Holt and Mrs Dwyer were not deemed capable of covering their tracks when visiting their husbands in the secret mountain hideaways.[46]

III

Tensions concerning Dolan may have been exacerbated by the heightened threat posed by informers during the later stages of the rebellion of whom many were women. Holt narrowly prevented his men from cutting the ears off a suspected female spy in late August and she was instead flogged with the cat-of-nine-tails. Athdown informers Mrs White and Mrs McGrath, furthermore, had considerable quantities of goods and livestock taken from them shortly afterwards as a punishment for their transgressions against the United Irishmen. Women within the camp posed a far greater threat than over-curious onlookers as they had access to details of rebel intentions which the military required to mount ambushes. The treachery of Peter 'Goodpay' Kavanagh's girl-friend resulted in an unexpected night attack on the rebels at Greenan in early September which might have proved disastrous if the military had not aimed high. One of those wounded by the Rathdrum yeomanry at Greenan was a young woman named Ann Byrne who was hit in the arm by a musket ball.[47]

On leaving Holt's force in late August Dolan returned to the largely destroyed village of Carnew where she was not immediately suspected of having had any direct involvement in the events of the rebellion. Carnew had been evacuated by virtually all its resident loyalist community during the first week of June 1798 and nowone was evidently then aware that she had accompanied the rebel patrol which had taken several local yeomen prisoner. Benjamin Stone claimed on 6 December 1799 to have been the 'only loyalist that rem[aine]d' in the village.[48] Indeed, she had no blood on her hands, but her imprudent volubility regarding 'everything she saw or heard' soon attracted the notice of the local loyalists. They were exceptionally aggrieved at the losses incurred at the hands of the rebels to their comrades, properties and livestock and were eager to make amends. Dolan's former associates also became cognisant of her conduct and she quickly gained a reputation as someone of 'very

46 Cullen, N.L.I., MS 8339, pp 198-20; Byrne, *Memoirs*, I, pp 297-8 and Dickson, *Dwyer*, pp 85-6.   47 Holt MS, pp 78, 81, 87-9.   48 *Trial of William Byrne*, p. 7. See also 14 November 1799, N.A., 620/17/30/41.

bad character'.[49] On 16 September 1798, less than a week after the military outcome of the rebellion had been settled by the defeat of French
at Ballinamuck, Dolan was arrested in Coolkenna by Captain William
Wainwright of the Shillelagh yeoman cavalry. Wainwright, a magistrate
and yeomanry officer, also managed the extensive south Wicklow estates
of the absentee Earl Fitzwilliam from Malton. Word of Dolan's willingness to speak freely of rebel excesses had evidently reached him and he
sent her to Rathdrum, the seat of his principal political ally, attorney
Thomas King of Kingston.[50]

The value of someone like Dolan was that their knowledge frequently enabled magistrates to invalidate the certificates of pardon
which had been granted to their enemies. Involvement in killings which
had occurred in cold blood, participation in house burning or having
acted as an officer in the rebel forces automatically nullified the vital
'protection' and rendered the holder liable to prosecution under Martial
Law. The exemption clauses were the principal chinks in the armour of
the otherwise comprehensive Amnesty Act which ultra-loyalists like
King and Revd Charles Cope so detested. Such men regarded Dublin
Castle's policy of 'measured severity' as misguided leniency which
threatened to unleash a revitalized United Irish threat. Invalidation of
pardons and the apprehension of fugitives dominated the agenda of
Wicklow's 'active magistrates', a task that was sharpened by the ongo-
ing state of insurgency in their home sector. The identification and
apprehension of those who had obtained 'protections' by subterfuge or
in error enhanced the role of informers. Their quarry were then pursued with determination for some years after the rebellion and often
into the south Dublin city streets where hundreds of Wicklow and
Wexford fugitives lived.[51]

King, the driving force in the Wicklow's magistracy's secret 'committee for receiving intelligence' since late 1797, was one of the central
figures in organizing post-rebellion court martials. When High Sheriff
Thomas Archer communicated the Viceroy's orders that all jailed suspects were to be brought to trial under the Rebellion Act of March 1799
it was King who managed the Rathdrum sessions. His influence spread
into all baronial sectors as the intimate pre-rebellion contacts with fel-

49 14 November 1799, N.A., 620/17/30/42.   50 *Trial of William Byrne*, p. 7;
Fitzpatrick, *Sham Squire*, pp 328-9 and 3 October 1799, N.A., 620/17/3.   51 See
Thomas King to Lieutenant-Colonel Stewart, 11 January 1801, N.A., 620/119/7; Diary
of Judge Robert Day, 11 August 1800, Royal Irish Academy, MS 12. W. 11, pp 107-8
and Byrne, *Memoirs*, I, pp 156-7, 352. On 11 November 1799 Dolan denounced a man
in uniform as a rebel veteran and a 'murderer' to Wicklow jailer William Carr. 14
November 1799, N.A., 620/17/30/41.

low hard liners Revd Cope and Wainwright of Shillelagh, Henry Moreton of Tinahely and Revd Edward Bayly of Arklow made for a county-wide role. He was consequently to be found on the panels which convened in Wicklow town where most of the county's prisoners were tried. Although Wicklow was a monolithically liberal county at Parliamentary level the United Irish crisis had vested the bulk of anti-insurgent duties in the hands of conservative extremists. King's conception of what constituted grounds for trial differed greatly from the Viceroy's by whom he was repeatedly rebuked for persecuting men whose relatively minor acts of sedition had been absolved by the Amnesty Act.[52]

Folk traditions that Dolan accompanied cavalry patrols from their temporary barracks at Rathdrum's Flannel Hall and directed them to the haunts of fugitives were probably well founded. Thomas Lewins of Kilmacoo, another former United Irishman who became an agent of King's, certainly fulfilled that role in late 1798. The degree of control exercised by Dolan over her escort, however, was probably not great, contrary to the popular record. It is also unlikely that her transformation from a raucous prostitute into a woman 'dressed like a lady, with habit and skirt' occurred at that time and the story was probably inspired by her later appearances at trial proceedings in Rathdrum.[53] When asked to explain how she was supported and 'furnish[e]d with clothes' in September 1799 Dolan replied 'by order of two magistrates [Thomas King and William Wainwright]'.[54]

More problematic is Cullen's assertion that many former rebels to whom Dolan 'had some dislike' were killed upon being pointed out by her.[55] Illegal killings of amnestied rebels by the Newtownmountkennedy yeoman cavalry had taken place prior to October 1798 and resulted in an important test case in which private Hugh Woolaghan was tried for murder. Killings were also widely attributed by Cullen's sources to the Rathdrum and Bray yeoman infantry some of which may well have been guided by informers. Yet the folk record for this is weak insofar as Dolan was concerned and only two men named Byrne were specifically named in connection with her. One of them had allegedly rebuked her 'undisguised immorality' in the rebel camps and was followed to his home upon being spotted by her after the rebellion. The Byrnes were

52 King to Edward Cooke, 10 January 1801, N.A., 620/10/119/2, 5 May 1799, N.A., 620/7/79/13, 16, Thomas Archer to Marsden, 24 March 1799, N.A., 620/49/88 and *Trial of William Byrne*, p. 11. 53 Fitzpatrick, *Sham Squire*, p. 329. See also Cullen, *Insurgent*, p. 71. See also Cullen, N.L.I., MS 9761, pp 165-8 and MS 8339, p. 190. 54 *Trial of William Byrne*, p. 7. 55 Cullen quoted in Fitzpatrick, *Sham Squire*, p. 329. See also Cullen, *Insurgent*, p. 96.

reputedly amnestied United Irishmen at the time of their deaths and were killed at their Ballymaurin farm when digging potatoes.[56]

The prospect of widespread or long-term persecution of retired rebels was curbed by a series of high-profile trials in late 1798 of yeomen suspected of murderous revenge attacks. The brunt of ultra-loyalist malcontents shifted, with some important exceptions, from the persons of their enemies to the religious infrastructure of Catholicism. By March 1800 loyalist arsonists had destroyed twenty-one chapels and priest's residences and murdered one if not two priests. The formal and legal aspect of the 'white terror' was waged concurrently against this grim backdrop in the courtrooms of Wicklow town, Rathdrum and Baltinglass where Dolan's talents were then deployed.[57]

Cullen ascertained that while Dolan had received an 'invitation' to appear as a prosecution witness she was more than willing to swear anything 'that she thought would please the Orange party, who supplied her with money and whiskey'.[58] This was evidently intended to undermine the suggestion raised at the trial of William Byrne that she was an involuntary witness who 'could not get [her] liberty without swearing against him' although Dolan denied having expressed such an opinion in William Manning's shop in Rathdrum. Outright bribery may have occurred given that one of Cullen's main sources was Rathdrum constable Tom Phillips who allegedly admitted having assisted King in Dolan's 'tuition' in advance of the trials. Phillips was certainly the man in whose 'custody' Dolan had been placed by Wainwright in September 1798 but the precise nature of his instruction to her is unknown.[59]

The detention of Dolan in Rathdrum, moreover, was not simply a matter of protecting her from vengeful former associates and it stands to reason that her close co-operation with the authorities was inspired by an understanding that it would be to her advantage. The controversial bestowal of clothes and material goods on Dolan during the trials implied that an informal *quid pro quo* arrangement had been entered into, an impression which her ultimate receipt of a government pension apparently confirmed.[60]

56 Cullen, *Insurgent*, p. 72. See also Fitzpatrick, *Sham Squire*, p. 329; Cullen, N.L.I., MS 9761, pp 9-10 and T.C.D., MS 1472, p. 206.   57 *SNL*, 7 November 1798; *FDJ*, 10 November 1798; *The genuine trial of Hugh Woolaghan* (Dublin, 1798); Troy to Marsden, 15 February 1799, N.A., 620/63/65; Cullen, *Insurgent*, pp 45-6, 76; William Hamilton Maxwell, *History of the Irish Rebellion in 1798* (London, 1845), p. 446 and Cloney, *A personal narrative*, p. 221.   58 Cullen quoted in Fitzpatrick, *Sham Squire*, p. 330.   59 *Trial of William Byrne*, pp 7-8.   60 Ibid., and John T. Gilbert (ed.), *Documents relating to Ireland, 1795-1804*, pp 54, 69, 76.

Much of Dolan's testimony was fabricated although allegations that powerful loyalist interests had conspired to concoct evidence in their vendetta against Byrne and others is less certain. On balance it seems likely that Dolan's merit in King's eyes was her ability to plausibly place known United Irishmen at the scene of genuine atrocities. Whether her statements to this end stemmed from magisterial encouragement, from duress or from her own initiative remains a mystery but the fact that King publically stood over her allegations, even after they had been discredited at Viceregal level, is indicative of his strong personal vested interest. Another loyalist insisted that Dolan's evidence had never 'been *justly* impeached'.[61] One of Dolan's most important assertions was made on 25 June 1799 during the trial of William Byrne when she claimed that his brother Garret had been present in Vinegar Hill on 21 June 1798 and at other camps before. That this was utterly false and open to cogent refutation by several key members of the Wicklow forces raises the question of why she had insisted it had been the case. Her description of a dispute between rival followers of Garret and William Byrne is also demonstrably untrue and had probably been suggested by an incident in which *Charles Byrne* of Ballyrogan had been deposed as commander of the Ballymanus Division's Redcross corps on the day in question.[62]

Garret Byrne did not, in fact, encounter the Ballymanus Division until the night of 21-22 June 1798 but went on to lead them in lieu of his younger brother until mid-July. The elder Byrne's negotiation of a pact with Major-General John Moore and the marquis of Huntley in Imaal shielded him from subsequent legal proceedings and Dolan's targeting of the family very probably reflected loyalist dismay at this circumstance. In early 1799 press reports that Garret was living a pleasant exile in Bristol in the south of England were galling to Wicklow loyalists who had suffered greatly in the rebellion and resented his State Prisoner status. Byrne's tangential association with the atrocities of the Wexford theatre, as delineated by Dolan, was exceptionally incriminating and had the desired effect of inflaming loyalist opinion in such a way that his chances of returning to Ireland were fatally compromised. Dolan consequently played no small part in attaining a moral victory for Wicklow's ultra-loyalists who succeeded in frustrating the intentions of Cornwallis and Hardwicke to rehabilitate Garret Byrne.[63]

61 14 November 1799, N.A., 620/17/30/42. See also Fitzpatrick, *Sham Squire*, p. 333 and *Trial of William Byrne*, p. 11. 62 *Trial of William Byrne*, pp 10-11. See also ibid., p. 54 and Dickson, *Dwyer*, p. 61. 63 O'Donnell, 'Rebellion of 1798', pp 361-5; Pelham to Hardwicke, 28 January 1803, P.R.O., H.O. 100/119/48; Cullen, *Personal Recollections*, p. 37; *Freeman's Journal*, 17 January 1799; Cloney, *Personal Narrative*, p. 234; Shannon to

Her contribution to William Byrne's death is more difficult to quan-
tify as several important unfounded depositions were made by other
prosecution witnesses, not least Mathew Davis' contention that Michael
Dwyer had ordered the shooting of three captive 'Orangemen' in
Mount Pleasant.[64] An earlier trial had heard Thomas Foy's claim in reference to the same incident that he had witnessed 'Billy Byrne ... dis-
charge three case of pistols into the breasts of [three] bloody
Orangemen'. Byrne understandably seized upon Davis' assertions in his
defence and, as might be expected from a man on trial for his life,
deflected the responsibility for the deaths unto Dwyer. Yet Davis' erstwhile commander in the Ballinacor Corps, James Doyle from that place,
informed Cullen in the early 1800s that he and Dwyer had been absent
from the camp when the executions had taken place and were angered
by the incident. Davis, therefore, had performed an important service
for his handlers by unfairly blackening Dwyer's reputation in that the
Imaal leader remained at large at the head of a dedicated and highly
dangerous rebel faction in western Wicklow. Any imputation of atro-
cious conduct on Dwyer's part was liable to lessen his standing amongst
his harbourers in addition to spurring Talbotstown's somewhat tardy
loyalist elements to engineer his downfall. Dolan was consequently simply one, albeit perhaps the most important, state's witness who functioned on behalf of local landed interests against their defeated
ideological opponents and, to some extent, against the liberally inclined
executive they distrusted.[65]

The Byrne trial is linked to Dolan's name more than any other as it
resulted in the death of a very popular and respected man on a Wicklow
town gallows on 19 September 1799, news of which was conveyed to his
former adherents who had been transported to New South Wales. The
naming of Dolan in the popular ballad 'Billy Byrne of Ballymanus'
ensured that some resonance of her 1799 notoriety was passed from
generation to generation. Yet it is difficult to assess what effect Dolan's
disclosures actually had on establishing Byrne's guilt given that equally
serious allegations were advanced by several other witnesses. Her most
pertinent contribution was to allege Byrne's presence at the piking of
Isaac Langrell in Gorey churchyard but this was not accepted at face

Boyle, 26 March 1799 in Esther Hewitt (ed.), *Lord Shannon's letters to his son, a calender
of letters written by the 2nd Earl of Shannon to his son, Viscount Boyle, 1790–1802* (Belfast,
1982); Garret Byrne to Cornwallis, 9 July 1801, P.R.O., H.O. 100/106/184; Cornwallis
to Pelham, 18 October 1802, P.R.O., H.O. 100/110/314 and Moore to Cornwallis, 1
September 1803, P.R.O., H.O. 100/119/40. 64 *Trial of William Byrne*, pp 31-2. 65 28
March 1799, N.A., 620/17/30/18. See also *Trial of William Byrne*, p. 70 and Dickson,
Dwyer, pp 137-8.

value by the panel. The court found Byrne 'highly blameable' for Langrell's death and accepted that he had been present but acquitted him of murder on the grounds that the execution had been ordered by a more senior rebel officer. Perhaps Dolan's principal value to the prosecution case was her ability to set the evidence of the other witnesses against Byrne in a vivid context, even if much of the detail conflicted. This may have helped dispose the panel towards imposing the death sentence which Cornwallis had little option but to uphold. Indeed, the cumulative weight of evidence had clearly shown that Byrne had functioned as a senior commander at a time when cold blooded killings had been carried out by his forces and was not legally entitled to the protection of the Amnesty Act. If anything, the testimony advanced at the 1799 trial underplayed Byrne's role in the Wicklow United Irish organization from 1797 and gave rise to an enduring myth of his chance involvement in the insurrection.[66]

Dolan's first trial appearances were made in Rathdrum in mid-1799 and, while no transcripts are extant, it is evident that most, if not all, of those she had prosecuted had their sentences quashed under the Amnesty Act. Notwithstanding this failure, Dolan was tasked with the prosecution of more vulnerable south Wicklow rebels who had been accused of complicity in the cold blooded execution of loyalists. Her November 1799 description of the killing of a captive yeoman and orangeman James Wheatly in Gorey on 8 June 1798 was typically sensational and detailed: 'Pris[one]r John Nowlan presented a gun and fired it at Wheatly. Wheatly was wounded and fell, but rolled about, the pris[one]r reloaded his gun and again discharged it at Wheatly but he was not kill[e]d thereby, the Pris[one]r Nowlan struck Wheatly on the head with the Breech of the gun, then gave his gun to ano[the]r person, and got a Bayonet screwed on a pole with which he stabbed said Wheatly'.[67] In 1793 Nowlan had become godfather to the daughter of Bridget Dolan nee Dunaghan of Croneyhorn (Carnew) whose name and parentage indicates a blood relationship to his main accuser six years later.[68]

The pedantic description of a makeshift pike, if accurately transcribed, seems calculated to ensure that the written record would be utterly unambiguous with respect to Nowlan's culpability. In general,

66 *Trial of William Byrne*, p. 74. See also Robert Walsh to Joseph Holt, 5 November 1803, quoted in George William Rusden, *Curiosities of Colonization* (London, 1874), p. 57, 3 December 1799, N.A., 620/17/30/82; Madden, *Emmet*, p. 124; Joseph H. Fowler, *Chapters in '98 History* (London, 1938), 'Leaflet no. 2'; Zimmerman, *Irish Rebellion*, p. 149; Dickson, *Dwyer*, pp 63-4 and Cullen, *Insurgent*, p. 94. 67 14 November 1799, N.A., 620/17/30/42. See also *Trial of William Byrne*, p. 11. 68 Catholic Baptism Registers, Carnew (Tomacork), p. 46.

Dolan's testimony was highly explicit and so focused in comparison to that of others as to suggest that it had been carefully rehearsed. This was very apparent to the defendants and Edward Neil of Carnew, a rebel charged with capital offenses, queried whether she had been induced by bribery to 'swear against' him. Allegations of this kind might ordinarily have been dismissed as the gambit of a desperate man but in Dolan's case it was bound to register a note of suspicion. Neil, moreover, like his close friend Nowlan, had known Dolan from her youth and had acted as a sponsor for members of her extended family at a Tomacork baptism in 1794.[69]

Administrative delays ensured that the Viceroy was incapable of reviewing Dolan's numerous November 1799 prosecutions until January 1801 at which time he had become convinced that her veracity was in grave doubt. Cornwallis determined that no death sentence could be carried out on the basis of Dolan's 'impeached testimony' unless it had been independently corroborated, an apparently unprecedented and unique proviso. Those who fell into this category had their sentences mitigated from death to transportation for either seven years or life (fourteen years) and most sailed to New South Wales on the *Atlas II* in October 1802.[70] Apart from Byrne's conviction, Dolan's evidence had helped secure at least six sentences of death and two of transportation in November-December 1799. On 7 December 1799 Dolan's evidence was crucial to the capital sentencing of John Doyle, James Fallon and Michael Doornen in Rathdrum for the murder of a yeoman in June 1798. Yet King's triumph was shortlived as Cornwallis ordered that the trio be released from custody on the sole grounds that Dolan's testimony had been 'completely ... discredited' on previous occasions.[71]

This censure did not dissuade the Wicklow magistracy and High Sheriff Thomas Archer from calling Dolan to appear at the resumed quarterly assizes on 2 April 1800. Michael Keally and Miles Byrne were then sentenced to death by Lord Yelverton for the murder of yeoman George Butler during the battle of Ballyellis on 30 June 1798. As the Viceroy avoided interceding in civil trials Dolan's role was not subjected to its typical close examination and her allegedly 'clear and satisfac-

69 14 November 1799, N.A., 620/17/30/41. Byrne noted that Dolan had been 'extremely minute in her evidence' yet prone to 'many flagrant inconsistencies', *Trial of William Byrne*, p. 52. See also Catholic Baptism Registers, Carnew (Tomacork), p. 38. 70 Cornwallis to ——, 19 January 1801, N.A., 620/17/30/42. 71 7 December 1799, N.A., 670/17/30/44. See also Dickson, *Dwyer*, p. 380. The 1799 defendants were John Nowlan, Patrick Murray, James Dempsey, Richard Carr, Nicholas Delaney, John Kavanagh, Patrick Stafford and Edward Neil. 14 November 1799, N.A., 620/17/30/41-2.

tory' evidence was, in this instance, supported by other witnesses. The standard of the evidence given could not have been great given that the engagement at Ballyellis was mistakenly reported to have been fought on 19 June 1798.[72]

Dolan followed up this success the following week in Wicklow town when she appeared at two courtmartials which proved to be her final outings. Matters seemed to be going according to plan when two more capital convictions were sustained against James Cullen and John Fowler but they were mitigated upon investigation. It must have been then apparent that the level of scrutiny elicited by Dolan's participation in military trials had become counter-productive.[73] Fowler, a Protestant rebel officer from Carnew, had successfully exploited Dolan's reputation in May 1800 with an argument that the unwillingness of the prosecution to disclose the substance of her accusations prior to the trial had hindered his cross examination. He had consequently failed to expose her 'contradicted' testimony and was apprehensive that her evidence 'may have more weight ... than it is entitled to and that the members of the court may have given credit to what she swore from their ignorance of her real character'. His fears were misplaced as while Cornwallis confirmed the verdict the punishment was altered to transportation for life on the basis that 'no reliance could be placed' on Dolan's testimony.[74]

When Wicklow's Grand Jury foreman William Hoare Hume MP, of Humewood (Kiltegan), recommended during the 1800 summer assizes that Dolan's services be considered by the Viceroy he was signalling that they would no longer be called upon. This proved to be an irreversible decision and a September 1800 application from Shillelagh yeoman that Dolan be summoned to prosecute John Hughes and Michael Byrne was ignored. Hume's promptings in mid-1800 probably led to the series of payments to her drawn from Dublin Castle's secret service funds which were often used to reward informers, pay bounties and to reimburse those connected with the legal system. A sum of twenty-two pounds, fifteen shillings was granted to Dolan on 10 March 1801, followed by an identical payment via Wainwright on 14 June 1802 and a third, possibly final, instalment on 14 July 1803. Other amounts may have been advanced from the same or other sources subsequent to that date but none are listed in the extant Castle accounts. Hume and

72 *SNL*, 11 April 1800. See also *Hibernian Telegraph*, 11 April 1800. 73 11 April 1800, N.A., 620/17/30/19, 28. 74 Petition of John Fowler, 31 May 1800, N.A., P.P.C., 409. Dolan's evidence was crucial as she was the only witness to place Fowler at the scene of Roger Pierce's execution in June 1798 and, moreover, had claimed to have observed the former Carnew resident giving the hapless yeoman 'sev[era]l stabs of [his] sword.' 1 May 1800, N.A., 620/17/30/19.

Thomas King were both reimbursed for the considerable amounts of
money they had passed to unnamed contacts but the fact that Dolan's
name appeared elsewhere in the ledger indicates she was not one of the
anonymous recipients.[75]

After her retirement as a prosecutor Dolan was permitted to return
to Carnew where she lived on her annual allowance from the Castle,
possibly with her father with whom she had resided when the rebellion
had broken out. It is not clear whether her pension was discontinued
after 1803 but Luke Cullen's sources alleged that she became reliant in
later life on the 'poor box in the Protestant Church' and the charity of
loyalist admirers.[76] This would appear to be essentially correct given
that she, alone of her extended family, was ultimately buried in
Carnew's Church of Ireland graveyard. While she lived Dolan was evidently quite unpopular and was said to have obtained a pair of bulldogs
for her protection. Nationalist accounts went further and claimed that
she was stoned and jeered by local boys on venturing into public and
became 'sour, reserved and morose' under the 'severe gnawing of a cor-
roding conscience'. Very little is known of her later life other than a
story that she became a single mother and raised a daughter.[77] She died
aged fifty on 29 October 1827.[78]

IV

As a pathetic decline into disease, madness, poverty and obscurity was
the near obligatory reputed fate of informers and 'active' magistrates in
traditional histories such sources cannot be relied upon for details of
Dolan's twenty-nine years of post-rebellion experiences. She was not,
for instance, buried in unconsecrated ground under a part of a Carnew
pavement where some refuse to tread. Dolan did, however, rapidly
become a hate figure in nationalist circles and was fortunate to escape
assassination at the hands of the Dwyer faction. Much to Thomas
King's consternation Mathew Davis, James Redmond of Clara, Patrick
Toole of Ballymanus and John Doyle of Greenan all succumbed to
Dwyer's death squads between December 1799 and April 1800. Dolan,

75 Dickson, *Dwyer*, pp 380-1; 18 September 1800, N.L.I., Kilmainham Papers, vol. 255
and Gilbert (ed.), *Documents*, pp 54, 69, 76-7. For Dolan's attempt to inculpate John
Synnott of Clonamonagh in the murder of Tinahely cobbler George Driver see
Information of Bridget Dolan, 7 January 1800, N.A., 620/17/36. 76 Cullen quoted in
Fitzpatrick, *Sham Squire*, p. 336. See also *Trial of William Byrne*, p. 7. 77 Fitzpatrick,
Sham Squire, p. 336. See also Church of Ireland Register of Burials, Carnew Parish, p.
3. 78 Church of Ireland Register of Burials, Carnew Parish, p. 3.

ensconced in the rebuilt loyalist centre of Carnew, was beyond the reach of the Talbotstown- and Ballinacor North-based insurgents and survived past the critical date of December 1803 when the outstanding rebels made terms with government.[79]

She may well have been reminded of the fate of her fellow witnesses by the widely sung ballad 'Billy Byrne', dated by Zimmerman as appearing in 1799 but probably composed a few years later. All published versions list the assassinated prosecutors and mention that the Devil had reserved 'a warm corner for ... Bid Doolin'.[80] Significantly, Dolan's name also headed a list of prominent state's witnesses in a vituperative rebel prison ballad collected, and almost certainly written, by the talented James Kavanagh of Roundwood in or before 1801. Hers, moreover, was the only name cited in full or in plain English and was correctly given as 'Bridget Dolan'. This reference was so formal in the context of the piece as to imply an ironic connotation, one which played on the remoulding of 'Croppy Biddy's' public persona. The prime target of Kavanagh's bitter sarcasm was Thomas Halpin who had denounced him as an active United Irishman but all Thomas King's main 'checkbook' witnesses were soundly excoriated.[81]

If the Wicklow rebellion had received similar attention to the events across the Wexford border it is likely that Dolan would have ranked in 1798 historiography with Madge Dixon of Wexford town who had helped organise the controversial piking of loyalist prisoners. Scant attention in the published writings of Cullen, Madden, Fitzpatrick and in more recent times, Charles Dickson, has insured that Dolan has faded from popular memory beyond her native south county Wicklow where 'Croppy Biddy' remains a term of abuse. She rates no entry in the 1996 *Women of Ireland, a biographical dictionary*. In the 1800s, however, sufficient was known of her exploits in Wicklow to give rise to unflattering stories which suited nationalist interpretations of the rebellion.[82]

One highly fanciful account has it that 'Bid Doolan' repeatedly shouted 'treason!' on viewing Lieutenant-Colclough Byrne's violent reaction to the execution of his brother William until dragged off by a

---

79 Cullen, N.L.I., MS 1472, pp 218-20 and N.L.I., MS 9762, f.2, p. 76; *Hibernian Telegraph*, 30 April 1800 and King to ——, 12 December 1801 quoted in Dickson, *Dwyer*, p. 206. 80 Padraig O'Tuathail (ed.), 'Wicklow traditions of 1798' in *Bealoideas*, V, 1935, pp 181-2; *Songs and ballads of '98*, p. 49 and O'Brien, 'The Byrnes of Ballymanus', pp 330-1. The version collected by Zimmerman says 'cursed Biddy Doolan too'. *Songs of Rebellion*, p. 149. 81 [James Kavanagh], 'The art of perjury, in three volumes, revis[e]d & correct[e]d by Tho[ma]s H[alpin] [*sic*] the P[ublic?] S[ervant?], Vol 1', n.d., 1801, N.A., 620/10/116/1. 82 Gahan, *People's Rising*, pp 201-3 and Holt, *Memoirs*, I, pp 70-1.

disapproving British soldier.[83] Another unfounded legend asserted that Dolan had 'swore away the life' of Michael 'Vesty' Byrne, Dwyer's cousin and brother of the celebrated Hugh 'Vesty' Byrne of Kirakee. The story may have arisen from the discomforting fact that Michael had not been tried for a political offence even though the folk account implied that it had been concocted to pressurise his fugitive brother.[84] The harsh reality was that Byrne had sexually assaulted the young Eleanor Phillips of Rathdrum and was capitally convicted by her 'lamentable testimony' at the March 1801 assizes. This ignominious crime probably steeled his brother to reject a proposed clemency deal on his behalf if the pair submitted to transportation for life.[85]

Dolan had no role whatsoever in the trial of Michael Byrne and was probably living in Carnew when the assizes were held. Yet her unenviable reputation was such that it could be invoked by nationalists to conceal certain facts which reflected poorly on the United Irishmen and their supporters. Bridget Dolan was not the sort of 'woman of '98' who attracted positive attention during the key commemorative anniversaries of the rebellion which did so much to revive interest in 1798. She had, however, probably spent more time with the active insurgents in the field than any other woman and was certainly much longer in the presence of such units than the conventional rebel heroines. Any claim to celebrity on this basis seems to have been invalidated by her alleged work as a prostitute, her evident lack of political motivation and her subsequent treacherous deeds. Such moral reservations are understandable but they reflect an unhistorical agenda which has served to denigrate one of the most interesting women to participate in the rebellion and its aftermath.

83 *Wicklow Star*, 26 November 1898. 84 Cullen, *Insurgent*, p. 94. See also *ibid.*, p. 130 and N.L.I., MS 8339, p. 37. 85 *FDJ*, 24 March 1801. See also King to ——, 8 April 1801, N.A., 620/49/99.

Protestant women of county Wexford and their narratives of the rebellion of 1798

John D. Beatty

The role of Protestant women with loyal or neutral sympathies in the rebellion of 1798 has received little attention from historians. In many ways the enormity of the suffering of Catholic women, raped and brutalised by invading English and Hessian armies at the close of the rebellion, has overshadowed and perhaps eclipsed any interest in the involvement of loyal women. Historians have tended to regard rebel women as a group, having no other recourse in the absence of contemporary narrative accounts written in their hand. With respect to Protestant women, the reverse appears to be true: a few did leave narratives of their experiences, but as a block, they have been neglected in rebellion historiography. In the accounts of Miles Byrne and Thomas Cloney, they remain almost invisible, and even though such loyalist historians as Richard Musgrave and George Taylor mention the sufferings of a few women specifically, they give little attention to their role as a constituent group.

Part of the difficulty arises from a lack of focus; historians have made little effort to study eighteenth-century Irish Protestant women in demographic, religious, or political terms. Such factors as fertility, life expectancy, child-rearing practices, religious piety, and the influence of their husbands' political activities on their own outlook have yet to be explored in any systematic or meaningful way. One could make the generalisation that in the South, these women remained overwhelmingly Anglican, with some dissenters including Methodists and Quakers. Religion played an important role in their lives, and it probably was the single most important factor affecting how they viewed the world. The non-violent views of a Quaker woman differed obviously from perceptions of Anglican and Methodist women, but the degree of piety may have differed within each group.

Literacy and socialisation also remain unexplored topics. Undoubtedly there existed a high rate of literacy among the gentry and upper

middle classes of all three Protestant denominations, although the number of lower middle-class women able to read and write is not known.
Protestant women of all social levels lived in a world that included a
wide range of social contacts with other Protestant women, both in their
own communities and in neighbouring towns. On the perimeter of their
social circle were many women of slight acquaintance, whom they knew
well enough to greet or identify from local gossip, but closer to home
was usually a smaller group of women with whom they socialised more
actively, usually having the same socio-economic status. The degree to
which those contacts were influenced by their husbands' political contacts remains unclear. Family and church connections also figured
prominently in defining a social circle.

The relationship of Protestant women to their Catholic counterparts
was more complex. Certainly they knew those Catholics who lived near
them, either as servants or relatives of servants, as tenants, or as cus-
tomers through the commercial activity in local shops and fairs. The
degree to which they entertained one another as social equals was probably minimal. Liberal gentry families such as the Richards of
Rathaspick, county Wexford, appear to have maintained close social ties
with Catholic gentry, such as the Tooles of Buckstown, but conservative
families probably had little social contact with their Catholic neighbours.

Even less is known about the political beliefs of Protestant women.
No doubt they felt loyalty to their king (though few of them wrote
about it), yet the average woman probably took little interest in local
politics, since she could not vote, and with the exception of the
Quakers, was denied a role in local church governance, the vestry. In
the absence of reliable evidence to the contrary, one must resist the
temptation of labelling a Protestant woman as 'orange' solely on the
basis of the known politics or military affiliations of her husband, father,
brother, or son. In fact, her attitude toward Catholics may have differed
considerably.

Another reason for historians' lack of interest in Protestant women
as a constituency of '98 may stem from the fact that women did not play
a military role in the rebellion. They were regarded by the United army
as non-combatants, along with the Quakers, and hence were not to be
disturbed. From the loyal claimant rolls of 1799, it would appear that
many women were robbed or reported stolen goods as a result of the
rebellion.[1] They do not appear to have suffered otherwise in large num-

---

1 'List of Claims for Relief as Suffering Loyalists', *Journal of the Irish House of Commons*,
Appendix [1800].

bers. 'In one point,' the Protestant historian James Gordon writes, 'I think we must allow some praise to the rebels. Amid all their atrocities, the chastity of the fair sex was respected. I have not been able to ascertain one instance to the contrary in the county of Wexford, though many beautiful young women were absolutely in their power'.[2] The biased Musgrave could have scored a major propaganda point by claiming that many loyalist women were murdered and many more raped by rebels, but he made no such claim.

This is not to suggest that Protestant women had total immunity from violence, as a few lost their lives in isolated incidents. A number of them died with their children in the terrible fire of the barn at Scullabogue. Several others were apparently murdered in their homes: Catherine Dale, who was stoned to death by children in county Kildare, and Hannah Manders, burned to death with several others in her house at Glassealy, also in county Kildare.[3] These women were not formal targets of the United army, but were the victims of local conflicts. In the Manders case, the burning appears to have been provoked. Indeed, United Irish leaders repeatedly warned their adherents against attacks on non-combatants, including women and children, a policy which was not mirrored on the British and loyalist side.[4] A few loyal women attempted to join their incarcerated husbands on Vinegar Hill and in the Wexford gaol, but they were always turned away by the rebel guard. There is no record of a woman being arrested by the United army and executed by military order. Musgrave relates a possibly apocryphal story of how the wife of a prisoner on Vinegar Hill attempted to offer her own life to save her husband, 'they seemed well disposed to kill her and would have done so, but that John Murphy, their captain, prevented them, having said that such a horrid deed would kindle a blush on the cheeks of the Virgin Mary'.[5]

Protestant women played their most important role in the rebellion as witnesses to the conflict, and a few, a very select number, left behind narrative accounts of what they saw. These accounts vary in content. A few were written during the rebellion or immediately after; most others were written long after the event. Those written by women specifically in county Wexford, seven in number, represent a fairly broad cross section of Protestant society in the county at that time, and taken together,

2 Revd James Gordon, *History of the Rebellion in Ireland in the Year 1798* (Dublin, 1801), p. 213. 3 For an account of these incidents see Richard Musgrave, *Memoirs of the Irish Rebellion of 1798*, 4th ed. Edited by Steven W. Myers and Delores E. McKnight (Indiana, 1995), pp 260, 690. 4 Kevin Whelan, 'Reinterpreting the 1798 rebellion in County Wexford', in Dáire Keogh and Nicholas Fulong (eds), *The Mighty Wave: The 1798 Rebellion in Wexford* (Dublin, 1996), p. 28. 5 Musgrave, p. 401.

shed some light on the attitudes of a small group of women toward the rebellion as they reacted to what for them was a period of terror and chaos. The significance of the narratives rests not only in the record they contain of the voices of women who lived two hundred years ago (a group that typically did not write their own history), but also because they reflect a candid, personal side of the rebellion with less of the hyperbole that one finds in the works of Musgrave, Taylor, and other male loyalist historians. Also significantly, these accounts provide rare descriptions of rebel women, and while these images are nearly always biased, they nonetheless have historical value. For all of these reasons, the narratives of loyalist women deserve a closer look, both by rebellion scholars and by students of Irish women's history.

I

The diary of Elizabeth Richards of Rathaspick offers an important, contemporary account of the rebellion. Elizabeth was born about 1778, the youngest of two daughters born to Thomas Richards and wife Martha (Redmond).[6] She came from a liberal, but loyal, landed gentry family and knew intimately well many other local gentry families, both Catholic and Protestant. Her father, who was deceased by 1798, had voted consistently with the liberals on several key votes of the late eighteenth century.[7] During the rebellion she lived in a large house at Rathaspick with her widowed mother and elder sister. She kept a diary throughout her adult life, and fortunately maintained a record of events between 26 May and 22 June 1798. She wrote in a vigorous style that seems remarkable for one so young and suggests that her diary was embellished or improved upon at a later date.[8]

Elizabeth's journal remains loyal in tone but also reveals evidence of her family's liberal reputation in county Wexford. As did most loyalists, Elizabeth reacted with horror to the news of the fall of Enniscorthy, and she expressed apprehension of the rebel army at Three Rocks and the occupation of Wexford, and her joy at the eventual loyalist victory at the end of June. At the same time she maintained close social ties

6 Bernard Burke, 'Richards of Macmine Castle', in *Genealogical and Heraldic History of the Landed Gentry of Ireland* (London, 1912), p. 591.   7 See Whelan, 'Reinterpreting the 1798 rebellion in County Wexford', p. 14.   8 The original mauscript of the Richards diary is believed to be owned by a descendant at The Hague, Netherlands. A copy of the diary is kept at Rathaspick Manor, county Wexford, while a second version, a copy made by Revd Thomas Orpen of a transcript by his brother Goddard Orpen, the noted historian of Norman Ireland, is housed in the National Library of Ireland (Microfilm 36486).

throughout the rebellion with several local Catholic families, including that of William Toole of Buckstown (Monaseed), and liberal Protestants such as the Le Huntes of Artramont. Three of Elizabeth's cousins, William Hatton, Michael Redmond, and John Cooke Redmond, were United Irishmen, though only Hatton maintained contact during the rebellion. One also finds throughout her journal the reports of friendly rebels giving the family news about the progress of the rising. These facts suggest that Elizabeth's family had much wider and perhaps more amiable contact with supporters of the rebellion than many other Protestants, and it may explain why the Richards' home was left virtually undisturbed.

In spite of her family's liberality, Elizabeth's diary is nonetheless replete with evidence of her fear, aggravated by a spurious rumour that she and her family would soon be murdered. On 30 May, after the fall of Wexford, a family friend came to their house with the news that all Protestants were to be murdered and that they must prepare for death. One is struck by the terror that she felt at that moment. Elizabeth wrote:

> I looked around me with horror. I felt there was no possibility of concealment or flight. The infernal pikes seemed already to glitter at our breasts. I shrieked and for a moment was all but mad … We could hear shouts or rather yells of joy from the town that struck terror into our hearts. I sat up late; death, I imagined, would have additional horrors if unthought of, and notwithstanding the assurances of safety that had been given to me, to that only did I look forward.[9]

Elizabeth reported attempts by several of the family's Catholic friends to convince her to convert to Roman Catholicism as a means of preserving their lives, but she remained steadfast in her Anglican faith. The most persistent was Mary Byrne, a Catholic who managed to coax the Richards to Wexford to meet with Fr John Corrin, the parish priest, but Elizabeth remained defiant. She wrote, 'I was too much exhausted to attempt arguing with her. I told her no force could induce me to change my religion, that it was not from the prejudice of education, but from conviction that I was a Protestant, that I could die, but not become Roman Catholic'.[10] Later Corrin arrived to reassure them that no massacre was intended and to offer the protection of his home.

9 Elizabeth Richards diary [Orpen copy, M36486], pp 7–8. 10 Elizabeth Richards diary [Orpen copy, M36486], p. 14.

This theme of attempted conversion recurs in several of these loyalist narratives as there seems to have been a prevailing view, shared by
the common masses of Protestants and Catholics alike, that all
Protestants who did not convert by the end of the rebellion would lose
their lives. Though one might see Mary Byrne as kind-hearted in her
effort to save her friends, Elizabeth remained contemptuous of her
efforts and in her journal called her a hypocrite, suggesting that she
feigned concern over the spiritual welfare of her family while at the
same time privately enjoying their predicament.

Elizabeth provides a fleeting and more disturbing glimpse of Irish
women at the end of her account on 22 June, when the rebellion was
being crushed by invading English and Hessian troops. The cries of distress from the Catholic women being raped in her neighbourhood
prompted Elizabeth to note cryptically, 'all the morning we listened to
the shrieks, the complainings of female rebels. They almost turned my
joy into sorrow'.[11] Here is evidence of her ambivalence: she was loyal,
but as a woman felt empathy for other suffering women.

II

The narrative of Dinah Goff of Horetown House, near Foulkesmills,
provides another landed gentry perspective of the rebellion in county
Wexford. Unlike the Anglican Richards family, the Goffs were Quakers
and hence were neither loyal nor rebel. Dinah and her family refused to
take sides and supported a non-violent outcome to the conflict. Aged
only fourteen in 1798, she was the youngest daughter in a large family
born to Jacob and Elizabeth (Wilson) Goff. Her family home was located near the rebel camps of Carrigbyrne and Corbett Hill about ten miles
from Wexford, and because of its location, she and her family were
given an unusual window on events of the rebellion. She was an eye-
witness of the Battle of Goff's Bridge which occurred on the family
property.

Her account was first dictated to a friend in 1850, and six years later
was published with some alterations as a Quaker religious tract.[12] The
lapse in time between its authorship and the rebellion itself may lead

11 Elizabeth Richards diary [Orpen copy, M36486], p. 38.   12 Dinah Goff's original
manuscript memoir, dictated perhaps to Mary Forster of Tottenham, is housed in the
library of Trinity College as Manuscript 5116. A slightly different version later appeared
under the title, *Divine Protection Through Extraordinary Dangers During the Irish Rebellion
of 1798* (Philadelphia, 1856). This latter version was reprinted in J.M. Richardson, *Six
Generations of Friends in Ireland, 1655 to 1890* (London, 1895).

one to suspect its accuracy, but Dinah's memories are detailed, and she seems to have had no hidden agenda in writing it except to illustrate how her family's Quaker faith sustained them in a period of adversity.

Because of their wealth and the location of their estate, the Goffs became a magnet for rebel activity. Dinah provides many valuable first-hand observations in her account, both of the United army and of rene-gade rebels or 'Babes of the Woods,' who were not part of the army. Her father's neutrality during the rebellion included his refusal either to join the yeomanry, own a working firearm, or take the United Irish oath. Instead, remaining true to the philanthropic tenets of his Quaker faith, he offered the hospitality of his home to both Hessian and United armies. Dinah, her mother, and her sisters baked bread and distributed it to the hungry, and dressed the wounds of the injured. They also offered a refugee Catholic family shelter in their house. At the height of the rebellion, many rebels took up residence in the Goff's yard. Dinah recalled how 'many hundreds were daily on our lawn, and our business was to hand them food as they demanded it'.[13] When told by a rebel that the Quakers would not be harmed but were to be driven into Connacht at the end of the rebellion to land worth two pence an acre, Dinah's mother had said cheerfully, 'give us a good portion, for we have a large family'.[14]

The neutrality of the Goffs did not shield them from experiencing a number of trials, both during and immediately after the rebellion. When they continued to attend their monthly meeting, they were jeered by their neighbours but allowed to pass. Dinah's father was threatened with death on many occasions and had several close calls. Once a band of renegade rebels led him into a field at gunpoint and placed a pistol at his head in an attempt to make him relinquish any hidden valuables. Dinah's sister had thrown her arms around her father in an attempt to shield him from a rebel sword. Still, he had offered no resistance to the threats made against him, and his death later that year from natural causes was blamed on these experiences.

Dinah related how her father narrowly escaped death on another occasion and provided at the same time a glimpse of rebel women, who seemed to play a positive role in blunting the violence of the men. She wrote:

> one day, about noon, a large company appeared on the lawn, car-rying a black flag, which we well knew to be the signal for death. My dear father advanced to meet them as usual, with his open,

13 Goff, *Divine Protection*, 13. 14 Goff, *Divine Protection*, p. 11.

benevolent countenance, and my mother, turning to me, said, with her sweet, placid smile, 'perhaps my stiff stays may prevent my dying easily'. On which the Roman Catholic who had taken refuge with us, said, 'have faith in God, madam; I hope they will not hurt you'. She quickly pushed forward and joined my dear father, who was surrounded by a large party. He observed to them, he feared they might injure each other, as their muskets were preparing for firing; when one of them replied, 'let those who are afraid keep out of the way'. My mother distinctly heard one of them say, 'why don't you begin?' and each seemed looking to the other to commence the work of death. Some of them presently muttered, 'We cannot.' At this critical moment some women came in great agitation through the crowd, clinging to their husbands and dragging them away. Thus a higher Power evidently appeared to frustrate the intentions of the murderers, and my beloved father was again graciously delivered.[15]

In contrast to this group of peace-making women were another group which Dinah found menacing. She recalled that after a group of rebel soldiers were thwarted by a United Irish officer from plundering Horetown, 'many wicked-looking women were outside, evidently waiting for plunder, and when disappointed, they made frightful faces and shook their hands at us as we stood at the windows. One of them was heard to say when [the soldiers] withdrew, "You are set of chicken-hearted fellows!"'

Like Elizabeth Richards, Dinah offered evidence of a gentle effort to convert her family to Roman Catholicism. She related the activities of an unnamed priest, who regularly visited the family, providing the following story:

he [the priest] said he came with good news – that we were now all of one religion the world over. My mother inquired what it was, as she believed there was only one true religion. He replied that an edict from the Pope had arrived, and that it proclaimed the universal Roman Catholic religion, adding that it was high time for her to put up the cross. She asked what he meant by the cross. He said, 'put up the outward sign on yourself and your children'. She answered, *that* they should never do; but she was thankful in believing that her heavenly Father was enabling her to bear the cross.'[16]

15 Goff, *Divine Protection*, pp 21-2.   16 Goff, *Divine Protection*, pp 12-13.

Dinah added that the priest was 'uniformly kind' and believed his presence was a positive influence on the minds of the rebels.

The Goffs' neutrality and non-violent stance served ultimately to protect them during the rebellion, but it was often a precarious shield. They did not promote the loyalist cause, but they obviously longed for the restoration of order that came with the conclusion of the conflict.

III

The narrative of Jane Barber of Clovass, county Wexford, offers the perspective of a girl from a lower middle-class family, which distinguishes it from the previous two narratives and makes it highly unusual, the only one known of its kind. It is not dated but was evidently written many years after the event when the author was middle-aged.[17] Jane was the daughter of Samuel Barber, a farmer, draper, and owner of a small textile factory at Clovass. Born in 1783, she was thus nearly the same age as Dinah Goff at the time of the rebellion. Like the Richards, the Barbers were Anglican, but their political views are not known with certainty. Jane's father did business with local Catholics, but the family had only two servants. When asked to join the rebel cause by one of his tenants, he had vowed his unswerving loyalty to the government. He was not an Orangeman, however, and indeed he may have held some liberal views. He had served in the Enniscorthy Yeoman Cavalry under the command of Solomon Richards, which had a more moderate reputation in dealing with Catholics than Archibald Jacob's Vinegar Hill Rangers.[18]

On 26 May Jane and her family fled their farm at Clovass for the sanctuary of Enniscorthy, where they witnessed the rebel victory over its yeomanry. Jane offers a graphic description of the ensuing chaos and the murder of her father on an Enniscorthy street. The family had attempted to disguise themselves as rebels by carrying a flitch of bacon at the end of a pike. After being separated from her father, Jane, her mother and siblings were given shelter with other Protestant refugees in the garden of William Barker, an Enniscorthy brewer and a captain in the United army.

17 The location of the original narrative of Jane Barber is not known. A typescript version is housed in the Wexford Library and in the National Library of Ireland. 18 See the claim made by Samuel Barber's widow Elinor in *A List of the Subscribers to the Fund for the Relief of Widows and Orphans of Yeomen, Soldiers, &c., Who Fell in Suppressing the Late Rebellion* (Dublin, 1800), n.p.

In addition to writing a lively account, Jane provided a detailed description of a rebel woman, relating how on setting out to find her missing father, she encountered Molly Martin, the mother of one of the Barber's servants. She wrote:

> The first person I saw was Martin's mother, dressed completely in new and excellent clothes, and in particular, a remarkably handsome beaver-hat. I was so astonished at this, for she was very poor, that forgetting for the moment all my anxiety and fear, I asked her who had given her the hat. She answered me sternly, 'Hush! tis not for one the like of you to ask me where I got it'. 'But Molly', said I, 'have you seen my father?' 'I have', said she, 'and he is dead'. I forgot what I said or did for some minutes after hearing this, but I then found that Molly Martin had drawn me away from the garden gate, lest, as she told me, my grief should tell my mother what had happened. I clung to her to take me to him that I might see him once more; at first she refused, but at last, to pacify my violence, she consented.[19]

When at last Jane discovered her father's corpse, she encountered another example of rebel intervention on her behalf. She wrote:

> I fell on my knees and, whilst kissing his forehead, broke out into loud cries, when one of the rebels gave me such a blow with the handle of his pike in my side as laid me breathless for a moment beside my father and must have broken my ribs, but for a very strong bodice I wore. He was going to repeat the blow, but then his comrade levelled his pike at him, crying with an oath, 'If you strike her again, I will thrust this through your body! Because this child is frightened, are you to beat her?' I now knew him to be one Jack O'Brien, who but the preceding week had purchased some cloth from my father at a fair … He spoke with kindness to me, and he and Molly Martin brought me back to the garden where I had left my mother, advising me not to tell her what I had seen lest she should perish with terror and sorrow.[20]

Jane's prior acquaintances with Molly Martin and Jack O'Brien proved instrumental in rescuing her from a difficult situation and illustrates the importance of such contacts during the chaos of the rebellion. By the

---

19 Jane Barber, *Recollections of the Summer of 1798* [typescript], pp 9-10. 20 Jane Barber, *Recollections of the Summer of 1798*, p. 10.

time the conflict concluded, the Barbers' house and factory at Clovass were in ruins and all of their possessions lost. An English army officer gave them a bed from the Vinegar Hill plunder, and they received a daily ration of bread from the troops. Nevertheless, Jane continued to treat suffering Catholics with kindness and refused to reveal to the authorities a group of rebels hiding in her barn.

IV

The diary of Mrs Brownrigg of Greenmount in the parish of Kilpipe, county Wexford, is well-known, having been published first in Musgrave in 1801.[21] The identity of Mrs Brownrigg has not been established with certainty beyond that she was the widow of Commissioner John Brownrigg of Greenmount, that she was middle-aged in 1798 and had two young children, a daughter Isabella and a son Henry John. She may have been identical to Isabella Stanford, who married John Brownrigg in 1789, according to the marriage licenses of the Diocese of Ferns, but this assertion has not been proved.[22] She appears to come from a mid-level Protestant Anglican family in county Wexford, a strata slightly below that of gentry, but wealthier than the Barbers.

This journal illustrates the difficulty of classifying loyalists neatly into liberal-conservative categories. As the possessor of a government post, her husband may have had a political alliance with the conservative Lord Ely and hence may have held Orange views. His widow seems to have been friendly with the Orange magistrate John Henry Lyster, to whose house she fled at the outbreak of the rebellion. She also had liberal ties, however, showing evidence in her account of an acquaintance with the moderate Le Huntes of Artramont. She remained on friendly terms with Dr Ebenezer Jacob, the liberal mayor of Wexford, in whose house she stayed during the rebellion, and with Bagenal Harvey, who gave her a letter of protection. As did most Protestants, Mrs Brownrigg maintained a wide circle of acquaintances, both liberal and conservative.

21 See Musgrave, 4th ed., pp 422-35. The first complete edition of the account appeared in two articles in 1895-96 with some errors, see Francis Joseph Bigger (ed.), 'Wexford in 1798: An Account of Events by an Eye-witness', *Waterford and South East Ireland Archaeological Society Journal*, vol. 1 (1895), pp 268-78; vol. 2 (1896), pp 16-22. The entire account, with the same errors, appeared again in H.F.B. Wheeler and A.M. Broadley, *The War in Wexford: An Account of the Rebellion in the South of Ireland in 1798 Told from Original Documents* (London, 1910), pp 162-99. 22 Ferns Marriage License index, National Archives of Ireland. The author has attempted to prove Mrs Brownrigg's identity by searching for her burial in the parish records of Bath, England, where she died in 1804, but he had been unsuccessful in locating her.

The Brownrigg journal begins on 26 May and ends on 3 June 1798, although much of the account written on the latter date was later expanded and enhanced by the writer after the rebellion, perhaps for Musgrave's benefit. The journal offers an important, first-hand account of the rebel occupation of the town of Wexford and the executions on Wexford Bridge. After leaving Lyster's house, Mrs Brownrigg and her children attempted to flee to Wales by booking passage on a ship in Wexford harbour commanded by Thomas Dixon, a rebel sea captain. Dixon, with his wife Margery, took prisoners of nearly all the men on board, and he announced, according to the narrative, that 'no woman or child should be killed, but that no man should escape except three he named'.[23]

Mrs Brownrigg harboured strong hostility for the rebels and perceived them as having evil intentions. Recalling her time aboard ship, she wrote, 'what ferocious savages then appeared, intoxicated with whiskey and victory, one woman brandishing the sheath of a sword and boasting of her exploits. She was a sister of Mrs Dixon and an old acquaintance of mine, as her husband had been killed at Artramont.'[24] She portrayed Captain Dixon in the darkest of terms for having forced her to view the corpse of John Boyd on the Wexford quay. Dixon's cohorts seemed demonic, but she and her young daughter engaged Dixon's wife in a friendly dialogue in an effort to diffuse what seemed a tense situation. They later left the ship when another man, 'more humane than the rest', offered his boat to take them safely to shore.[25]

Despite suffering lengthy periods in a state of terror, Mrs Brownrigg was treated reasonably well by the rebels throughout her ordeal. Though she lost most of her clothes in her trunk to Mrs Dixon, she found sanctuary with Dr Jacob, where she found some stability until Wexford fell back under loyalist control. The chaos taking place around her at times seemed almost incomprehensible, and she remained pessimistic about the lives of her friends, noting that 'all my friends in town were loyal and I supposed were murdered'.[26]

Some rebels seemed hostile (Edward Fitzgerald gave her a ferocious look), yet others showed her much respect. This was particularly true of many in the United Irish political leadership in Wexford. Bagenal Harvey, she wrote, 'spoke with great kindness, seemed greatly struck by

23 Brownrigg narrative in Wheeler and Broadley, 169.   24 Brownrigg narrative in Wheeler and Broadley, pp 169–70. Mrs Brownrigg's reference here to Artramont is further evidence of her association with the Le Huntes. Daniel Stanford, a Dublin attorney admitted as a freeman of Wexford in 1776, served as executor of the will of Richard LeHunte in 1779.   25 Brownrigg narrative in Wheeler and Broadley, p. 172.   26 Brownrigg narrative in Wheeler and Broadley, p. 171.

the misery he must have felt he had caused, and gave me a paper ... at the same time saying he had no real command'.[27] Matthew Keugh behaved as a gentleman and promised to help her obtain passage for her family on a ship, but was unsuccessful.

Her account of the execution of Protestant prisoners on Wexford Bridge on 20 June remains one of the few eye-witness accounts extant. She provided a poignant description of what she saw:

> I thought some alarm had induced [the rebels] to leave the town and sat eagerly watching till I beheld, yes – I absolutely saw a poor fellow beg for his life and then most barbarously murdered. To give a minute account of this hellish scene is beyond my strength ... I saw the horrid wretches kneel down on the quay, lift up their hands seeming to pray with the greatest devotion, then rise and join other murderers. Their yells of delight at the suffering of their victims will ever, I believe, sound in my ears. To describe what we all suffered would be impossible. I never shed a tear, but felt all over in the most violent bodily pain.[28]

Mrs Brownrigg concluded her narrative with a description of the retaking of Wexford by a group of yeomanry, whom she portrayed in heroic terms with no hint of its excesses. She remained confident and unswerving in her loyalist outlook, and with the exception of Harvey, she had no sympathy for any of the rebel leaders. Her narrative, though not overtly political, supports the prevailing conservative loyalist view that existed in 1799, when many Protestants regarded the events of the previous year with anger and consternation.

v

The narrative of Barbara Lett of Killaligan, county Wexford also takes a conservative, anti-Catholic view of the rebellion, but in some respects is more complex than the Brownrigg narrative. The Lett account has been described as a diary, but in fact was written in 1859 when the writer was aged eighty-two.[29] Barbara (Daniel) Lett was born in 1777,

27 Brownrigg narrative in Wheeler and Broadley, p. 173. 28 Brownrigg narrative in Wheeler and Broadley, p. 186. 29 There are two nineteenth-century versions of Barbara Lett's narrative, virtually identical, one being MS 4472-73 in the National Library of Ireland, the other being MS 2066 in the library of Trinity College Dublin. The former version was used as the basis by Joseph Ranson in editing 'A 1798 Diary by Mrs. Barbara Newton Lett, Killaligan, Enniscorthy', *The Past*, 5 (1949), pp 117-49.

the daughter of William Daniel of Fortview, county Wexford. Her father served as Surveyor of Excise in Enniscorthy, a political appointment which suggests he held conservative views and owed his position to Lord Ely. He was among the prisoners piked to death on Wexford Bridge. In 1794, Barbara had married Newton Lett, son of Joshua Lett of Killaligan, a liberal Protestant and farmer, whose family was better off than the Barbers but perhaps not quite as wealthy as the Brownriggs. The Letts were Anglican but as a family were divided in their sympathies during the rebellion. Newton Lett remained loyal, but his brother Stephen Lett of Newcastle, whose wife was a niece of Bagenal Harvey, became an active rebel supporter.[30] As with Mrs Brownrigg's journal, the Lett account reflects a strong anti-rebel tone, but unlike the others remains critical also of the excesses of the loyal army.

At the beginning of the rebellion, Barbara and her husband fled their home and journeyed to Enniscorthy, where, like Jane Barber, they witnessed the fall of that town and the chaos that followed. She became separated from her husband during the battle, and later stood weeping in the streets until being consoled by a rebel named Williams, who offered her his personal protection and conducted her to his own home for safety. Williams' action seems extraordinary on the face of it, for, unlike the other accounts of loyalists helped by rebels, Barbara apparently had no prior acquaintance with Williams. Later, when she asked for shelter from her sister-in-law Mary Lett, a rebel sympathiser, she was turned away.

Whilst under Williams' protection, Barbara also reported an attempted conversion experience. She wrote: 'Mrs Williams suggested that our better plan would be to send for the priest. She said that if we were christened by him, they would no longer look upon us as heretics. In this she was mistaken, for after submitting to this form, our enemy were not less cruel.'[31] She met with Fr James Doyle, parish priest of Davidstown, who spoke to her with kindness and offered what protection he could give.

---

30 Kevin Whelan asserts that the family of another brother, William Lett of Rathsilla (Kilgibbon) 'were among the earliest Orangemen in the county', attending an Orange lodge at Enniscorthy and adorning themselves and their horses in Orange insignias (Kevin Whelan, 'The Religious Factor in the 1798 rebellion in county Wexford', in Patrick O'Flanagan, Paul Ferguson, and Kevin Whelan (eds), *Rural Ireland 1600-1900: Modernisation and Change* [Cork, 1987], pp 69, 79.) This fact may have influenced the rebels' treatment of Newton and Barbara Lett, leading to the burning of their home. There is no evidence, however, that Newton Lett was an Orangeman.   31 Lett narrative, MS 4472-73, NLI.

Indeed, throughout the remainder of the rebellion, Barbara found assistance from benevolent rebels, often people whom she knew slightly. Martin Fenlon, a rebel leader but also a childhood friend, delivered a letter from her imprisoned father in Wexford. She wrote 'he assured me that if my father were at Enniscorthy and under his protection, no one should injure him'.[32] At Fenlon's urging, she applied for a pass from Captain William Barker, who treated her with courtesy and gave her the necessary document. At the jail, she compared some of the guards to demons, but was nevertheless treated politely by a few and allowed to see her father on several occasions.

Barbara used the terms 'bloodthirsty' and 'barbarous' to describe many of the rebels whom she encountered, and in many instances her depiction of the government soldiers were no less charitable. The North Cork Militia, she admitted, was 'badly disciplined,' and the Hessians, 'were as merciless as the rebels they came to subdue, who fired indiscriminately upon unoffending women and killed the suffering loyalists who escaped the other party'.[33] She related the story of Mrs Pounden and John Devereux, who rushed out to greet their deliverers in Enniscorthy, only to be mistaken for rebels and shot dead in the street by crown troops. Later, when seeking protection from the English in Enniscorthy, her husband was seized, threatened with death, and briefly imprisoned after being mistaken for a rebel. She wrote:

> upon entering town, we were interrupted by a military guard, one of whom seized my husband with the one hand, with the other drew his bayonet, swearing vehemently that he should die that moment for a croppy villain. In vain I pleaded that we were suffering loyalists, who were plundered and persecuted by the rebels and had flown to them for protection.[34]

An officer on horseback ordered him released, but he was later seized again by another group of soldiers. Barbara attempted to obtain his release from Colonel Bligh of the Dublin Militia, but was rebuffed and called a hypocrite. Only after she showed him the letter written by her father from prison did he soften his views and believe her. She returned to the countryside with a group of women who earlier had entered Enniscorthy 'decked with orange lilies, the symbol of their Order' which they later hastily removed upon hearing a rumour that the rebels were returning to destroy them.[35] This statement is the only one in any

---

32 Lett narrative, MS 4472-73, NLI. 33 Lett narrative, MS 4472-73, NLI. 34 Lett narrative, MS 4472-73, NLI. 35 Lett narrative, MS 4472-73, NLI.

of the narratives reflecting the support of Protestant women for the
Orange Order. It is clear from Barbara's statement that the Letts were
not members.

After suffering these experiences it is not surprising that Barbara
was filled with bitterness and remorse at the rebellion's close. Her home
was destroyed, her father was killed on the bridge, and in 1799, the
Letts' claim for compensation was rejected, perhaps on account of the
rebel sympathies of Newton Lett's brother and father.[36] On seeing the
heads of Harvey, Keugh, and Grogan impaled over the courthouse in
Wexford, she admitted, 'the human heart was turned to stone at that
time ... My great revenge had stomach for them all'.[37]

VI

Compared with the previous accounts, the narrative of Alicia Pounden
of Monart is a much shorter work, and like that of Lett and Goff was
written many years after the rebellion.[38] Alicia was born in 1772, the
daughter of John Colley of Ballywalter, near Gorey, county Wexford, a
prominent member of the local gentry. Later she became the wife of
John Pounden of Daphne in the parish of Monart.[39] Pounden, a liberal
member of the Wexford gentry who served captain in Solomon
Richards' moderate Enniscorthy Yeoman Cavalry, was killed in the
Battle of Enniscorthy on 28 May.[40] Following his death, Alicia and her
children had attempted to escape Wexford by ship, but like Mrs
Brownrigg, were prevented from doing so when the ship's crew pro-
fessed loyalty to the rebel cause. In describing the different standard of
treatment that women received, Alicia agreed with Brownrigg and
recalled, 'we remained in the ship till Thursday, when parties of the

---

36 'List of Claimants for Relief as Suffering Loyalists', *Journal of the Irish House of
Commons*, Appendix [1800], ccclxxxvii. 37 Barbara Lett narrative, MS 4472-73, NLI.
38 The original account of Alicia Pounden is preserved as manuscript T.720, Public Record Office of Northern Ireland. It was reprinted in Simon L.M. de Montfort (ed.), 'Mrs.
Pounden's Experiences During the 1798 Rising in Co. Wexford', *Irish Ancestor*, 8:1
(1976), pp 4-8. 39 See 'Pounden of Ballywalter House', *Burke's Landed Gentry of Ireland*
(London, 1912), p. 572. 40 John Pounden's brother Joshua was persecuted for his liberal views by his more conservative neighbours. See Kevin Whelan, 'Politicisation in
County Wexford and the Origins of the 1798 Rebellion', in Hugh Gough and David
Dickson (eds), *Ireland and the French Revolution* (Dublin, 1990), pp 162-3. Their maternal grandther, Revd Joshua Nunn, was among those 'cherished by the rebels because of
their universal reputation as charitable men'. See Whelan, 'Religious Factor in the 1798
Rebellion', p. 75.

Rebels went out in boats and took all the men prisoners, but told the females they should not be injured in honour of the Virgin Mary'.[41]

In spite of her sufferings, which were not as severe as those of Barbara Lett, Alicia remarked throughout her narrative on the kindnesses shown her by various rebel neighbours. After her husband was killed in battle, a tenant of theirs named John McGuire obtained a coffin and had the body buried in the churchyard. Later, with her in-laws, she found shelter at the home of a Catholic family in Enniscorthy. Her house at Daphne was not burned, but received a note of protection signed by a list of United Irish leaders.

Alicia's assessment of rebel women seems less charitable after she returned at last to her own home and found it occupied by another family. She wrote:

> the first night I went, they had a dance and fiddle, the sounds of which were most distressing to me; the servants said it was cruel, just as the poor Mistress had come, but the women of the before mentioned family said – 'if she does not like it, we will turn her out'; indeed, these were amongst the few instances where any incivility was offered, as the numerous persons who were assembled at my place during the rebellion, were particularly respectful and said that no one should have injured Mr Pounden, if he had not been killed in the battle'.[42]

This statement illustrates the loyalty felt by the Poundens' Catholic tenants in contrast to the sentiments of those rebels unconnected with their estate.

The liberal reputation of the Poundens may have further influenced the rebels' treatment of Alicia and her family. Whilst she seemed happy to see the appearance of English troops at the close of the rebellion, she also praised the fact that at Vinegar Hill, when the army had the opportunity to kill all of the rebels and allow no route of escape, 'humanity triumphed and the orders were issued 'to disperse, but not kill'.[43]

VII

One of the most intriguing and complex of the women's narratives from county Wexford is that of Jane Adams of Summerseat House. Dated

41 'Mrs. Pounden's Experiences During the 1798 Rising in Co. Wexford', p. 6. 42 'Mrs. Pounden's Experiences During the 1798 Rising in Co. Wexford', p. 7.   43 'Mrs. Pounden's Experiences During the 1798 Rising in Co. Wexford', p. 8.

between May and August, 1798, it was apparently written as a diary, although much of it was evidently rewritten or embellished after 1801 as the author makes an allusion to Musgrave's history. The account was first published in 1823 in T. Crofton Croker's *Researches in the South of Ireland*.[44]

Jane (Owen) Adams was a native of Dublin, the sister of the Revd Roger Carmichael Owen, prebendary of Tombe in county Wexford, a land agent and a clerical magistrate with a notorious reputation for pitchcapping.[45] In 1773, Jane had married the Revd Tobias Adams in Dublin, but after having three children, the couple became estranged, with Adams moving alone to county Cork to become rector of Cloyne.[46] Jane and her two daughters had settled with her elderly father at Summerseat, three miles from Wexford town. The family was part of the professional-middleman strata of Protestant society on a par with that of Mrs Brownrigg, a level just under that of landed gentry but slightly above the large-farmer level of the Letts.

The political stance of the Owen family in county Wexford remains more difficult to ascertain as its members were not necessarily of one mind. As a clerical magistrate, Roger Owen identified himself with the conservatives, treated Catholics under his control in harsh terms, and may in fact have belonged to the Orange Order, though no direct proof has yet been found. Hence he was much despised by the Irish at Camolin and Gorey. His father was too old to be political in 1798, however, and as a Dublin native was probably regarded as an outsider by older families in Wexford. Sister Jane was, by contrast, non-political and appears to have treated her Catholic neighbours and servants in a strikingly different manner from her brother.

On the Monday after Whitsunday, Jane fled with her family to Cora island in the south of Wexford Harbour, but was later persuaded to return home. Although she heard a variety of threats made against Protestants, she nonetheless met a number of rebels who offered assistance, often on the basis of some prior contact. Laurence Butler, a rebel captain and former coachman of a neighbouring family, offered her the protection of his guard because she had once offered him a warm drink

44 See T. Crofton Croker, *Researches in the South of Ireland*, 2nd ed. (Shannon, 1969), pp 347-85. The original account, Add. MS 21,142 in the British Museum was significantly bowdlerized by Croker, much as he did with Holt's memoir. Some clauses were shuffled around and some added, but the memoir was not otherwise significantly changed. 45 See Miles Byrne, *Memoirs of Miles Byrne* (Paris, 1863), I, p. 33. 46 See for example W. Maziere Brady, *Clerical and Parochial Records of Cork, Cloyne, and Ross* (Dublin, 1863), II:16. See also Canon James B. Leslie, 'Biographical Succession List of the Clergy of Dublin Diocese' (ms., Representative Church Body Library, Dublin), I, p. 340.

on a cold day.[47] Hayes, one of Jane's servants, managed to keep her family fed during the rebellion, despite having rebel sympathies and being permitted to pass freely through various camps. On another occasion, when a group of pikemen found her disconsolate on the side of the road, they offered comfort and escorted her safely to her home, promising to return again in the evening to stand guard at Summerseat.[48]

These periods of rebel protection were brief. At other times, Jane recounted having to endure the waves of rebel parties that raided her house, one of which took her elderly father into custody at the jail in Wexford. Several Catholics had made it clear to her at the time that her failure to convert to Roman Catholicism was the reason for her father's imprisonment. She quoted a servant as saying, 'ah! my dear mistress, if you had allowed yourself, my master, and the young ladies to be christened, it would not have come to this'.[49] Said another more hostile rebel officer: 'Mr Owen has been favoured more than any gentleman in the barony: you should have sent for a priest long ago.'[50]

Jane offered herself as a prisoner with her father, but was told there was no room for women. Refusing to accept the matter passively, she engaged several rebels in a dialogue and eventually persuaded a sympathetic official to intervene. After explaining that her father was ill and advanced in years and that the imprisonment would prove fatal to him, she obtained a pass from Matthew Keugh to return with her father to Summerseat. Having gone without eating, she became hungry on the road back and begged for bread. A rebel soldier threw her a large piece of his own bread and cheese, refusing to take any money in compensation.

The ordeal of Jane's brother Roger proved an even greater trial than that of her father, yet it prompted her to take the initiative by engaging the rebel leadership in a constructive dialogue. Roger was arrested, pitch-capped, and suspended over the market house in Gorey, and then led barefoot to the jail in Wexford. The experience drove him to the point of insanity. By the time he reached Wexford he was dancing in the street, exclaiming and singing that he was an Orangeman. He sent his sister a note from prison, stating that he was never merrier in his life and that he desired fresh vegetables and cucumbers. Upon hearing this news, Jane returned to Wexford and boldly sought his release from several officials. She received threats from the crowd, but was received courteously by William Kearney, who had charge of the Wexford jail.

47 *Researches in the South of Ireland*, p. 352. 48 *Researches in the South of Ireland*, pp 368-69. 49 *Researches in the South of Ireland*, p. 355. 50 *Researches in the South of Ireland*, p. 355.

She could not at first obtain his release, but succeeded in getting some provisions to him. She persisted in her appeal to Kearney and later convinced him to give his permission to take her brother into her own custody at Summerseat. When a party of rebels returned later that day to demand him, she refused to give him up, reading to them Kearney's letter of protection and saying, 'at your peril, lay a finger on him!'[51] Because he was not in the jail at the time the executions took place on Wexford Bridge, Owen's life was spared.

None of these experiences left Jane hardened with prejudice; she continued to behave with humanity toward her neighbours and local Catholics. Near the end of the rebellion, a young rebel soldier was brought to Summerseat with a badly wounded arm. Jane ordered him taken immediately to a bedroom, where she permitted the local priest to administer the sacrament. Jane had wanted to relieve the boy's suffering by sending for a doctor, but she was prevented from doing so by the boy's mother. Finding the woman's behaviour incomprehensible, she wrote:

> I really dreaded the scene that I thought must have ensued, but she strutted into the room with an air of effrontery that astonished me, and turning to him with more command than tenderness said, 'what signifies your arm, if you suffer death it is in the good cause, your Saviour suffered for you'. I was shocked at her countenance, but assured her he was in no danger, except from his wound, and urged her to let me send for Doctor Johnston, which she refused very bluntly, and desired her son to take her arm and come home, that 'all was not over with them yet'. This horrid woman frightened me so much that I most gladly saw her departure, and pitied extremely the poor young man, whom I offered to keep till he was better.[52]

This encounter reflects another tantalising element in Jane's account: how the rebellion influenced the relationship of rebel women to loyalist women. Her account suggests that it affected that relationship more dramatically than that of rebel men and loyalist women. The gallantry shown to her by several United Irish army soldiers was not mirrored in the behaviour of the women whom she encountered, and she offered several stories and illustrations. Once, when begging for a morsel of food from a group of women feeding the rebel soldiers, she was rebuffed and told there was none to be had.[53] Later in the course of the

51 *Researches in the South of Ireland*, p. 371. 52 *Researches in the South of Ireland*, p. 377.
53 *Researches in the South of Ireland*, p. 358.

rebellion, after seeing her brother in prison, she suffered an emotional breakdown and fainted after entering a Wexford ale-house. When she revived, she noticed

> four women were sitting in a corner of the room at breakfast, all this time unmoved, though my darling Susan repeatedly begged of them to give her mamma a glass of water; but to the disgrace of our sex, she called in vain, till two men came into the house and rendered me every assistance in their power, and scolded Judy for not asking the lady to take a cup of tea.[54]

Rebel women in county Wexford may have perceived the rebellion, even in its early stages, as a revolution in the social order, freeing them from the constraints and formalities of the old system. When a party of rebels suggested to Jane's faithful servant Ally that her role with her mistress was now reversed, it prompted an emotional reply:

> the same persons were quite abusive to my faithful Ally for smoothing some muslin handkerchiefs of mine, and asked her did she still think of herself as my servant? that she ought to make me change places with her – she had the *right* to command me. This shewed me how impressed they were with the idea that they were really to *change places*, as they said, and all become gentlemen. My excellent Ally burst into tears, and said she would die before she would *command* me'.[55]

As the rebellion concluded, it apparently left Jane without the same bitterness that Barbara Lett and Mrs Brownrigg experienced. Her account harbours no cry for vengeance. Instead, she had reached a more pragmatic view of the events, offering in tangible ways her gratitude to the many local Catholics who had shown kindness to her family. She wrote letters of protection for many Catholic neighbours and instructed them to nail the cards on their cabin doors. She invited Fr Roderick O'Connor, the local parish priest of Rathmacnee, to dinner at Summer-seat out of gratitude for assisting her in getting her father released from prison. She also wrote a letter in praise of his humane conduct and interceded on his behalf with the English commanding officer. These were not the actions of one sympathetic to the Orange Order, and they illustrate the difficulty of labelling a family as 'conservative' or 'bigoted' on the basis of the views of only one of its members.

54 *Researches in the South of Ireland*, p. 368. 55 *Researches in the South of Ireland*, p. 369.

Taking these women's narratives together, are there some general themes that present themselves in them that would allow one to reach some general conclusions about the attitudes and condition of Protestant women in 1798? The answer is cautiously affirmative, but any such conclusions must remain tentative due to a number of factors. The existing accounts, whilst coming from a cross-section of Protestant society in county Wexford, are nevertheless too few in number to be considered a sufficiently large statistical sample to make any definitive or sweeping statement. Moreover, there is always a danger that the authors have embellished their accounts in ways that cannot be verified, especially those written long after the rebellion when memories had dimmed and events may have appeared more sensational or their own actions more heroic.

One must also consider the author's motive for writing the account: Dinah Goff's attempt at religious edification; Barbara Lett's venting of anger against both the rebels and the British, or Alicia Pounden's autobiographical sketch for her descendants. Each of these factors may have influenced the tone of the narrative, although none of the writers appear to have had a political agenda or distorted facts in an overt manner.

The overriding feature of these narratives remains the strength of women, each trying to cope with a period of confusion, terror, and chaos. The terror had different sources for the writers. Elizabeth Richards feared being forced to abjure her religion or face death. For Dinah Goff, Jane Barber, and to a certain extent Mrs Brownrigg, the threat came from renegade rebels or Dixon's sailors, none of whom were governed by the discipline of the United army. For Barbara Lett, the conquering British army and the local yeomanry posed additional terrors, mistaking loyalists for rebels, confiscating provisions, and dispensing summary justice without evidence. Several writers reported being robbed, but only Jane Barber was assaulted.

Rather than shy away from the ordeal, most of the women described how they met the challenge of the rebellion in a forthright manner. In resisting attempts to convert her, Elizabeth Richards engaged in a debate with several Catholic acquaintances. Dinah Goff's sister threw her arms around her father when threatened with death by robbers. Jane Barber persuaded a rebel to help find her father's corpse, then acted as leader of her family in the weeks following his death. Mrs Brownrigg engaged Harvey, Keugh, and Mrs Dixon in dialogue, in an attempt to leave the prison ship and later Wexford itself. Barbara Lett walked into rebel-held areas, obtaining passes from Martin Fenlon and William Barker for her safety and persuading hostile jail officials to allow her to see her father. Alicia Pounden remained confident returning to her home, even though it was occupied by rebels, some of whom were hostile towards her. Faced with losing her father and brother, Jane Adams negotiated at length with William Kearney for their release, then defied those rebels who demanded her brother's reimprisonment. None of the women were content to accept the situation in which they found themselves; rather, through their assertiveness, they attempted to improve their condition, if only in small ways, through tactful dialogue.

Accounts of attempted religious conversion appear frequently in the narratives, and they offer evidence that a rumour circulated widely in county Wexford, believed by Catholics and Protestants alike, that non-Catholics would forfeit their lives during the rebellion if they refused to convert. Although the county's United leaders made no attempt to promote the canard, they did little to discourage it. Catholics urged their Protestant neighbours to go to chapel and renounce their faith in order to preserve their lives, and some appear to have viewed the rebellion more as a war for religious purity than of political independence. The accounts illustrate how some Catholics attempted to win conversions, often with the tacit support of local priests.[56]

In addition, the narratives reflect the extraordinary cooperation that existed among some Protestants and Catholics in 1798, especially those with some prior acquaintance or connection. High-ranking United Irish officials and officers such as Barker, Kearney, and Keugh treated women with respect, with Barker even opening the grounds of his house in Enniscorthy as a shelter for Protestant refugees. Some United Army soldiers also behaved with gallantry: the soldier sharing his bread with Jane Adams and another group of pikemen comforting her when they find her crying on the road; the rebel named Williams sheltering Barbara Lett after the Battle of Enniscorthy at considerable personal risk, and another offering protection to Jane Barber after the death of her father, since he had known her father through business. A Catholic friend of Alicia Pounden retrieved her husband's corpse from an Enniscorthy street and had it properly buried. That Protestant women often reciprocated is evidenced by Jane Adams and her cards of protection, and Jane Barber's sheltering of injured refugees from the Battle of Vinegar Hill in her outbuilding. Personal contacts between Protestants and Catholics established before the rebellion made an important difference in helping each group cope. For many, humanity proved stronger than bigotry. Old kindnesses were often repaid with new ones, perhaps as often as old grudges were avenged.

56 See Whelan, 'The Religious Factor in the 1798 Rebellion', pp 75-6.

Finally, what of the Catholic rebel women as seen by their Protestant counterparts? Here, the image presented is often distorted by caricature and prejudice. Most of the Protestant women viewed their female counterparts with fear and distrust: the crones staring into the windows of Horetown House in the hope of pillage; the angry Catholic mother removing her injured son from Summerseat; the family friend entreating the indignant Elizabeth Richards to convert; the rebel sister-in-law refusing help to Barbara Lett. If many rebel men in the United army treated Protestant women with the respect afforded to non-combatants, the evidence suggests that many rebel women did not feel the constraints of such decorum.

The narratives of this small group of county Wexford women challenge historians to continue taking a broader view of the rebellion. They reveal a conflict waged as much by pragmatists as ideologues, where family members held differing political opinions and where women's views sometimes differed from men's. Even if we reject the hostility some obviously felt toward the cause of Irish nationalism, their words compel us nonetheless to listen and feel empathy for their sufferings. Through their eyes, we find a rebellion inhabited by heroes and villains on both sides of the conflict. We see altruistic Protestants and Catholics, loyal and rebel, behaving with humanity and decency. We also see evidence of inhumanity on both sides. Most of these women seem unusually candid in relating what they saw. What we are left with is a more complex picture of the rebellion – a picture which, in turn, may lead all of us to a more honest appraisal of the events of 1798.

Mary Shackleton Leadbeater:
Peaceful rebel

Kevin O'Neill

This essay explores Irish politics of the 1790s from the perspective of one rural Irish woman, Mary Shackleton Leadbeater.[1] While this may seem a rather narrow perspective to some, the complexities involved have provided more than ample challenge for this writer. The difficulties for the modern historian stem from two separate but related problems. First although the revolution of 1798 was an overwhelmingly rural event, our knowledge of rural political mobilisation during the 1790s has been hampered by historiography. The victors who wrote the first histories of the rebellion wished to impose a partisan sectarian interpretation upon the revolution.[2] This paradigm, created in the aftermath of the rebellion, when the voice of republicanism was silenced by failure and terror, presented the rebellion in stark images that located the meaning of the revolution in stories of rebel atrocity. Later-day defenders of republicanism have been largely concerned with disproving this charge by exploring the high politics and theory of the United Irish leadership. Beyond the obvious problems of objectivity posed by such a dialectic, the focus upon these two theatres of history – desperate acts of violence and high urban politics – has left the study of rural political mobilisation relatively untouched until recent years.[3] The second problem posed is more germane to the subject of this volume, the difficulties posed to those who would explore the participation of women in public life during the late eighteenth century.

1 Born Mary Shackleton 1758, married William Leadheater 1791. She is best known as Mary Leadbeater; I refer to her here as Mary Shackleton Leadbeater. 2 See Kevin Whelan, '98 After '98: The Politics of Memory', in Kevin Whelan, *The Tree of Liberty: Radicalism, Catholicism and the Construction of Irish Identity: 1760-1830* (Cork, 1996). 3 The list of county scholarship is growing very rapidly. For good examples see: Kevin Whelan, 'The Catholic Community in Eighteenth Century Wexford' in Power and Whelan (eds), *Endurance and Emergence: Catholics in Ireland in the Eighteenth Century* (Dublin, 1990), pp 156-78; L.M. Cullen, 'Politics and rebellion in Wicklow in the 1790s' in Hannigan and Nolan (eds), *Wicklow History and Society* (Dublin, 1994), pp 411-501 and Daniel Gahan, *The people's rising: Wexford, 1798* (Dublin, 1995).

Concerns regarding the selectivity of history are not the creation of late twentieth-century academics. Mary Shackleton Leadbeater devoted her literary life to chronicling the communal and domestic life of rural Ireland. And, true friend of historians that she was, she frequently copied into her diary compelling thoughts or observations from her current reading. One such excerpt from Arthur Young's *Tour in France* illustrates the sort of revisionist agenda which she wished to assist:

> To a mind that has the least turn after philosophical enquiry, reading modern history is generally the most tormenting employment that a man can have; one is plagued with the actions of a detestable set of men, called conquerors, heroes & great generals; & we wade through pages loaded with military details; but when you want to know the progress of agriculture, of commerce, & industry, their effect in different ages & nations on each other – the wealth that resulted – the division of that wealth – its employment – & the manners it produced – all is a blank.

Young's quote points to the problematic linkage between gender, rurality and popular politics that students of the 1790s face. Moments of dramatic political violence often obscure the role of women in political culture even more than the normal gender filters imposed by government and institutional biases. And even among the gender conscious there is an obvious attraction to the simplicity of the premise that as violence in patriarchal societies was primarily a male sphere of action, so violent moments were primarily 'male moments'. But political violence does not necessarily emerge out of the 'normal' realms of male aggression. The process by which ordinary people, male and female, overcome their everyday rational reluctance to engage in an unequal contest with the ascendancy needs to be more fully explored.[4] This process of political mobilisation in late eighteenth-century Ireland was a complicated one, still the one thing that has seemed clear from the existing documentation is the predominance of men in its more public and formal aspects. The United Irishmen, the Defenders, the Orange Order, and their prolific pamphlet and broadside publishing activity were overwhelmingly male in their production, orientation and 'market focus'. But it is not so clear that the consumers of this literature, or of its ideological message were quite so exclusively male. And, it is not at all clear that our difficulty in documenting women as political participants

---

4 The use and abuse of this term has recently been highlighted by S.J. Connolly in *Religion, Law and Power: The Making of Protestant Ireland 1660-1760* (Oxford, 1992). Its use here is a limited one: the Church of Ireland, propertied, politically entitled population.

reflects an absence of female participation in politics. The likelihood of women's participation in popular politics was, perhaps ironically, multiplied in pre-democratic societies where most people, male and female, participated in politics not as 'citizens' but as 'subjects'. In communities where most people were denied formal political power both male and female voices were exercised in non-institutional ways about which we know little. And there is at least a theoretical basis for supposing that the gender and rurality filters that obscure our subject are closely connected; the further away from urban centralised authority a community was, the more likely it was that it offered women individual and corporate opportunities to exercise public influence and power. But a cautionary note is needed – we know so little about the village and townland level of political discourse in eighteenth-century Ireland that any presumptions must be treated with extreme caution.

One of the most productive ways in which we can enhance our understanding of the social and gender dimensions of the rebellion of 1798 is to widen our view and focus not upon the dramatic event of violence itself, but to consider the process which produced the rebellion. This project is already well launched and promises to alter considerably our understanding not only of the rebellion of 1798, but also the post-rebellion reactions and realignments which helped to shape the nature of sectarian relations during the early nineteenth century.[5] Such studies are by nature labour-intensive and are most efficiently carried out on the very local level where we can see ordinary women and men in action and thought and where we can follow things from their perspective. And, of course, the best way to begin to broaden our gender dimension is to rely upon women's words as our major source of information. For these reasons this paper will focus upon the events leading up to May 1798 rather than the rebellion itself. It will attempt to open one small window into the effervescent local politics of the pre-revolutionary decade. Because of space limitations I have chosen to focus primarily upon the years 1793 to 1797, the period during which Mary Shackleton Leadbeater witnessed her village move from a period of politicisation to one of revolution.

I

The small Irish village of Ballitore, county Kildare is located in the triangle of southern Kildare where Wicklow, Carlow and Kildare converge. The village took an active role in the Leinster rebellion of May

5 For examples see op. cit. Cullen, Gahan, Whelan.

1798. Unlike the more famous rebellion of Wexford, the Kildare rebellion was the result of years of United Irish preparation. For this reason the local politics of Ballitore are of considerable interest to the student wishing to understand the relationship between the urban-centred United Irish leadership and the rural communities which would serve as the base of the United Irish rebellion. Fortunately it is also one of the rare places and moments in which we can attempt to explore the process of politics from a woman's perspective because Mary Shackleton Leadbeater, a lifelong member of the community of Ballitore has left us remarkably vivid accounts of the 1790s in her diaries and letters.

Mary was forty years old in the year of the rebellion, the mother of three children, the author of a book of children's stories and a poet. She was also the wife of William Leadbeater, a farmer, house builder and proprietor of a livery service. Later in her life she would become better known as a rural chronicler and several of her works achieved considerable success in the nineteenth century, especially the posthumous *Annals of Ballitore*.[6] Readers who are familiar with these works may be surprised by the discussion of her politics that follows. For, while Mary Shackleton Leadbeater was a lifelong member of the Society of Friends, a committed pacifist and the author of works which strove to ameliorate social and sectarian confrontation in Ireland, her sympathies and hopes were in close alignment with radical republicanism during the years of upheaval. And more surprisingly, she along with her husband, neighbours and fellow Friends, placed their lives and property in grave risk by providing assistance to the most radical local members of the United Irishmen, and by engaging in negotiations with the French government that might well have led Mary and William Leadbeater to emigrate to France in 1794.[7]

One of the most defining characteristics of Mary Shackleton Leadbeater and the village of Ballitore was their shared Quaker identity. Mary was a member of the Society of Friends from birth, and her husband William Leadbeater became a member of the society as a young adult. The small village of Ballitore on the Kildare/Wicklow border was founded by Friends in 1707, but became a predominately Catholic community with an important Quaker leavening.[8] The social and political

6 Mary Leadbeater, *The Annals of Ballitore*, in *The Leadbeater Papers: A Selection From the MSS and correspondence of Mary Leadbetter*, vol. 1 (London, 1862). 7 See below for the a discussion of the Leadbeater's French possibilities. 8 The formal name of this religious community is the 'Religious Society of Friends'. In this essay I refer to the church as 'The Society of Friends' and to individuals as 'Friends'. For simplicity I have chosen to use the term 'Quaker' as an adjective.

'place' which Mary Shackleton Leadbeater inhabited as a Friend provides readers of her work an unusual and revealing perspective from
which to view Irish rural society. Members of the Society of Friends did
not fit into the normative social and political categories and hierarchies
of eighteenth-century Irish society. Although they were 'Protestant',
members of the Society of Friends, were never part of the Protestant
Ascendancy. Quaker landlords were even rarer than Catholic landlords,
and no Friend could accept the sectarian Penal state that might have
privileged them. They, themselves, had been the objects of active persecution during the seventeenth century, and they remained targets of
harassment and periodic violent attacks by the established church population throughout the eighteenth century. Their refusal to recognise
Anglo-Irish linguistic, sartorial, and gender distinctions of class and
power, and their subversive refusal to serve as jurors, or to swear an
oath, separated them from both the formal and informal apparatus of
ascendancy in Ireland. More dangerous still, they refused to pay tithes;
and to confirm their isolation and alienation from their Anglo-Irish
neighbours, their principle of non-violence made it impossible for them
to join or support the Volunteers, the militia or the yeomanry – the institutional symbols of the ascendancy during the late eighteenth century.[9]

Clearly Friends did not belong to the Anglo-Irish ascendancy. Yet,
despite the considerable political and economic distance that these factors created between the Friends and the Ascendancy, Friends were
culturally more 'Anglo' than the 'Anglo-Irish'. They were generally of
more recent English decent than the Protestant population as a whole,
and they maintained closer family connections with the Big Island than
all but the most spectacularly elite of the Anglo-Irish. Members of the
Society also believed it important to attend the London General
Meeting of the Society if they were able to do so. And many Friends,
especially women, often spent considerable time travelling and preaching among English Friends. Several Ballitore women, including Mary's
sister, spent prolonged periods in this type of ministry. Perhaps more
surprising, Irish Friends remained in close communication with, and
frequently exchanged visitors with North American and Caribbean
Friends. When all of this is considered, it is doubtful whether any other
group of Irish people was as widely informed, or personally familiar
with the world-wide Anglo community. In some ways they represent
the most distilled product of eighteenth-century Anglo culture in
Ireland. Yet, paradoxically, at least from the perspective of traditional

9 See Maurice J. Wigham, *The Irish Quakers: A Short History of the Religious Society of Friends in Ireland* (Dublin, 1992).

discussions of the Anglo-Irish, these most Anglo of the Irish had an unusually intimate and positive relationship with their Catholic neighbours. From a Catholic perspective the Friends of Ballitore were neither landlords, magistrates, soldiers, or tithe collectors – the normal rural functions of the Anglo-Irish. Instead, they were farmers, teachers, millers and most of all, neighbours. In a similar fashion, Friends viewed their Catholic neighbours not as dangerous idolaters or treacherous tenants, but as farmers, artisans, and neighbours. This notion of shared communal identity was one of the most valued earthly achievements among Friends.

In Ireland both family and neighbourhood bonds were severely tested by the effects of the French Revolution. Mary's early response to the French Revolution parallels that of most Friends; like most 'ordinary' people she was slow to recognise the import of the Revolution and only gradually came to understand its implications for Ireland. This gradualism is an important element of Mary's engagement with the new radicalism. Emphasis must be put upon the 'new' aspect of the French influenced radicalism in Ireland as members of the Society of Friends had long been on the radical edge of Irish politics. The commitment to equality which Friends demonstrated daily in their clothing and speech exceeded the most zealous Hébertist or United person. Their belief in the common weal of all people, regardless of class or sect was the creed which the Friends had preached since their inception. From their perspective it was not a case of being 'radicalised' by the French Revolution, but of being encouraged and uplifted by the seemingly miraculous way in which two of the principals upon which their faith and lives were founded, equality and community,[10] were suddenly central passions shared by so many Europeans. There was, of course, a powerful and worrisome counterforce, for while the revolution offered so much hope for a new egalitarian society, the political violence it engendered posed a direct challenge to another central Quaker principal – the principal of Peace. Friends could not accept the legitimacy of violence from any quarter. Yet violence threatened to engulf them. A pair of short notes from Mary's diary for the autumn of 1795 catch the dilemma in stark visual terms. She and William had gone to Dublin for the Yearly Meeting. While there they went to call upon a friend in order to deliver a poem that Mary had written:

> W[illia]m & I ... joined Hannah Haughton at D. Thomas's ... Debby seems very comfortable ... They have here a little model

---

10 By 1789 Friends had already recognised the gender limitations of 'fraternity'. In 1784 women Friends had sought and achived autonomy for the Woman's Yearly Meeting.

of a guillotine in ivory & in that she fixed my verse – So near
allied sometimes are Love & Murder said to be.[11]

On the journey home to Ballitore they passed through the town of
Naas, county Kildare:

> On the top of the Jail at Naas is fixed the head of [O']Connor the
> school-master, who was hanged for being a Defender, & who
> shewed on his trial a spirit worthy of a better cause, the wretched
> spectacle was shocking to humanity.[12]

The juxtaposition of these images of state violence and Mary's comments upon them serve well to illustrate the tension which existed
between Friends and the revolutionary atmosphere of the 1790s. There
was no neutral space – terror and murder were primary components of
both the old and new orders. And, while modern readers may now have
difficulty seeing the guillotine as 'humane', there is little difficulty in
joining Mary in her recognition of the extraordinary nature of brutality
underlying Anglo-Irish 'justice'. Mary's comment on O'Connor's spirit
being 'worthy of a better cause' points to an even greater potential isolation of Friends. Those whom Friends might have joined in opposition
to the hierarchical state were already engaged in activity that posed
grave dangers to the fragile peace of the countryside. The cause of
Defenderism was frightful to Friends because of the threat it posed to
the sectarian equilibrium of rural communities. They feared that
Defenderism would both author its own violence and provoke an extension of state brutality into rural areas that were largely outside the day-
to-day interest of the government. Even so, Mary and many other
Friends sympathised with the spirit that animated the humble schoolmaster as he articulated the injustices that his community suffered. To
Friends the truth was found in the spirit.

The model of a guillotine as a souvenir presents intriguing opportunity for discussion, but its simple presence suggests that despite their
well-known public neutrality on 'party' political issues, many Friends
went beyond simply recognising the similarities between their own the-
ological life and the new republicanism which complicated the lives of
their neighbourhoods. Mary's citation of the nearness of love and murder carries an ironic undertone that is ambiguous. Perhaps it criticizes

11 National Library of Ireland, The Diary of Mary Shackleton Leadbeater (Diary),
October, 1795. 12 Diary, October 1795. Lawrence O'Connor was arrested and executed
in Sept. 1795 as a Defender organiser.

Debby Thomas for being callous, perhaps it does not, but it very clearly expresses Mary's understanding of the difficulty that Friends had in
finding their way during this crisis. Many Friends attempted to find a
way to engage with the new secular promise of liberty, community and
equality while maintaining their enthusiasm for the Quaker Principle of
Peace. That this path was fraught with dangers did not deter Friends –
it merely confirmed their continuity with the seventeenth-century
founders of the Society. Friends were conscious of the common connections which they and all republicans shared with seventeenth-century English Republicanism and the Enlightenment philosophers who
had transmitted much of this thought into eighteenth-century language.

The Society itself had a dynamic and complicated relationship with
Enlightenment thought that prepared them in some ways for this new
encounter with republicanism. Friends shared a profound confidence in
the progress of the human race. This faith in the future was predicated
upon a belief in the universality of human and divine virtues and graces.
Friends rejected Calvinist notions of 'election' and 'covenant' with their
division of humankind into 'saved' and 'damned' peoples. Instead they
believed in the universality of an inner light which was the expression
of the bond between divinity and humanity. It was this belief in universality that led them to recognise their Catholic neighbours as fellow
travellers on the pathway to salvation rather than as followers of the
anti-Christ. And, because they believed that the entire human race was
moving towards a greater understanding of the truth, both divine and
human, they accepted as an article of faith that human understanding
was in the process of convergence with divine truth. Most Friends
believed that science and other branches of philosophy were useful tools
in the acceleration of this process. They especially welcomed technological innovations that might prove useful in the improvement of material
life. And always they believed that there could be no excuse, temporal
or spiritual for the state's violation of the divine laws of simplicity,
equality and peace.

For all these reasons most Friends were excited by the egalitarian,
anti-monarchical, anti-aristocratic, anti-clerical elements of Enlightenment philosophy, and had positive, if more complicated, responses to
Enlightenment ideas about human reason and science. Yet, there was
one deep and seemingly insurmountable obstacle which prevented
Friends from becoming full supporters of the Enlightenment project –
they could never accept that human reason could stand alone, apart or
especially in contradiction to Divine Truth. They could not entertain
ideas that placed reason or science as forces superior to the inner light.

What Mary Shackleton Leadbeater called the 'poison' of extreme rationalism was merely a new form of idolatry. But, as Irish Friends were optimistic believers, they generally focused upon areas of common experience and agreement between themselves and the followers of the Philosophes. With their belief in the universality of the inner light this was rational: Many Paths – One Truth.

In the two decades before the revolution of 1798 Ballitore Friends had many opportunities to engage with political and philosophical radicalism in their eighteenth-century European and American manifestations. Their reactions to these encounters reveal a great deal about the complexity and shifting nature of the community of Ballitore and its specifically Irish politics during the crisis years. In her diary Mary Shackleton Leadbeater never presented a systematic explication of her political philosophy. She would have considered such an explication a vanity. But we can come very close to an understanding of her politics as it evolved during this period by exploring the relationships that she formed with other actors upon this stage. Her relationship with one young Catholic radical, Theobald McKenna, provides a window into this dynamic, for McKenna represented both the radical rationalism of the Scottish Enlightenment and the particular political interests of her Catholic neighbours.

Mary first took note of the young McKenna in August, 1787, when she was twenty-eight and he but twenty-three. She records in her diary that she had heard a pamphlet read aloud that was 'rather political, written by McKenna a student of Edinburgh, an Irish young man he seems to have wonderful powers of genius'.[13] This brief reference carries a good deal of meaning. The simple fact that Friends were reading controversial political literature aloud indicates that at least some Friends took a rather liberal view of their society's restrictions against party politics. The fact that they were reading the work of a young Catholic writer who was beginning an active career as a champion of Catholic Emancipation, and subsequently of Irish republicanism, places these Kildare Friends on the radical edge of Irish politics on the eve of the revolutionary era.

In September 1787, William Lecky, a close family friend and a member of Mary's Monthly Meeting, brought McKenna with him on a visit to Ballitore. Mary was impressed with McKenna, and especially his respect and love for his early schoolmaster, Thomas Chaytor. She also noted that he 'seems to possess a brilliant understanding'.[14] Over the following three years Mary formed a social and intellectual relationship

13 Diary, August 1787. 14 Kildare County Library, PP1/12/19.

with McKenna. They exchanged writings, and conversations in Clonmel, Ballitore and Dublin. A brief humorous note demonstrates how easy their interaction became; in her Diary of March 1790 she noted that McKenna 'had been reading my verses advising me not to write so many Elegies, lest my book be called a Poetical Church-yard'.[15] But at the heart of her connection to McKenna lay a deep anxiety that his commitment to rationalism was dangerously extreme. In that same month she wrote that while McKenna was 'possessed of distinguished talents, & amiable dispositions' she was worried by his rationalism and

> lamented ... at hearing the character of infidelity which he bore in Clonmel – not but I can make some allowance for young & inquisitive minds being led astray by the inconsistencies of the professions of Christianity ... through which the Vulture eye of human wisdom cannot pierce.

She hoped that he might escape from this religious scepticism, 'the poison with which an Edinburgh education is so apt to taint the mind'. In a query based upon the Quaker notion of the convergence of natural, human and divine affairs she wondered how could a heart 'so sensible of the fine feelings of Nature, revolt against the convictions of Grace?'[16] She answered her own query, in a letter to her most intimate correspondent of the time, Elizabeth Grubb of Clonmel. In it she explained her feelings for McKenna:

> he looked so friendly & goodnatured, that my heart warmed yet more to him, & I thought much of him, & wished (but O that it was an availing wish! for) I say I wished for his reformation, & recovery from the howling wilderness, into wch the false light of human wisdom I fear has led him, for that perfidious glare is not able to dispel the mind, which beclouds the glorious name of Christianity.[17]

It is clear from this language that in 1790 Mary placed her emphasis upon spiritual not rational or political salvation. Yet despite this anxiety regarding McKenna, Mary continued to read his work, and sympathetically follow his career as he authored [in 1791] a new declaration urging Catholics to move from a posture of supplication to one of radicalism, and later still as he played an important role in forging the link between Catholics and the United Irishmen.

15 Diary, March 1790. 16 Diary, March 1790. 17 Kildare County Library, PP1/12/42.

Mary also read widely among French and English political philosophers from Burke to Wollstonecraft. She adored the person of Edmund Burke, her grandfather's pupil and her father's classmate, but found the most compelling intellectual arguments in the work of Burke's antithesis, William Godwin. As noted earlier, Mary often entered passages of particular interest to her in her diary: The most quoted work of the decade was William Godwin's *Political Justice* which Mary read in 1794. A few of the quotes that Mary choose illuminate her growing awareness of the convergence of Quaker and secular radicalism. At the heart of this convergence was the absolute value of an equality that was social, economic and cultural. Equality was the focus of her citations from Godwin's work. In Godwin's view equality was not a commodity that could be given or taken, but a competitive environment that would be as demanding as it was beneficial:

> The virtues that grow up among us are cultured in the open soil of equality, not in the artificial climate of greatness. We need the winds to harden as much as the heat to cherish us.[18]

The heart of Godwin's argument, as Mary perceived it, was his passionate attack upon the excesses of the wealthy, and his presentation of a social pathology of poverty and crime. Both arguments resonated deeply in Mary's Ballitore and Quaker experience and discourse:

> What can be more injurious than the accumulating upon a few every means of superfluity & luxury, to the total destruction of the ease, & plain, but plentiful subsistence of the many? ... Is it well that so large a part of the community should be kept in abject penury, goaded to the commission of crimes & made victims to the merciless laws which the rich have instituted to oppress them.[19]

But Godwin was not simply restating familiar Ballitore or Quaker truths in a more modern fashion. His logic moved beyond the social and economic pathology of society – with which most Friends would have been comfortable – towards a direct attack upon the state as a brutal agent of inequality.

> The more there is in any country of inequality & oppression, the more punishments are multiplied. The more the institutions of society contradict the genuine sentiments of the human mind,

18 This and the following quotations are from Mary's diary of 1794.   19 Diary, July 1796.

the more severely it is necessary to avenge their isolation. At the
same time the rich & titled members of he community, proud of
their fancied eminence, behold with total unconcern the destruction of the destitute & the wretched.

Friends had always been suspicious of the state, and sought to insulate
themselves as best they could from its operations and corruptions. But
it was difficult for many Friends to escape a new sense of urgency created by the convergence of secular rational arguments such as Godwin's
s with their own spiritual beliefs. In assessing the impact of such reading upon Mary it is worth recalling her comment upon seeing Lawrence
O'Connor's head upon a spike — a moment still some months in the
future when she first read Godwin. The horror she expressed on that
occasion may have fused the 'simple' shock occasioned by the sight of a
severed human head with the shock of recognition occasioned by
Godwin's explanation of such brutality: extreme State brutality was a
confirmation of extreme State deviance.

Such shocks might have crushed a weaker faith in the future. But
for Friends there was no possibility of retreating on the principals of
equality and community and most, at least through 1796, kept their traditional focus on the positive possibilities of the moment. This perse-
verance was supported by the joy with which Friends met the eruption
of traditional Quaker principals into the broader and especially Catholic
popular politics. The period leading up to the outbreak of war in 1793
was one of increasing enthusiasm for the possibilities of the new age. So
much so that even after the outbreak of war, and an increasingly repres-
sive climate, Mary's Ballitore neighbours nicknamed her close friend,
Thomas Bewley (who held a transparent passion for all things French
and republican) 'The Citizen'.[19]

Mary's wide-ranging reading in political economy and theory were
important to the formation of her personal politics as well as the wider
political discourse of Ballitore, but to contain this discussion within a
narrow definition of politics would be to ignore one of the most potent
forces of discourse in Ballitore, religion. For Friends there was no fire-
wall between political and religious discourse, and because of their
rejection of any sort of regular clergy or ministry, any Friend, male or
female, rich or poor, local or foreign, had direct access to the discourse.
Many Friends, especially women, felt compelled to travel as witnesses,
and this tendency frequently brought visitors to the small village of
Ballitore. Along with their religious testimonies these visitors carried
secular news and ideas acquired in their travels. A number of American
and Irish Friends who visited France during the early days of the

Revolution brought such first-hand uncensored news to the village. Among Irish Friends Sarah and Robert Grubb were the most engaged in this Franco-Irish ministry.[20] But without question the most efferves-cent and provocative testimony was brought to Ireland and Ballitore by the Rhode Island Friend, Job Scott. Ironically, it was an Irish Friend and Shackleton family friend, Samuel Neal, who had awakened Scott's own religious enthusiasm decades before while Neal was in America bringing his testimony to American Friends. As a fitting return of Neal's efforts in America, Scott's testimonies were a voice of revival to the Irish Society. His prophetic teaching brought the words and images of the seventeenth and eighteenth century very close together and demonstrated that the intersection of popular politics, new radicalism, and Quaker faith could become powerfully eschatological.[21]

Scott spoke with the vividness and clarity of the early Friends, and with their same lack of regard for audience response! He deeply alienat-ed many Catholics who had begun to attend Friends' meetings through his sustained criticism of 'superstition' and of all forms of clergy. But his most controversial testimonies bore directly on the crisis posed by the French Revolution. His fiery evocation of Quaker principles opposing hierarchy resonated both with traditional Quaker teaching and with republicanism. His American origins, and recent travels in France gave him the ability to draw connections that even a dim-witted parson would have found difficult to miss. In her diary Mary records some of the energy of Scott's testimony:

> He spoke sublimely of the Duty before Creation – & professed how inconsistent with his mercy was the idea that he would cre-ate any to be eternally miserable. Were this true it would make the Creator worse than our great Adversary Satan, who goeth about as a roaring Lion, it would even excuse him, & excuse man, & throw the fault upon him who created to destroy, & even those who were destined for happiness would find it much allayed by the consideration of the doom of their fellow creatures, by a par-tial & unjust Creator.

If the notion of such a God was unthinkable to Friends, Scott's teach-ing on law and order was equally unthinkable to the Ascendancy:

20 See below for their mission to France. 21 For a valuable discussion of seventeenth-century Quakerism see Phyllis Mack, *Visionary Women: Ecstatic Prophecy in Seventeenth-Century England* (Berkeley, 1992). The evidence presented here suggests that the marked decline in Quaker prophetic spirit that Mack documents left a resevoir of energy that could be taped by later day Friends.

> At Ballycane meeting, Job Scott spoke beautifully, & as I never
> heard before ... & clearly shewed the Law, & all typical observa-
> tions, were forever abolished by Jesus Christ making a shew of
> them openly, blotting out the handwriting of ordinances, & nail-
> ing them to his cross.[22]

His denunciations of privilege and its protecting law, and his prophetic
proclamation of an approaching 'overflowing scourge' in Ireland placed
both Scott and the Society in danger. While his friends were too
respectful of his message and person to directly urge caution upon him,
they did reveal their concerns for his safety to him. Scott responded to
one influential Friend's dream portending harm, by declaring that
despite his many travels he 'had never felt his life in so much danger as
since he came into Ireland'.[23]

It is uncertain how long Scott's rhetoric would have been tolerated
for after contracting smallpox he died in Ballitore in November 1793.
Scott's reawakening of the prophetic passion among Friends compli-
mented the work of a remarkable Quaker couple, Sarah and Robert
Grubb, who dedicated themselves to the tradition of Quaker activism.
Together they travelled through France and the Netherlands during
1790 observing and preaching. After Sarah's sudden death in 1790
Robert spent time in Ireland working among Friends to win support for
an anti-slavery boycott of sugar. Grubb was a cousin to Mary
Shackleton Leadbeater and a valued friend and mentor. An account
from her diary of 1790 describes their attendance at a meeting in
Waterford and reveals Grubb's characteristic enthusiasm and activism.

> Robt Grubb, when the meeting was about to separate, men-
> tioned, that in no age was more evinced the promise that male &
> female are all one in Christ; ... he had some printed copies of the
> Self discourse, he gave one to a man in the street, who saying he
> could not read, Robt. read it for him, & another man who came
> up; they were sober & attentive, & said they were 'Fine words'. I
> was glad to be witness to so benevolent a scene.

Robert Grubb also introduced Mary to direct participation in the anti-
slavery movement. In 1791 Grubb left Mary and her sister Sally a pamphlet on Slavery. She comments in her diary upon listening to her sister
read the pamphlet aloud.

> I did really hear the little book, especially when the strong argu-
> ments in favour of individual forbearance from the use of the

22 Diary, July 1793. 23 Diary, October 1793

produce of Slavery are produced we are called upon in a civil capacity to beware of being accessory to murder & robbery.[24]

The importance of reading aloud is worth noting. Just as she first heard Theobald McKenna's words read aloud, this encounter with anti-slavery discourse was a social rather than a private moment. Despite the highly literate nature of Mary's family and intimate social circle, this remained an intensely oral political culture. It is obvious how such social readings facilitated the dissemination of radical political publications in a semi-literate society, but it is much less clear how and why such readings functioned for literate groups. Perhaps they represent a transitional moment in a communities acquisition of literacy – for while Mary and her family were all literate others who visited and worked with her family were not. When such moments involved radical political texts they also helped to create a sense of unity in struggle which in turn might help to provide a sense of security in an environment that was becoming increasingly marked by censorship and state aggression against its subjects. It is also important to note that this orality was not a lower order of communication – an end point of a chain of communication which lead from literate urban elites to oral rural people.

After being moved by this pamphlet read in Ballitore, Mary gave it to her visiting Dublin friend, Molly Bewley, so that it could be reprinted in the Metropolis. The two women then worked to distribute the pamphlet through their network of women Friends, and in turn one of them sold it on to itinerant peddlers for sale throughout the country. In this way the pamphlet which Grubb brought to Ballitore was multiplied and recirculated throughout the capital and the countryside where it was no doubt read aloud in other households. In a letter of 8 January 1792 to her friend Elizabeth Grubb Mary comments upon its success in Ballitore. 'What think you of the pamphlet relating to the Slave-trade? It has wrought & is likely to work much reformation hereway[?]'.[25] The following day Mary received a letter from Molly Bewley relating the impact of the reprinted pamphlet in Dublin and noting its movement back to the countryside:

> What think you of the revolutions that have taken place here by that Pamphlet I borrowed from you, I think it was worth my while to go for that only, there is a prospect of its being very useful, almost every day we hear of members leaving off sugar by reading – *our Rachel* is warm in it and distributes many & sells to

24 Diary, December 1791. 25 Kildare County Library, PP1/12/50.

the people who buy alamanacks to carry about the country –
Dear Richard Pike I believe will give up selling it [sugar] but it
is not quite determined. Jacob Barrington is resolved to give it
up. Tommy came home last night, and brings account that this
pamphlet has also had a good effect on many in MtMelick, that
even our dear little John wont take sugar in his tea, since he
hears that the poor little black boys is hurt in getting it for us.[26]

These letters demonstrate an almost casual approach to political
publication. They also describe the speed and efficiency with which
such informal networks of Quaker women could be mobilised for political purposes. I have been unable to further identify 'Rachel' but she
clearly played a critical role in connecting the political with the commercial, as well as the urban with the rural; a most Quaker-like role –
but one not normally recognised as a female one.[27] Quaker women also
had more formal and corporate methods of advancing their political
agenda. At a Women's Quarterly Meeting held in September 1793 the
meeting took up the issue of the anti-slavery boycott and discussed
whether the boycott should be extended to include cotton. Jane Watson
urged the women to do so, arguing that consistency required it:

> [She] mentioned the use of cottons & calicoes which so much
> prevails, & which are even brought into meetings: she understood
> that in gathering & plucking[?] the cotton, the Negroes suffered
> as much oppression as in most employments. She ... recom-
> mended the use of woollen manufacture, according to the prac-
> tice of our ancient friends, which would save much trouble in
> washing ... Mary Ridgeway spoke sweetly against oppression.
> Went to the adjournment, at the close of which Sarah Newland
> warned us against too much conversation about what had passed
> in meeting this day about the cotton, in humility & love.[28]

It is unclear whether Sarah Newland's warning was occasioned by fear
of causing division within the Society, or of bringing the Women's
meeting to the attention of the forces of reaction. In either case it points
to the growing awareness by Quaker women of the oppositions that
their actions might engender.

Anti-slave agitation was not explicitly linked to republican radicalism. But among Irish Friends there was little separation between the
causes or the individuals involved in them. While Robert Grubb con-

26 Kildare County Library, PP1/13/38. 27 The most likely candidate is Rachel Jackson.
See Diary, February 1792. 28 Diary, September 1793.

tinued to promote these anti-slavery efforts he was also becoming more and more interested and involved in French politics. He travelled between Ireland and France during the early months of 1793 and was in France at the time of Louis' execution. Mary records that 'many are sorry for the King's fate', but she does not indicate how she felt. Instead, she notes that she looked forward to Robert's return so that she and others could have 'a real account how things are'.[29] Grubb was in France with ambitious plans for a collaboration between Irish Friends and the French government. His goal was the creation of a Friend's technological school in France. With the sponsorship of Madame Roland and the partnership of Jean Marsillac of Congénies, Grubb was close to an agreement with the Department of the Loire et Cher to launch a school at Chambord, a confiscated Royal chateau. In addition to educating 150 French adolescents gratis and another 300 for a fee, the establishment was to house 80 to 100 workshops where 'new trades and particular cultures possessed until now only by England' would be taught.[30] This project promised to fulfil several goals dear to radical Friends. It would help to provide revolutionary France with the technological equality with Britain that Friend's believed necessary for the revolution's success. Just as importantly it would allow Friends to exercise a moral influence upon the revolution. Among the very few guarantees that Grubb sought for the school was an exemption from military service for those students who wished to join the Society. Grubb and Marsillac saw the school in terms larger than pedagogy. True to Quaker tradition, they believed that the presence of Friends would 'witness' not only the virtues of equality and community, but also of Peace. It is hard to imagine that Robert Grubb did not have this in mind when he read in the Minister of the Interior's endorsement of the project that '[these Friends] would soon have the happiest influence on the whole Republic'.[31]

Mary's husband, William, was a shareholder in the proposed venture, and both husband and wife planed to settle in France.[32] Grubb's support for gender equality had insured that women could enrol in the school, thus creating an opportunity for both William and Mary to continue the Shackleton tradition as schoolmaster missionaries. The outbreak of war in 1793 forced a postponement of the plans. And before peace could provide a new possibility the climate for co-operation deteriorated in both countries. Jean Marsillac fled to Ireland during the terror – most probably because of this close co-operation with British

29 Kildare County Library PP1/12/53.   30 *Quakerism and Industry Before 1800*, Isabel Grubb (London, n.d.), p. 144.   31 *Quakerism and Industry Before 1800*, Isabel Grubb (London, n.d.), p. 144.

subjects. While in Ireland Grubb's position became increasingly uncomfortable as his motives came under question. It was likely questions about Grubb and his loyalties that caused a rare argument in the Leadbeater household that Mary noted in Novernber 1793. 'Brother & Sister, John Bewley & J. Beale to sup. Some dispute about politicks, rather unpleasant.'[33] In a letter to Elizabeth Grubb of the following month Mary makes clear her concern for both Robert and their community. After expressing her difficulty in diverting her mind 'from dwelling on gloomy thoughts [my mind] like a troubled sea!' she lightly touched upon the subject:

> Between us in confidential friendship, I believe I might touch upon a subject which is of a delicate nature; & that is my concern that cousin Robt. Grubb should have betrayed any weakness, to lessen him in the view of his friends, which I very lately heard was the case, & yet I cannot but love & respect him much ... I think it is a great favour to be preserved, however weak & small our number, in love towards each other.[34]

William Leadbeater also had difficulty putting the school project out of his mind – even his subconscious mind. Mary records in her diary a dream which William had in October 1794:

> He imagined himself in Paris, where the order & tranquillity which reigned there surprised him – no appearance of hurry & bustle, no gazing at him & his companion, no stately publick edifices, as in Dublin, but simple & plain wch surprised him in so great a City as he expected to find it & the citizens going quietly about their business – He wanted to see the palace but did not – however going into a large chapel in shape like an L he perceived it a school, where a great number of sweet-looking boys were taught, who seemed improving fast: though not friends, they were as plain in their dress wearing no capes to their coats, dressed man alike, but not in uniform: the Teachers appeared of a piece with them, & sweetness was sensibly felt among them.[35]

William's ability to level the grandeur of Paris demonstrates that even Friends had limitations to their powers of prophetic observation. But this should not detract from our recognition of the fusion of Quaker and French principals that this dream suggests.

32 *Annals*, p. 204. 33 Diary, November 1793. 34 Kildare County Library. PP1/12/55. 35 Diary, September 1794.

II

It was just as the Chambord project was postponed that Mary's and William's lives began to converge with two Ballitore brothers, Peter and Malachi Delany. The Delany brothers were sons of a prosperous Catholic farmer. As a young man Malachi had fled the country to escape a murder charge arising out of a dispute with his father's landlord over turf-cutting rights. After some six years in the Austrian army he returned to Ireland in 1788. Upon his return he was already 'a violent anti-aristocrat' who had left the Catholic church – though he refused to join another. In 1793 Peter Delany took a lease on the Ballitore mill owned by Mary's brother Abraham Shackleton. He was soon joined in Ballitore by Malachi who had already become a revolutionary determined to abolish what little separation remained between the local rural politics of Ballitore and the high violent politics of the larger Europe. Writing in the 1820s, with a distance made possible by twenty years of peace, Mary could report with a touch of humor that though Malachi Delany was 'a great talker, and qualified to handle various subjects, he confined himself to two – religion & politics. His mode of treating the first consisted of rating [*sic*] at the clergy, and the last in abusing the government.' But despite this slightly mocking tone, she was careful in all of her published comments about Delany to present a consistent defense of his honesty and decency. She ends her assessment of him by noting that 'he was not a secret enemy, and he had at least the merit of sincerity'.[36] In the more violent and dangerous days of the 1790s Malachi Delany was much more to Mary and William Leadbeater than a character of humour, and he was anything but their enemy. During the critical years of Ballitore radicalisation Malachi Delany was a friend and confidant of both Mary and William.

Delany spent much of his time between 1793 and 1795 outside of Ballitore, mostly in Dublin. His return to residence in Ballitore in March 1796 signaled the transition in Ballitore from politicisation to preparation for revolution. It also marked the intensification of the relationship between Delany and Mary and William Leadbeater. Over the next fifteen months Delany was a frequent guest at the Leadbeater household calling in for breakfast, dinner, supper and tea – becoming such a part of the family that he received a very rare first name only reference in Mary's diary.[37] Between these visits to Mary's household Delany was busy swearing in United men in the triangle formed by Ballitore, Blessington and Baltinglass.

36 *Annals*, p. 206. 37 Diary, September 1796.

Mary describes him on these visits as a 'great talker' and 'full of politics as usual'.[38] But she records nothing more specific. Perhaps the 'as
usual' was enough of a reference in a diary where the author carried the
full text in her own memory. But there is also increasing evidence that
Mary was becoming concerned about the dangers which her words
posed to herself and her family. While her diary continues to record
local events in detail as the situation spiraled towards war, she provides
little overt political commentary in her diary, and even more tellingly we
have markedly fewer letters to assist us in understanding these months.
This may be because she wrote fewer letters during this increasingly
chaotic period; or it may be because she and her correspondents collaborated in destroying all evidence of disaffection. There is likely some
truth in both of these explanations. As early as November 1793 Mary
Bewley writing to Mary about earlier letters issued this request:

> I must request that thou will destroy these letters that I have
> wrote to thee of late – for I fear I have shown too much anxious-
> ness in them, thou would oblige me by doing so ... do tell me in
> thy next that thou hast burnt them, I won't be satisfied other-
> ways.[39]

The 'anxiousness' that Mary Bewley wished to hide was her response to
the brief but fiery appearance of Job Scott in the community. In other
times Scott's preaching and Mary Bewley's emotional reaction to his
words might not have been dangerous, but with the advent of war with
France and increasing tension at home, Friends were becoming wary of
political exposure. This caution becomes increasingly clear in Mary's
world early in 1794.

In January of that year Mary wrote to Elizabeth Grubb explaining
that her husband William was not willing to send Elizabeth a requested
copy of a paper which he had written – an unusual act of resistance by
Mary's cooperative spouse. The contents of this rare literary effort by
William Leadbeater was not discussed in Mary's letter but the context
and dates of the letter suggest that William was putting together a com-
pendium of Job Scott's testimony. Whatever its contents, William
would not risk entrusting it to the post, or even copying it in his own
hand. Instead, he offered to allow Elizabeth to read the paper if she
would come for a visit. Mary hints at the extent of William's concern,
and the difficulty that the request created. 'The larger conversation I do
not like so well, & would not ask a copy [even] for myself.'[40]

38 Diary, August and December 1796. 39 Kildare County Library, PP 1/13/52

But the most demonstrative evidence of the increasing apprehension of Mary and her friends is the simple silence of the correspondence between these women after 1795. Mary Bewley's last surviving letter to Mary Shackleton Leadbeater was dated February 1794; and Mary's Shackleton Leadbeater's last extant pre-revolutionary letter to Elizabeth Grubb was written on Christmas day, 1795.[41]

There was no other comparable period of silence in Mary's long and active life as a correspondent. It can only be explained by the destruction of letters, or by a level of disturbance in daily life that bordered upon chaos. Unfortunately for those seeking clarity, we have evidence of both. The period of 1795-8 was one marked by a military occupation of Ballitore that included the billeting of troops in the Shackleton Leadbeater home, frequent houses searches in the village and, of course, the massive violence of May-June 1798. Clearly letter writing would have been difficult for the most dedicated friend and writer, but Mary was both, and it is most likely that she did manage to send and receive some letters during this period, it was their protection that likely proved impossible. Two small pieces of evidence suggest how most of her correspondence during this period disappeared. In the *Annals of Ballitore* she describes an incident in which her family narrowly escaped government reprisal through a stroke of luck. She had carelessly thrown 'one of the squibs then privately circulated, which in very tolerable poetry avowed disloyal sentiments' into her desk. The house was subsequently searched by a patrol seeking such evidence of disloyalty, but by a lucky accident it was not discovered. Mary's response was instantaneous: 'I started at the danger it was so near to bringing upon us, and thankfully flung it into the fire.'[42] Letters that did not perish in the fire, may simply have been lost in the turmoil of revolution. The first post-revolutionary letter to Elizabeth Grubb that does survive, dated almost a year after the rebellion, suggests this and confirms that there were prior letters written that do not survive. 'I have looked much for thy last letter & cannot find it, having lost much of my former regularity by having my papers & c so often ransacked & tost about.'[43]

These images of broadsides flung into fires and papers ransacked and tossed about represent the very real transition taking place in Ballitore and Irish politics. The period during which open political debate and mobilisation was possible at the local level was giving way to a period of escalating violence and repression. Mary and her fellow Friends would continue to play important roles in their communities,

40 Kildare County Library, PP1/12/56.　41 Kildare County Library, PP1/13/55 and PP1/12/62.　42 *Annals*, p. 224.　43 Kildare County Library, PP1/12/63.

but these roles were shifting from an active and positive engagement with radical ideas that characterised the early 1790s to an increasingly moderate stance as the society moved closer to its terrible moment of violence. The Society expressed its fears of impending civil strife officially at a national level early in 1796 by taking the aggressively peaceful step of insisting that every Quaker household destroy its arms – regardless of the purpose of those arms. The instructions were quite explicit, arms were to be destroyed, not sold, or given away, in order to insure that Friends were not involved – even indirectly – in the violence they saw approaching. This national decision was vigorously enforced, and the only Friend in Mary's monthly meeting who resisted was disowned by the society.

In one of her last letters to Elizabeth Grubb before the revolution Mary gives voice to her growing apprehension, and identifies its source – the growing militarisation of society:

> my cowardice proceeds much from a cause which thou seems not to be afflicted with, I mean publick calamity, for when I look on the sweet, peaceful scenes, the cattle grazing quietly in their own pastures, the country people following their business unmolested, & the other marks of peace, I am apt to contrast this with the terrible view of a ravaged country, & an unbridled army spreading desolation wherever they go.[44]

Such actions and images were anything but alarmist as 1796 came to a close, At Christmas time of that year the attempted French invasion at Bantry threw loyal Leinster into disarray and even panic. Mary and William were in Carlow town for their Monthly meeting when the news of French ships appearing came through on 27 December:

> Snow had fallen last night ... The passing of Expresses, the various reports, & above all the uncertainty increase the panick. Tom P. come from Ballitore, informs us that our house had been thronged with soldiers last night on their march, & more expected. Under these tumultuous impressions we went to meeting. Mary Ridgeway spoke of, when the judgments of the Lord are in the earth the people learn righteousness ... John Grubb spoke of the coming of the day of the Lord ...
>
> After meeting it really was a confused scene! Friends, some going, some endeavouring to go, & others concluding upon stay-

44 Kildare County Library, PP1/12/60.

ing, their horses being prest, & no carriages to be had, the weath-
er very cold, the soldiers thronging into town, & those who part-
ed uncertain whether they should be permitted to meet in quiet
again.[45]

III

The French did not land and the moment Mary feared was still over a
year away. In Ballitore things were quiet, if uneasy, under a now constant military occupation. Surprisingly this military presence did not
hinder Malachi Delany's recruitment efforts. Ignoring the watch of
militia men and regular troops, he continued to move in and out of
Ballitore, and in and out of the Leadbeater household. It was not until
June of 1797 that the peace was permanently disturbed by the governments opening of active repression of Ballitore. Mary recorded the
moment:

> Last night we were wakened out of our deep sleep by a party of
> horse galloping by who searched Welsh's, O'Hara's & Delany's
> for arms, I suppose suspecting them to be united Irishmen. Peter
> Delany fled in his shirt to Mullamast; I suppose, & Malachi took
> himself clean away: we hear a price is set upon his head. Tonight
> a party of highlanders; searched the poor people's houses for
> arms. Dick Miles told them they were Quakers & had none.[46]

These raids dramatically increased the temperature of the village, and
were soon followed by United Irish raids to capture weapons from the
local gentry. This in turn prompted further military repression and further popular resistance, a cycle distressingly familiar to the disturbed
areas of Leinster. In June of 1797 there were three attacks upon
Ballitore homes carried out by United men, and one retaliatory raid led
by the Yeomen. In September there was another incident of home invasion, and the first serious case of arson. In November the Leadbeater
house grew bleaker still when an old friend William Bennet was murdered by assailants unknown.

In January, 1798, the first arrests of local men for United activity
took place when James Doyle and Mat Bulger were arrested for one of
the weapons raids that the United men were carrying out. Billeting also
became more oppressive, with the numbers of soldiers placed in each

45 Diary, December 1796. 46 Diary, June 1797.

house increasing, and all female households that had been exempted were now subjected. Mary noted her closest neighbours who actually rented a part of the Leadbeater house being subjected to the billeting:

> Oppression! a billet for 40 nights for two soldiers; on M[ary]. & A[nn]. Doyle. The officer, the billet-master applied to in vain. The dear girls bear with patience, & endeavour for content.[47]

The spiral towards war accelerated early in April when the Kings County militia were rotated out of Ballitore, and the Tyrone militia, notorious for its Orange behaviour, entered. Mary reports that when the Tyrone militia entered Ballitore her husband, William, 'burst into involuntary tears prophetic perhaps of the calamities awaiting Ballitore'.[48] William's tears were not long dry when their prophesy was fulfilled. Before the month was out the village was subjected to a confiscation of the people's provisions, and regular army units arrived to carry out further arrests, interrogations and reprisals. Ominously the army's first action was to disarm the Yeomanry – supposedly the most 'loyal' of the government-sponsored military organisations. Mary knew why, she explained in a diary entry.

> The Regular army arrive to disarm the Yeomen ... some of whom had been seduced by Delanys efforts the soldiers proclaim that every man woman & child in Ballitore were United Irishmen.[49]

This was an ominous proclamation and it would prove deadly. On 4 May the Suffolk Fencibles arrived and arrested Tom Murray and Owen Finn, along with their blacksmith's tools, and took them to Athy. On 11 May, in an effort to terrorise the villagers into informing upon each other the Suffolk Fenecibles began to set fire to houses and flog local residents. The following morning Mary visited the worst afflicted and recorded the atmosphere in the village, and her own dismay with the army's methods:

> The horrours of yesterday begin to subside tho ... the executioners threaten to come again, & the village was quite in alarm, many dreading the burning of their houses, & lashing of their backs Dear Sister Peggy left us for Athy. Shall I ever see her again? ... I called to see Paddy Murphy it seemed melancholy to see a man in his full health reduced to a painful condition, &

47 Diary, January 1798. 48 Diary, April 1798. 49 Diary, April 1798.

confined to his bed by his fellow man, & without any proof of guilt but to make him confess some, but without effect.

On the 18 May two cart loads of Ballitore men were sent off to prison for further interrogation:

> The noon exhibited a dismal scene ... The street lined with people waiting for the prisoners to come out. At length they came on two cars, followed by their weeping wives & children, & under a strong guard, a sight so unusual here, deprest our spirits. I went to Mother's.

Three days later the yeomen who had been arrested were sent off to Dunlavin 'with their coats turned'.[50] They would be executed there a few days later.

On 24 May, as a part of the secret United Irishmen's plan for revolution, Malachi Delany led approximately 200 United men and women from Ballitore and the surrounding area in three skirmishes with Militia and regular army forces. For three days the rebels would hold Ballitore arid launch attacks upon loyalist forces in Narraghmore and Castledermot. On 27 May the army retook Ballitore, put it to the torch, and summarily killed suspected sympathisers of the United Irishmen. Those days of violence lie beyond the scope of this paper. They mark a tragic transition in the communal life of Ballitore and the larger world of which it was part. The violence that Friends had so feared did just as they had feared: it destroyed not only lives, but also the connections between the different religious and social groups of Ballitore, and it halted, at least for the moment, the progress towards a free and moral society in which Friends had so invested. But Friends did not dwell upon failure, and it would be a mistake to conclude that the radical changes in thinking and action which the 1790s had occasioned would be simply defeated by the horror of this violence. Mary, her family, and her neighbours would rebuild Ballitore; and she and the other Friends of Ballitore would spend the rest of their lives in efforts to undo the damage caused by the systems of inequality and exploitation that were their targets during the 1790s.

The evidence available in Mary Shackleton Leadbeater's diaries and letters provide an image of a woman and community actively engaged in political life. Her involvement in pamphlet production and distribution indicates a high level of political awareness and action, while her

50 Diary, January 1798.

involvement in the Chambord project and her moral and logistical support of the United Irish organiser Malachi Delany provide evidence of a far deeper engagement in the revolutionary politics of the 1790s than other sources would lead us to expect from a woman in a small Kildare village. It would not be too much to suggest that during that tumultuous decade Mary Shackleton Leadbeater was in fact a peaceful revolutionary. During these years, in word and action, she was an advocate of radical equality in Irish society. Her equally radical commitment to peace prevented her from being a revolutionary in the meaning normally deployed in Irish discourse. But perhaps as we learn more about the history of 1798 we will come to recognise that the peaceful legacy of republicanism was ultimately more subversive of ascendancy hierarchy than any pike. The tragic fact that peaceful revolution was impossible in the Ireland of her time should not deflect our attention and recognition from the unexpected facts revealed in Mary's diaries and letters. She and a number of other women were commited advocacates for their most cherished ideals of equality and community. They were women most political.

Lord Edward's aunt: How Louisa Conolly and her sisters faced the rebellion

Eleanor Burgess

It is over thirty years since I first met Lady Louisa Conolly through her letters to her sister Sarah. They formed the bulk of a collection of about 600 that Hubert Butler had been asked to find a home for in Ireland. Typically he thought that before being absorbed into the bowels of a library or museum they should be transcribed and suggested that, in spite of being a two-finger typist, I should do it, with the hope of being remunerated by the lucky recipient of the originals. Eventually when Desmond Guinness bought Castletown so that it could be a museum for the Irish Georgian Society, this seemed to be the perfect home for them and they are now in the Society's possession.

For me Louisa became a kind of pen-friend, but living in another age rather than another country. Gradually I got to know her, the numerous members of her family and her circle of friends. Had there been space there are many pertinent passages from these letters I would like to have quoted.

I

Louisa was the wife of Tom Conolly of Castletown. Her two sisters who were still alive in 1798 were Lady Sarah Napier and Emily, duchess of Leinster. At the time Louisa and Sarah were living in County Kildare, but Emily was in England. They were daughters of the second duke of Richmond, who was grandson of Charles II, and his mistress Louise de Kerouaille. Nevertheless, they were intimately connected with and deeply involved in Ireland. For Emily came to live at Carton in 1747 following her marriage to the earl of Kildare. Her departure for Ireland came three years after her elder sister Caroline had blotted her copy book in the eyes of her parents by eloping with Henry Fox, who became Lord Holland. Louisa was only born in 1743, to be followed by Sarah two years later. Cecila the youngest child of the family was born in 1750 but, at about the same time, their father died suddenly and his wife survived him by just a year. However he had made provision for the three little girls in his will. They were to live with Emily at Carton until they were fifteen and then go to Caroline at Holland House on the outskirts of London.

As it turned out, Louisa never did join Caroline's family for, in December 1758, she married her neighbour. Thus she became wife of the richest man in Ireland and mistress of the largest house, built in the 1720s by the renowned Speaker William Conolly. Tom, his great-nephew, had inherited it in 1754 along with other estates in Ireland and England.

Speaker Conolly died in 1729 before completing Castletown and it was left to Louisa to put flesh on the bones of the bare structure. In this way both the house and grounds became her creation. She poured her heart and soul into them and, whenever she had to be away, was always anxious to be back in her beloved Castletown. Her letters are full of detailed instructions about its enhancement as well as her enjoyment of the place. This snippet for example from 29 June 1764:

> You say in your letter do I think there are no liars but in London? I think they are in every great town, and I therefore detest a town, and wish to live as little as possible in them. I must only describe to you my delightful pleasant situation. I am sitting in an alcove in my cottage with a porch before it, in the wood three-quarters of a mile from the house, a lovely fine day, the grass looking very green, honeysuckle and roses in abundance, mignonette coming up, seringa all out, the birds singing, the fresh air all about, Mrs Staples playing upon the guitar in the porch ... Therefore you may please yourself with the thoughts that I am at this minute as happy and as pleasant as can be.[1]

There was however one sadness. She and Tom had no children of their own. But the Fitzgerald children next door were an endless source of pleasure and concern. There were also the children of Tom's six sisters, three of whom actually came to live at Castletown and, of course, she took a great interest in the family of her closest sister Sarah, one of which, another Emily, she actually adopted.

Again the letters are full of descriptions of many of these children, their doings, their characters and their illnesses. But right from his early days Edward Fitzgerald stands out as being somebody very special. He was born in 1763 and nine years later she wrote:

1 Louisa to Sarah, 29 June 1764, Irish Georgian Society Archive.

You say you suppose the Eddy's nose is out of joint. No indeed it is not for 'tis the sweetest of all creatures, and I should be the most ungrateful mortal upon earth if I did not adore him, for his love for me is quite astonishing, not at all like a child's but that of a steady friend and I assure you I do depend upon it as much as if he was grown up.[2]

Louisa not only lavished her love and care on her relations but on the local inhabitants as well, her 'Paddys' as she called them. She was pleased that during the winter of 1771 Tom was involved in providing for the poor and writes on 28 November:

Upon looking back at what I have said I find I have not told you a word of the business which is about the poor of this country. It is to make some provision for them, as the poor wretches have really none. I am vastly happy at Mr Conolly's being the person to undertake it, for I do think it so much a duty in the people who have the power to do such things to do it.[3]

A similar concern for the plight of the poor was reflected in a letter written a month later:

I do assure you that it is not possible to live in this country without perpetually feeling distress on account of the greatest number of its inhabitants which are poor.[4]

Conolly's concern was reflected in his introduction of a Poor Bill in the House of Commons.[5]

II

Louisa realised that trouble lay ahead, she frequently mentioned the state of the country. In 1782 during the American War of Independence, she wrote:

Added to all this I have the agreeable prospect in my own mind that we shall have a rebellion: it is really *my* opinion from all that I have seen and heard these two years past, and from what is now before us; only think that at this moment (in Dublin) there are people who are rejoicing at the loss we have had of our 47 West

2 Louisa to Sarah, 26 August 26 1772, ibid. 3 Louisa to Sarah, 28 November 1771, ibid.
4 Louisa to Sarah, 31 December 1771, ibid. 5 Louisa to Sarah, 5 February 1772, ibid.

India men and 4 East India men outward bound taken by the
combined fleets! What can they mean, but Rebellion? Is it not a
positive declaration of ill will towards Britain?[6]

But when rebellion did come she and Tom were perplexed and started
to panic. Reports of events in France worried them. In January 1793
Louis XVI was guillotined. What would happen in Ireland? According to
Sarah, Tom terrified Louisa 'with his croakings and when she wakes up
she expects Robespierre or Danton to guillotine her before night'.[7]

In 1795 there was much fear and speculation. The United Irishmen
were arming, the point of no return had been reached. Negotiations
were going ahead for help from France. Sarah again in a letter described
Louisa's fears:

> Dear Louisa still expects the French and to be guillotined
> because Paddy and Larry and Derby will tell the French 'Kilt dat
> man for he's rich, kilt dat woman for she has lands – destroy all
> dat family, for they are no good and they are quality' – and so
> she thinks the French will implicitly destroy all they are bid to
> do. Conolly assures me he has proofs (and I own they are fright-
> ful) of the common people above the mere mob trying to seduce
> the soldiers to teach them the use of arms and to join them, and
> all longing for the French to come. He is (with reason) very anx-
> ious to support the militia and form it into a useful body for
> internal defence as the regulars are taken away.[8]

In July 1795 150 Defenders, who by that time had begun to merge with
the United Irishmen, marched to Sarah's house in Celbridge. The leaders fired shots at the upper windows and demanded arms. Sarah was
away but the housekeeper acted as her mistress would have wished and
armed with a pistol refused them entry. They went away. Louisa, on
her own at Castletown, panicked for her brother-in-law Colonel
Napier's weapons had been hidden there. She feared the house would
be the next target. Accordingly, Castletown was put in a state of defence
with every gun primed and loaded. With the house secured, she went
round Celbridge knocking on doors:

> [speaking] to every poor person to explain the nature of this mis-
> chievous manner of proceeding, [and] entreated them to desist

6 Louisa to Sarah [n.d. 1782], ibid. 7 Sarah to … 1793 cited in Fitzgerald, *Lady Louisa
Conolly, 1743-1821*, p. 158. 8 Sarah to … 1795, cited in Fitzgerald, *Lady Louisa Conolly,
1743-1821*, p. 163.

and repose some confidence in two such friends as Mr Conolly
and myself, who never had or would deceive them.[9]

She made a list of those prepared to commit themselves to her:

> I have all their names down and of course shall be more likely to
> find out our strength if anything happens. The housekeepers
> seemed vastly pleased at this sort of association that I have set on
> foot and I think it can't do any harm and may do good.[10]

But Louisa found it hard to understand what was going on, that there
might be shades of grey between the hostility and faithfulness of her
servants and tenants. Perhaps their alliances were expedient. In her
mind she confused disaffection towards the government with disloyalty
towards herself – those that were not with her must be against her.
Their apparent ingratitude broke her heart especially after twelve of her
servants and workmen along with Sarah's footman were arrested as
housebreakers and United Irishmen.

Louisa had always thought of herself as Irish and disapproved of the
way the country was being governed and she had done what she could
to alleviate the situation. The prince of Wales had even come to see her
when she was in London in February 1797 specially to question her
about Irish politics and, in Emily's words, 'butter her up'. However she
and Tom were part of the social hierarchy and most of their huge
income came from Irish land which might be lost if the revolution was
successful. Hence her quandary.

To lose Castletown was an unthinkable catastrophe but hardest of
all to bear would be the loss of her tenant's love and respect. It seemed
to her that this was the case:

> My feeling so much as I did arose from the very great mortifica-
> tion I felt in having spent forty years (in what I considered a
> laudable pursuit) in vain. After having shown the greatest good
> will to the different classes around me, without ever once having
> been conscious of a moment's pride or severity towards them,
> and not even suffering my amusements to be independent of
> their advantages, I had flattered myself with the hope of possess-
> ing their friendship and confidence and then when ill-advisers
> came to them with new proposals, that they would at least have
> consulted me before they engaged in so deep a business.[11]

9 Louisa to 3rd duke of Richmond, 20 July 1795, cited in Tillyard, *Aristocrats*, p. 373.
10 Ibid. 11 Louisa to ... cited in Tillyard, *Aristocrats*, p. 378.

On the other hand the Napiers could remain detached. Unlike the
Conollys they had little to fear and little to lose, having no income from
land, estates or government offices.[12] They were in a sense outsiders.

Sarah had not spent her whole life in Ireland for at fifteen she had
gone to live with Caroline. The prince of Wales, who was about to
become George III, was attracted to her and entertained hopes of marriage, but these were thwarted by his mother and Lord Bute who disapproved because she was Henry Fox's niece. So it was that Charlotte
of Mecklenburg became queen of England; Sarah's pride may have been
hurt but not her heart. After various flirtations she married Sir Charles
Bunbury of Barton in Suffolk. But he neglected her for his horses and
the Turf and so she became bored there. Eventually she gave birth to a
daughter but it transpired that the father was Lord William Gordon.

To the horror and consternation of her family and society in general Sarah eloped with him. However within a year she left him and for
the next twelve years lived in penitent seclusion with her daughter,
Louisa, on her brother's estate at Goodwood. She was divorced in 1776
and eventually found happiness and fulfilment when five years later she
married George Napier. She valiantly rose to the challenge of rearing a
large family on his meagre army pay. She was thirty-seven when
Charles, the first of their eight children was born. On the birth of their
second son, George, Louisa persuaded Sarah, partly to help with their
finances, to let her bring up their daughter Emily. In 1787 the Napiers
bought a house near the gates of Castletown which had the advantage of
being close to both Louisa and their daughter. With their five boys they
moved in three years later.

At Christmas 1796 a storm had defeated the French invasionary
force in Bantry Bay. But another was threatened the following year and
so Napier thinking the poor of Celbridge were being incited to revolt,
started garrisoning his house and Castletown. He dug parallel ditches in
the fields of loyal tenants and threw up earthworks on the periphery
from where sentries could watch for attack. His boys had an early initi-
ation into the art of war, which may account for their renowned careers.
They did not have to play at soldiers, for this was the real thing.

Sarah did not allow her house to be searched as Louisa had. She
could remain cool and objective, retain her composure, hold her head
high and present herself as a model military wife. She was able to
regard the situation dispassionately and did not think the political order
was threatened by the local rebels. She considered the Dublin administration, its cruelties and oppressions, the chief cause of the disaster. She

12 Cited in Tillyard, *Aristocrats*, p. 379.

blamed it for the disaffection as it had offered no hope of emancipation and repeal of the penal laws. All the same, while the rebellion was explicable, she remained a monarchist.

There was, however, another aspect that worried all three sisters — that was the involvement of Lord Edward Fitzgerald. They had been in constant anxiety about his political activities throughout the decade. He had been dismissed from the army for attending a revolutionary dinner in Paris when he renounced his title. Then in 1796 he joined the United Irishmen and as head of the military committee had more than 300,000 men under his command. His mother Emily wrote, 'as all Edward's intentions are good, I must be satisfied, tho' I wish him more moderate'.[13]

Far away in England where she lived throughout the 1790s Emily was becoming more and more anxious about Irish affairs. It appears that Louisa in her letters managed to hide her own disquiet and state of mind for in January 1797 Emily wrote to her daughter Lucy, who had gone to Ireland to be near her favourite brother Edward:

> Dear Louisa has never been the least alarmed. She helps too to give me spirits on the subject ... Be as easy as you can make yourself about me, for indeed I am wonderfully well and am even surprised at myself. I don't listen to any of the stories, and your dear Papa contrives, I see, to have it as little talked about as possible before me.[14]

Papa was William Ogilvie, not Lucy's father. He had been employed by Emily, an admirer of Rousseau, to educate her children as far as possible on the lines of *Emile*. Then after the death of the duke of Leinster in 1773 she had married him.

As the 'fatal year', as Emily called it, drew near, helpless in London she could only wait and hope. Inspite of not being able to dissuade Edward from his treasonable aim, she first thought of him as a hero but later as a martyr, for a reward for his capture of £1,000 had been set on his head.

One of Thomas Conolly's nieces was married to Lord Castlereagh, who suggested the family should use its influence to persuade Edward to leave the country and go to America. Louisa wrote accordingly to Emily and Ogilvie and unsuccessfully tried to coax him. Emily had taken care of Lord Edward's son, but there was also Pamela, his wife,

13 Emily to Ogilvie, June 1792 cited in Fitzgerald, *Emily Duchess of Leinster, 1731–1814*, p. 199. 14 Emily to Lucy, 4 January 1797, cited in Fitzgerald, *Emily Duchess of Leinster, 1731–1814*, p. 233.

for the sisters to worry about. After he had gone into hiding she remained in Dublin with her newly-born daughter. The government became suspicious. Once more Castlereagh was commissioned to inform Louisa that there was information against Pamela, nevertheless they would give her ten days to leave the country. Having broken the news to Pamela, Louisa transmitted this information to Ogilvie so that he could inform Emily as gently as possible.[15]

III

When in May 1798 a ferocious campaign of disarming reached Celbridge and a Scottish regiment plundered at will and threatened to burn the houses, Louisa went all round Celbridge trying to persuade the angry, frightened inhabitants to give up their arms:

> I have spent days in entreaties and threats to give up the horrid pikes. Some houses burnt at Kilcock yesterday produced the effect. Maynooth held out yesterday, though some houses were burnt and some people punished. This morning the people of Leixlip are bringing in their arms, Celbridge as yet holds out, though five houses are burning. Whether obstinacy or that they have them not I cannot say. But you may imagine what Mr Conolly and I suffer. He goes about entreating to the last – spent yesterday out among them and to-day is gone again. He goes from Maynooth to Leixlip and Celbridge and begins again and again to go round them. We have fortunately two most humane officers, that do not do more than is absolutely necessary from their orders. At present I feel most prodigiously sunk with all the surrounding distress, but I am determined to exert myself, for the little use I may be of. It would grieve you to see Mr Conolly's heart so wounded as it is.[16]

Thus she wrote to Ogilvie on 21 May 1798 but the news in the earlier part of her letter was much more personally devastating. She described in detail Lord Edward's capture, how he was taken to Newgate prison and how Emily Napier and her step-sister Louisa were at the theatre when they heard the news being imparted to the Lord Lieutenant in the next-door box.

15 Louisa to Ogilvie, 18 May 1798, Terling Essex. 16 Louisa to Ogilvie, 21 May 1798, cited in Fitzgerald, *Lady Louisa Conolly, 1743-1821*, p. 172.

Two days later she wrote to the husband of Charlotte, Edward's sister:

> He was taken on Saturday night last, at nine o'clock in a house in Thomas Street, where three of the town magistrates accompanied with a guard seized him. He made great resistance, is himself wounded and wounded two of the magistrates – none of the three wounds are now considered to be dangerous. Edward had two balls lodged in his shoulder which are not yet extracted, but the two surgeons that attend him, Stewart, the surgeon general, and Doctor Lindsay, the family physician, say that they will be got out. The last tells me that his mind is quite firm, and that tho' he suffers a good deal of pain, that he bears it well. It has been such a decided order, since the first taking up of persons upon this unhappy business that none of the friends should be admitted to see the prisoners, that I could not obtain leave for poor Lady Edward to see him. The heartbreaking scene, that it is with her, is past description. For in addition to the misfortune of having him taken up, and not seeing him, it is thought necessary to send her out of the Kingdom, and I need not picture what the feelings of a wife in such a tryal must be. I can hardly stand it, but am determined to show her every friendly office in my power to the last, am therefore now in town, waiting to put her on board the packet.[17]

No one but Lucy, his sister, considered Edward's wound dangerous. Their chief concern was that he would be tried for high treason. So Emily did not set out immediately for Dublin, thinking she could be more use seeking support from influential friends. The trial was set for 11 June and she was only told of the wound on 28 May. Then she tried at least to get it postponed till he had recovered.

Meanwhile back at Castletown after putting Pamela on the boat Louisa had another fright. At 3 a.m. on 26 May she saw from her bedroom window 200 rebels armed with pikes silently, apart from clinks and rustles, crossing the lawn in front of the house. Although they harmed no one, closed the gates behind them and disappeared into the night Louisa decided to have all the doors locked, the windows shuttered and the servants armed. News from Wexford of rebel successes and atrocities on both sides increased her misery.

Then news came that Edward was dying. Emily, her niece and constant companion, has left an account of how Louisa finally got permis-

17 Louisa to Joseph Strutt, 23 May 1798, Terling Essex.

sion to see him. She describes how they set off immediately to see Lord
Camden in the Phoenix Park. Louisa went in to him but in less than
half an hour she was back in the carriage saying to Emily 'order them to
drive home. I have knelt at his feet and the Brute has refused to let me
see my dying Edward.'[18] At Emily's suggestion they decided to try Lord
Clare and drove to Ely Place. Louisa was instantly admitted and Lord
Clare agreed to take her to Lord Edward himself and on the way they
would pick up his brother, Lord Henry. The two of them were the last
members of the family to see Edward alive.

This is how Louisa described her sad interview in her letter to
Ogilvie:

> I first approached his bed. He looked at me, knew me, kissed me
> and said (what will never depart from my ears) 'It is heaven to
> me to see you.' And shortly after, turning to the other side of the
> bed he said, 'I can't see you.' I went round and he soon after
> kissed my hand and smiled at me, which I shall never forget,
> though I saw death in his dear face at the time. I then told him
> that Henry (his brother) was come. He said nothing that marked
> his surprise at his being in Ireland but expressed joy at hearing
> it, and said, 'Where is he, dear fellow?' Henry then took my
> place and the two dear brothers frequently embraced each other
> to the melting a heart of stone; and yet God enabled both Henry
> and myself to remain quite composed. As everyone left the room
> we told him we only were with him. He said: 'That is very pleas-
> ant.' However he remained silent and I then brought in the sub-
> ject of Lady Edward and told him I had not left her till I saw her
> on board; and Henry told him, having met her on the road well.
> He said, 'And the children too? She is a charming woman', and
> then became silent again.[19]

On waking the next morning Louisa received a note from the surgeon,
dated 6 a.m. 4 June 1798, to say he had died soon after they left. She it
was who arranged the funeral. It was to be at St Werburgh's Church at
night to avoid rioting. No relations were present.

Louisa received a letter dated 7 June from her brother the duke of
Richmond describing the effect her melancholy news to Ogilvie had had
on them all. He praised his nephew:

18 Emily Napier's account of the death of Lord Edward Fitzgerald (August 1832),
P.R.O.N.I. 19 Louisa to Ogilvie, cited in Fitzgerald, *Lady Louisa Conolly, 1743-1821*, p.
174.

A more generous, good-hearted soul I believe never existed than poor Edward possessed. His faults were errors of imagination, but I am sure no man acted more from principle (mistaken as it was) than he did.[20]

Then he informed her that Emily with Edward's son had set out for Dublin the previous evening. She had hoped that by being there she could postpone the trial. A messenger was sent with the letter to overtake Ogilvie, who had followed Emily at dawn. Richmond hoped he would catch up with her at Lichfield and went on to say:

Nothing can exceed the fortitude of mind which my poor sister has shown in this dreadful trial of her nerves. Her composure has been beyond anything that one could have conceived, from one whose whole soul one knew to be so enraptured as hers was in Edward, till the night before she set out, I never saw her sink, and then it was from fatigue at the repeated exertions she never ceased one hour to make, to retard his trial which was all we thought it prudent (in the then stage of the business) to aim at. I must say that from the prince of Wales and the duke of York who both saw her, she had at least the satisfaction of knowing, that they interested themselves much in favour of her wishes.[21]

But how was Louisa bearing up? She wrote to Emily:

I have had no time for indulgence, nor can I allow it myself yet, but go on like a machine from morning till night, catching at the little momentary enjoyments of fresh air, the smell of mown grass and flowers. And now and then a moment's attention to the harvest coming home. But the eagerness and delight that used to attend these occupations is so mixed with pangs of grief, that I sometimes fly from them and endeavour to occupy myself with the stupid details of house economy where no happy or pleasing remembrances can mix.[22]

Fighting continued through the summer. The Napier family, afraid Celbridge might be burnt, moved in with Louisa who wrote on 10 July:

I make it a rule to believe as little as possible all that I hear, yet these histories of cruelty I cannot at all times avoid. I confess candidly that I hear of them on both sides and they equally fill

20 3rd duke of Richmond to Louisa, 7 June 1798, Terling Essex. 21 Ibid. 22 Louisa to Emily, 1798, cited in Fitzgerald, *Lady Louisa Conolly, 1743-1821*, p. 175.

me with horror. But I am determined to pursue, as long as I possibly can, the plan of standing my ground; for I really do not apprehend personal danger, but sufferings. The miseries of the country pursue me day and night, for I have at times most terrible dreams ... Our house is a perfect garrison. Eighteen soldiers sleep in our saloon, and we are all blocked up and shut up except the hall door and one door to the kitchen yard, and are frequently ordered into the house upon the alarm being given of the rebels being near Celbridge. Thank God they have never been in a body since the military company came into it, or else there would have been some battle which is the thing I dread. Lord Cornwallis would have a Proclamation inviting the rebels to come in, and although it has not been as decided as I am sure he would wish it to be, yet many are daily coming in to Mr Conolly, begging protection, which you may imagine he gives them with the greatest pleasure. I have opportunities of conversing with these poor people, from whom I find that many are forced into rebellion and of course are grievously to be pitied. I verily believe that many of them are heartily tired of it.[23]

To Louisa's relief Cornwallis, more humane and experienced as a soldier, had replaced Camden. A week later by 18 July there was a general amnesty.

In spite of her sadness and worries about Edward's wife and children Louisa could at least look forward to a resumption of her previous relationship with her 'Paddys'. Indeed she devoted the remainder of her long life to improving their lot. Three years after Tom's death she refused an invitation in 1806 to live comfortably at Goodwood with her brother, so that her time and energy could be spent helping her poverty-stricken tenants in every way she could. Aided by her faithful niece Emily, she continued ministering to them and started up a school of industry.

Her sisters, Emily and Sarah, died in England in 1814 and 1826 respectively but Louisa lived on at Castletown until 1821, when she died aged seventy-eight. At the time George Napier came to support his heartbroken sister Emily. The detailed memoir he wrote for his children included a description of the grieving tenants coming to pay their last respects. Louisa could have wished for no greater reward.

23 Louisa to ... 10 July 1798, cited in Fitzgerald, *Lady Louisa Conolly, 1743-1821*, p. 175.

Before the day came when it would be necessary to place her remains in the coffin, the poor labourers and others of the village wished to be allowed to see the body, to which of course I consented. I watched from a recess where I could see without being observed, the various persons as they came in singly, and went to the bed where she lay with a countenance so serene, so beautiful, that you could scarce believe she was not alive. As every poor person after seeing her passed on to another room and (not seeing me in the recess) conceived themselves alone and unobserved, I had full opportunity of witnessing their natural feelings, and if ever gratitude for benefits conferred and deep affection, nay I may say despair for the loss of a parent, was depicted in the countenance of human beings, it was so in those of these poor Irish Catholics. One old white-headed man took her cold lifeless hand and, kissing it on his knees, sobbed out, 'Oh my dear, my sweet lady, my long tried, my only friend, why, why have you left your poor old creature to die alone. You who used to come to his bedside when he was sick, and cheer him up with your good word, and give him the drop of soup, and the bit of meat, and tell him to have comfort, and now you're gone before me after all. But I'll not stay long, I'll follow you, for you'll clear the way for a poor old sinner like myself, and God will receive me from you.' Then he crossed himself, laid her hand gently down, kissed it again and then still turning his white head to take a last look and his face streaming with tears he tottered out of the room.[24]

At dawn on the day of the funeral, from far and wide, crowds started to gather in front of the house and wait patiently to see the coffin come out. Then having prayed for the soul of their Protestant friend, this Catholic multitude followed the remains of her, whom they almost revered as a saint, to the family tomb. Emily and George remained on at Castletown for three months to ensure that Louisa's school of industry continued on a firm and lasting basis. Before they left, the Roman Catholic inhabitants of Celbridge showed their appreciation by presenting an address to them, wherein they stated that in Louisa

> the poor have lost a comforter and protector, the middle classes a patroness and adviser and the higher orders an amiable lady and an inestimable friend. The recollection of her virtues and goodness generally shall ever command our admiration, whilst her kindness particularly to the poor of our persuasion shall never be

24 Emily Napier, 'Extract from my brother's memoirs', Irish Georgian Society Archives.

erased from our memories: of her goodwill towards us she has
left a lasting and speaking monument in the School of Industry
at Castletown.[25]

FURTHER READING

Stella Tillyard, *Aristocrats* (London, 1994).
Brian Fitzgerald, *Emily Duchess of Leinster 1731-1814* (London, 1949).
Brian Fitzgerald, *Lady Louisa Conolly, 1743-1821* (London, 1950).
Edith Roelker Curtis, *Lady Sarah Lennox, 1745-1826* (London, 1947).

25 Address of the Roman Catholic inhabitants of Celbridge to Colonel and Miss Napier,
22 October 1821, Irish Georgian Society Archive.

'The Noggin of Milk': An Old Testament legend and the Battle of Ballinamuck

Maureen Murphy

Late in the summer of 1798, a small fleet carrying French troops sailed under English colours into Killala Bay, county Mayo. It was the beginning of the last invasion of Ireland.[1] The French came at the request of the United Irishmen, but Napoleon gave only a token response to the Irish call for help. Had he committed his forces to Ireland instead of pursuing his Egyptian campaign, it might have changed the course of European history. Instead, he supplied the Irish with 1,000 muskets, some artillery and 1,000 men under the command of General Humbert.

In spite of their small numbers, the unexpected landing in the west and the local support that varied between 1,000 and 3,000 men resulted in three quick victories at Killala, Ballina and Castlebar. The Castlebar engagement became known as the 'Races of Castlebar' because the Kilkenny and Longford militias fled in confusion. Some militiamen turned coat and joined the Irish and French.[2]

The rebels established a provisional government in Castlebar and lingered in the area for ten days before heading north as far as Collooney and then east intending to join the major force of United Irishmen at Granard, county Longford. The Irish and French continued on the offensive. The tone of alarm in Viceroy General Charles Cornwallis's dispatches, and the concern in the contemporary press indicate that the threat posed by a small force of largely untrained

---

1 Richard Hayes used the title *The Last Invasion of Ireland* (Dublin, 1939) for his study of the French campaign. 2 The records of the Longford militia at Castlebar list one sergeant and twenty-three rank and file killed, nine rank and file wounded and one captain, one lieutenant, one ensign, one staff, eight sergeants and 146 rank and file missing. Sir Henry McAnally, *The Irish Militia 1793-1816. A Social and Military Study* (London, 1949), p. 137.

troops in a countryside garrisoned by 100,000 Crown soldiers was
regarded very seriously.

The delay in Castlebar and the rebel march first north and then east
gave the Crown forces time to cast a net around the rebel army.
Cornwallis marched west with 26,000 troops intending to contain the
Irish and French at the Shannon while General Lake was ordered to
pursue the rebels, to snipe at their rear guard and to cut their line of
retreat. On the evening of 7 September 1798, the Irish and French, now
hard-pressed by the Crown forces, stopped to rest at Cloone, county
Leitrim. *Saunders's News-Letter and Daily Advertiser* for 14 September
1798, reported that the Irish and French had marched eighty-seven Irish
miles or one-hundred and ten English miles in four days. Both General
Lake and a French officer, Jean-Louis Jobit, refer to the exhausting
marches in their letters and journals. Lake's letter from Ballinamuck
camp on 8 September 1798 mentions 'four days and nights of most
severe marching'.[3] Jobit's account describes the exhuasted and dispirited
Irish leaving Cloone; 'à 5 heurs du matin, nous nous remîmes en
marche, nos soldats extrêment fatigués et presque en partie décourages
par la nouvelle des grandes forces de l'ennemi que les harcelait'.[4]

The delay at Cloone to let the harassed rebels rest closed the noose
around them. The next morning, 8 September 1798, the Irish and
French, pinned between the pincers of Lake and Cornwallis, were overtaken at Ballinamuck, county Longford. While the Battle of Ballinamuck was a short one with only token French resistance, there were
three engagements. First, at Kiltycreevagh Cross, Colonel Crawford's
troops overpowered the French rear guard forcing General Sarazin's
surrender. The main encounter was on Shanmullagh Hill where
Humbert and his main body of French troops put up a fight till their
line was broken by Lake's troops and Humbert surrendered. Oral tradition suggests that the English were shown the way by an informer,
sometimes described as an old crone. A desparate last stand was made
by the Irish, probably near the present Gaigue Cross; however, oral tradition tends to put the rebels at the Black Fort, a site on the western
slope of Creelaughter associated with local folklore and history.

Ninety-six French officers and 746 French rank and file were taken
prisoner, brought to Dublin and exchanged for British prisoners of war.
No provisions were made for the captured Irish. The luckier rebels ran

---

3 Hugh Pearse (ed.), *Memoir of the Life and Military Service of Viscount Lake* (London,
1908), p. 270. 4 Jean-Luis Jobit, *Journal de L'Expedition D'Irlande Suivi de Notes sur le
General Humbert qui L'a Commande*. MS 44, Bibliotheque Municipale de Brest, in Nuala
Costello (ed.), 'Two Diaries of the French Expedition, 1798', *Analecta Hibernica*, XI
(July, 1941), p. 29.

for their lives; the rest were treated as traitors. A first batch was exe-cuted immediately; a second group was forced to draw lots. Those with the fatal tickets were hanged.[5] Local oral tradition supports the lottery accounts. Most of the Irish casualties were men from the west; locals escaped into the bogs where the cavalry could not pursue them and the infantry was too exhausted to take up the chase.[6]

The facts of the Battle of Ballinamuck suggest that it was one of those battles that was an accident of history, the place where two armies met. In reality, however, the place had the markings of the fulfillment of the millenarian Prophecy of Collumbkille, also called Pastorini's Prophecy, which predicted an Armageddon in the Valley of the Black Pig 'in the year of the eight or the nine' when the Irish would triumph. The name Ballinamuck, the Mouth of the Ford of the Pigs, is associat-ed with the lore of the Valley of the Black Pig.

A letter from Maria Edgeworth written from Edgeworthtown, coun-ty Longford, on New Year's Day, 1798, alludes to 'the old prophecy found in a bog' and its prediction that an earthquake would bring down Slievegaulry on Edgeworthtown. 'Almost all the people in this town,' she wrote, 'sat up last night to receive the earthquake.'[7] While it was not collected in North Longford, an anecdote recorded by Miles Byrne about the Wexford insurrection suggests that the Prophecy was linked to Napoleon and French help. Byrnes said after the Vinegar Hill disas-ter, he was hiding with his men in the Wicklow Hills where he met a northern United Irishman called Antrim John. When asked by Byrne why he and his men did not support the rebels at the Battle of Arklow, Antrim John replied that according to the Prophecy, Ireland could not be freed before the autumn of 1798 when help would arrive from France and England would be defeated.[8]

Although no accounts have been collected to support a direct con-nection between the Battle of Ballinamuck and the Prophecy, it is pos-sible that the local people thought that the fulfillment of the Prophecy was at hand: a battle between the Irish helped by Napoleon's men and the English, fought on the feast of the nativity of the Blessed Virgin Mary, the eighth day of the ninth month, in the year 1798, in the town whose very name conjured up the myth of restoration, the myth of the Valley of the Black Pig.

5 In his history of 1798, W.H. Maxwell, who was not sympathetic to the rebels, report-ed that seventeen rebels in this lottery system were hanged. *The Irish Rebellion* (London, 1845) pp 243-4. 6 'Extract from a Letter of an Officer of the Kerry Militia', *Faulkner's Dublin Journal*, 13 September 1798. 7 Augustus Hare (ed.), *The Life and Letters of Maria Edgeworth*, I (London, 1894), p. 154. 8 Miles Byrne, *Notes of an Irish Exile of 1798* (Dublin: Maunsel, n.d.), p. 228.

While the fate of the Irish in the rebel army has been recorded in dispatches, diaries, journals, letters and comtemporary newpapers, it is only in oral tradition where one finds accounts of what happened to the local people around Ballinamuck during and after the battle. The folklorist Richard M. Dorson's pioneering essay, 'Oral Tradition and Written History', suggested five areas where oral tradition can supplement the standard sources of historical scholarship: as a source for popular attitudes, prejudices and stereotypes; as an insight into the concepts of myths, symbols and image; as an method of helping to separate fact from fancy; as a means of verifying incidents, and as a way of providing data about minority groups.[9] Folklore is especially important to accounts of 1798 where contemporary written accounts are biased.

According to tradition, most of the population fled to places of safety in the area: to caves and dugouts, to Clonback fort, to Sallagh Lough or Keeldra Lough, but most of all, like their local rebel counterparts, they took to the bogs of Clonback and Edenmore. Local stories describe women carrying children on their backs to family or friends in Leitrim or in Cavan. Safety was the chief concern. A Duignan family story describes a great-grandmother who was a flaxen-haired girl hiding in Clonblack fort. When she would raise her head over the top of the fort, others would say, 'Keep down or they will see your white head'.[10]

People lived on oaten bread or oatmeal. One account describes women from the townland of Fardromin standing in Sallagh Lough breaking up large cakes of oatmeal bread, moistening them into a doughy consistency and handing pieces around to others.[11] They also hid their livestock in the bogs. These accounts are corroborated by written sources, such as Musgrave's history of 1798 which describes the deserted houses around Ballinamuck and the need for the troops to forage.[12] One woman who had taken her infant from Cornakelly to Mullach Bán in county Cavan returned to ransom her husband with money in her dress and was forced to kill her chickens to feed soldiers.[13]

Ballinamuck produced its own '98 heroes: Gunner Magee, Art McQuade and Robin Gill. Magee is the traditonal epic hero who died fighting to the last against overwhelming odds. Out of ammunition, he fed his cannon with broken pots. When the gun carriage collapsed, two

9 R.M. Dorson, 'Oral Tradition and Written History', in *Journal of The Folklore Institute*, i (1964), pp 200-34.   10 Recorded in 1938 by Peter Duignan from John Duignan, Kiltycreevagh, Ballinamuck parish who heard it from his father Patrick Duignan. Account given to Maureen O'Rourke, 1964.   11 Kate Kelly, Crouch Hill, London. Recorded by Maureen O'Rourke in 1966.   12 Sir Richard Musgrave, *Memoirs of the Different Rebellions in Ireland*, 3rd ed., II (London, 1802), pp 177-8.   13 Department of Irish Folklore, MS 1430, pp 91-5.

brave lads offered their backs and were killed by the cannon's recoil.[14] In some accounts Magee dies at his cannon during the last engagement of the Battle of Ballinamuck; in others, he is hanged: at Bully's Acre in Ballinalee, at the hands of Captain Dukey Crawford or over the back of the notorious Hepenstall, the 'walking gallows'. In his poem 'An Gunnadóir Mac Aoidh,' Eoghan O'Tuairisc introduces the details of the legend and ends with the traditional consolation offered to Irish heroes: that his deeds will be remembered. 'Ach ar éacht an Ghunnadóra beidh trácht go lá an bhráth' (But there will be talk of the Gunner's deeds till Judgment Day).[15]

Art McQuade and Robin Gill are the resourceful rebels, men on the run who overcome their stronger adversaries by their intelligence and courage. Their daring escapes anticipate the men of the flying columns in the Irish War of Independence. McQuade, a renowned runner, meets a trooper or Hessian who is killing a child a woman carries on her back. McQuade unseats the trooper from his horse by cutting the reins and finishes him with his own sword.[16] Gill's similar exploits are remembered in local legend and in a folk ballad of twenty-four stanzas. Gill kills the Hessian who shot his friend Prunty. Shot himself by two soldiers as he escapes, Gill stops only long enough to stuff moss into his wounds in the manner of the old Irish heroes.[17] Gill kills a second soldier like Synge's Playboy: he clefts his head in two with Michael Columb's loy. The ballad ends with the reminder of the myth of restoration. An eighty-five year-old survivor of the Battle of Ballinamuck, Gill concludes, 'boys, keep your pikes well-sharpened. They may serve another day'.[18]

Gill's exploit killing a soldier with a blow to the head is probably grafted from Ballinamuck's widely collected legend of the lone woman

14 Recorded in 1936 from James O'Neill (80), Crowdromin and Patrick Dolan, Kiltycreevagh Cross, Ballinamuck parish by Richard Hayes, *Last Invasion*, pp 235, 229. Department of Irish Folklore, School MS 758, p. 434. Recorded in 1938 from Mick Grimes (86), Kiltycreevagh Cross by James McKenna. School MS 758, II, p. 58. Recorded in 1938 from John Brady (72), Crowdromin by Frances Brady. Recorded in 1964 from Patrick Duignan (59), Gaigue Cross, Ballinamuck parish and in 1966 from Kate Kelly (57) Crouch Hill, London by Maureen O'Rourke. 15 Eoghan O'Tuairisc, 'An Gunnadóir Mac Aoidh', Seán O'Tuama (ed.), *Nuabhéarsíocht* (Baile Atha Cliath, 1950), p. 97. 16 Department of Irish Folklore. School MS 758, II. Recorded in 1938 from Patrick Brady (75), Gaigue, Ballinamuck parish by Frankie McQuade and in 1964 from Patrick Duignan (59), Gaigue Cross by Maureen O'Rourke. 17 Cuchulain to Sualtaim, 'Dry tufts of grass are stuffed into my wounds'. Joseph Dunn (ed.), *The Ancient Irish Epic, Táin Bó Cuailgne* (London, 1914), p. 299. 18 'The Ballad of Robin Gill', Department of Irish Folklore. School MS 758, pp 446-7. Collected in 1938 from Patrick Gill (45), Edenmore, Ballinamuck parish by James Mc Kenna.

who kills a soldier.[19] Eleven versions of the story of the lone woman
appear in Ballinamuck tradition. In its usual form, a horseman rides up
to a cottage and asks the woman of the house who is alone to give him
a drink. She goes into the house and returns with a noggin, a wooden
vessel, of milk, buttermilk or cream which she hands to the soldier. As
he raises the noggin to drink and tips his head backwards, she takes a
beetle or a pounder from behind her back and delivers a fatal blow to
the soldier's throat or head killing him instantly. She hides the body till
she she disposes of it in a lake or in an unmarked grave.

Half the versions of the story name the narrator. Reilly, a common
name in the district, is the heroine in four versions of the story while
the narrator of another version claims his great-grandmother Mrs Brady
as the courageous woman.[20] Along with the variation in local names, the
location of the episode moves around the district. Since location has the
least bearing on the story, the incident has been shifted around the
townlands without damaging its dramatic or logical integrity.

Victims vary from soldiers to horsemen to yeomen and to Hessians,
Baron de Hompesch's Mounted Riflemen or Hompsech's Dragoons,
continental mercenaries whose ferocity was remembered well into the
nineteenth century. Around Ballinamuck the people thought the
Hessians were men of extraordinary size because of their tall hats and
the expression 'He's a big Hussian of a man' or the word 'Mahussian'
to describe a large person continued in circulation to our own time.[21]

---

19 There are two versions of this legend in Wicklow '98 tradition. When a yeoman tried
to molest Susie O'Toole, the daughter of a Wicklow blacksmith, she killed him with a
blow of her fist. Collected in 1964 from Caoimhín O'Danachair, Department of Irish
Folklore by Maureen O'Rourke. Anne Flood, another Wicklow woman, was washing
potatoes in her kitchen when a Hessian appeared and asked whether she had seen a red-
coat passing. She said she had and pointed the way. When the Hessian turned his head,
she hit him with a mallet and killed him. Department of Irish Folklore. MS 437, pp 132-
3. Collected in 1937 from Mrs. John Carroll (65) of Assegart, Cullenstown, county Wexford by Thomas O'Gardha. 20 Reilly versions: Department of Irish Folklore, MS 758, p.
447. Recorded in 1938 from Mick Grimes (86), Kiltycreevagh, Ballinamuck parish by
James McKenna; recorded in 1964 from Patrick Carty (75), Drumbad, Ballinamuck parish
by Maureen O'Rourke; recorded in 1964 from Peter Duignan (59), Gaigue, Ballinamuck
parish by Maureen O'Rourke. Brady version: Department of Irish Folklore, School MS
758, II, p. 47. Recorded in 1938 from John Brady, Crowdromin, Ballinamuck parish by
Frank Brady. 21 The nearest to a tall story in Ballinamuck tradition incolves a Hessian
victim. When Manus Deveney kills a Hessian in single combat, he notices a fine pair of
boots on the soldier. Tugging to get the boots off the dead man, Devaney pulls his legs
as well as his boots off. Department of Irish Folklore. School MS 758, II. Collected in
1938 from John Dolan by Michael Connolly. Richard Dorson pointed out that the taking
of boots and legs off a dead soldier is similar to a legend told about the Battle of Culloden.
Both are versions of folktale type AT 1281A 'Getting Rid of the Man-eating Calk'.

The major distinction between versions of the legend is whether or not there was a motivation other than that the horseman is an enemy soldier. One informant questioned the morality of killing a man, even an enemy, in such a deceptive way. Patrick Carty said, 'twas a loss of honour giving a man a drink and killing him with a stroke. I wouldn't think there'd be much honour in that'.[22]

Where motivation is provided, it does not have to do with the woman's personal safety but with her concern to protect a rebel hiding in her house. The woman believes she must choose between the soldier and the young rebel who will certainly be killed. A woman in Lettergeeragh saves her own son who is hiding in a loft; a Mrs Hart in Lettergullion acts to protect her nephew.[23] One woman protects the local hero Robin Gill, and two other women hide unidentified rebels behind staves of flax.[24]

The other motive is revenge. Two accounts, which differ only in location and attributed to the same informant, tell how Mrs Reilly recognizes a suit of frieze that the horseman carries under his arm as that of her son, and she kills the soldier.[25] Another woman, unnamed, living south of Ballinamuck village near Corn Hill, breaks the neck of a soldier with a pounder because her two sons had been killed and she was 'desperate'.[26]

The lone woman who kills a soldier may be an Irish version of an Apocryphal legend that can be traced back to the story of Jael and Sisera which is told twice in the Old Testament Book of Judges (4:17-22 and 5: 24-27). In 4:17-22, Sisera, commander of the Canaanite army flees before the Israelites and takes refuge in the tent of the Jael, the wife of Heber the Kenite, because there is peace between the Canaanites and the Kenites. He asks for a drink and shelter. Jael gives him a drink, but while he sleeps, she takes a tent pin and drives it into his temple.

22 Recorded in 1964 from Patrick Carty (75), Drumbad, Ballinamuck parish by Maureen Murphy.   23 Recorded in 1936 from James O'Neill (80), Crowdromin, Ballinamuck parish by Richard Hayes. Hayes, 236; The Brady anecdote was printed in *The Longford Leader*, 29 December 1928, p. 2.   24 Recorded in 1964 from John Lenihan (59), Gaigue Cross, Ballinamuck parish by Maureen O'Rourke. Department of Irish Folklore, MS 758, p. 446. Recorded in 1938 from Mick Grimes (86), Kiltycreevagh, Ballinamuck parish by James McKenna. Department of Irish Folklore, MS 1457, pp 656-657. Recorded in 1956 from Patrick Connell (84), Drumlish, Drumlish parish by James Delaney.   25 The informant was Patrick Grimes (86) of Kiltycreevagh, Ballinamuck parish. The Clonelly version was recorded in 1938 by James McKenna, Department of Irish Folklore, MS 758, p. 447; the Shanmullagh version was recorded in 1964 from Peter Duignan (59) by Maureen O'Rourke.   26 Recorded in 1964 from Kate Kelly (58), Crouch Hill, London, by Maureen O'Rourke.

In 5:24-27, a version dated earlier, there is no mention of peace between the Canaanites and Kenites, and Jael is called blessed for avenging Israel. The scenario is the same:

> He asked water, and she gave him milk;
> she brought forth butter in a lordly dish.
>
> She put her hand to the nail, and her right
> hand to the workman's hammer; and with the
> hammer she smote Sisera, she smote off his
> head, when she had pierced and stricken through
> his temples.

Like Patrick Carty, who viewed Mrs Reilly's killing the soldier as dishonourable, some Biblical scholars have criticised Jael's deception as immoral; however, they allow her action was justified by her intense feeling for the Israelite cause and their defense against oppression.[27]

The story of Jael is often linked with the Book of Judith which describes the beautiful, devout widow taking her maid and going to the camp of Holofernes, the leader of the Assyrian host who has taken the strategic town of Bethulia on the road to Jerusalem. Winning Holofernes's confidence, Judith is invited to a feast in his tent. When the other guests leave, the drunken Holofernes falls asleep. Judith seizes his sword, decapitates Holofernes and gives the head to her maid who puts it in a bag. The women slip away and return to Bethulia with their trophy. Leaderless, Holofernes's army is routed and the Jews pursue the army to Damascus.

Artists have been drawn to these Old Testament women. Medieval drawings portray Jael with a mallet raised ready to drive a tent pin into the temple of the sleeping Sisera. Gustave Doré's nineteenth-century engraving places the dead Sisera lying in the foreground and a tall, powerful, impassive Jael raising the tent flap to show his body to his waiting army.[28]

Painters, including Matteo di Giovanni, Andrea Mantegna, Sandro Botticelli, Lucas Cranach, Giorgione da Castelfranco, Raphael, Peter

27 George Arthur Buttrick, et al. (eds), 'The Book of Judges', *The Interpreter's Bible*, II (New York, 1953), pp 537-8. James Dixon Douglas, 'Jael', *The New Bible Dictionary* (Grand Rapids, 1967), p. 596. 28 Medieval drawings include the English miniature from the Queen Mary Psalter in the British Museum (Royal 2B vii, Folio 33) and the pen drawing after the Master of Flémalle in the Herzog Anton Ulrich Museum in Brunswick. A later drawing by Lucas van Leyden is in the collection of the Museum Boyman van Beuningen, Rotterdam.

Paul Rubens, Joachim Antonisz Wtewael, Artemisia Gentileschi, Rembrant, and Gustav Klimt, have been particularly attracted to the story of Judith because it offered them the opportunity to portray their ideal of feminine beauty in the context of traditional iconography: Judith represented with a sword holding head of Holoferenes while her maid attends her with a open sack.

A fifteenth-century miniature from the *Champion des Dames* of Martin Le Franc conflates the tradition of Judith and Joan of Arc by having the two women appear outside Holofernes's tent. Judith holds a head and sword; Joan carries a lance and shield emblazoned with the cross of Lorraine.[29] More important is the earlier fourteenth-century link made by the Dominican, perhaps Ludolph of Saxony, who wrote the influential *Speculum humanae salvationis* (The Mirror of Human Salvation) that used drawings of Jael and Sisera, Judith and Holofernes and Queen Tomyris with the Head of Cyrus to establish the connection between those traditions and the victory of the Virgin Mary over Satan by thrusting a vexillum into his gullet.[30]

Like the heroines of Judeo-Christian tradition, the lone woman who kills the soldier in the Ballinamuck legend is a model of a woman who acts courageously and independently and who uses her wit to defeat the power of an oppressive or evil opponent. Such action against these forces was not considered gender specific, and later stories of local nationalist encounters feature plucky local women. No doubt the '98 legend would have inspired the girls and women who acted with daring in the Drumlish land war in 1881.[31] During the War of Independence, when Ballinamuck men formed a company of the 'Blacksmith of Ballinalee' (Sean Mac Eoin's North Longford Brigade of the I.R.A.), the women of North Longford risked their lives carrying messages and offering safe houses to men on the run.

These narratives of women's autonomy were important in creating positive attitudes about the value of women to the independence movement. The narratives demonstrate that women could be counted on to take bold action to protect local rebels. The narratives had another function that was gender-free: they helped prepare girls for emigration.

29 *For Joan of Arc. An Act of Homage from Nine Members of the French Academy* (New York, 1930). 30 Robert W. Berger discusses this point in his 'Rubens's 'Queen Tomyris with the Head of Cyrus', *Bulletin of the Museum of Fine Arts Boston*, 77 (1979), pp 5-10. Marina Warner also mentions the Old Testament origins in *Alone of all Her Sex. The Myth and the Cult of the Virgin Mary* (New York, 1983), p. 55. The well-known Freudian interpretation of the beheading motif is that it is a substitution for narratives of castration anxiety. 31 An Irish Priest, *A Short History of the Land War in Drumish in 1881* (Dublin, 1892), pp 21-2.

Combined with versions of folktale type AT 956B, 'The Clever Maiden
Alone at Home Kills the Robbers', a tale widely collected in the west of
Ireland and in print as early as 1834 in the *Dublin Penny Journal*, and
with a text like 'Grace Darling', the story of the lighthouse keeper's
daughter who gallantly initiated the rescue of the surviviors of a ship-
wreck that appeared in the *Fourth Reading Book* (1909), the legend of
the lone woman provided an important role model to North Longford
national schoolgirls. The example of courageous, independent action
would have been a valuable one to girls emigrating alone to begin lives
of domestic service in America.[32]

32 The subject invites the kind of feminist literary analysis as Lee R. Edwards developed
for his study of English and American novels in *Psyche as Hero. Female Heroism and
Fictional Form* (Middleton, Ct, 1984).

Nineteenth-century perspectives: The women of 1798 in folk memory and ballads

Anna Kinsella

When asked, before the Secret Committee of the House of Lords in 1797, what number he thought the United Irishmen amounted to throughout the Kingdom? Dr MacNeven replied 'those who have taken the test do not, I am convinced, fall short of 500,000 without reckoning women and old men'.[1] Clearly women were perceived in the same category as old men. Yet, Ireland is spoken of as a woman; names such as Dark Rosaleen and Caithlin ni Houlihan were frequently used while in the 1790s the Shan Van Vocht was the title of a popular ballad heralding the coming of the French to set her free. Ironically however, there is little mention of women in the written histories of the revolutionary period. Their contribution in the Insurrection of 1798 is often discounted, and for an insight into their role we must rely largely on their own accounts, on folk memory and on ballads.

I

Many of the events of '98 would have been consigned to oblivion had it not been for the efforts of women like Barbara Lett, Jane Barber, Jane Adams, Elizabeth Richards, Mary Leadbetter and Dinah Wilson Goff who recorded their experiences of that fateful summer.[2] Apart from these accounts, discussed elsewhere in this volume, little survives to chronicle the role played by the women in the rebellion yet a number of

---

1 James McCormick 'The Irish Rebellion'; The Black History of Ireland (Dublin, 1844), p. 72; Report of the Committee of Secrecy of the House of Commons (London, 1798). 2 Jane Adams of Summerseat, Wexford; Dickson, The Wexford Rising, p. 44; Barbara Lett. Memoir MS 2066 (s. 3. 18) TCD; Jane Barber, Recollections of Summer of 1798, Xerox copy of typescript 22pp (i. r. 920041) p. 7, N.L.I.; Dinah Wilson Goff of Horetown House, Divine Protection through extraordinary dangers, 3rd ed. (Dublin 1871).

the ballads contain fleeting references to their courage and sacrifice. All too often, however, their memory became victim of the late nineteenth-century paternalism, which could not accommodate their story. An indication of the Victorian attitude to women is provided by Madden's failure to interview Matilda Tone when he was researching his monumental study of *The United Irishmen; their lives and times*. Expressing surprise, she wrote to *The Nation* on 17 December 1842, 'I am told that Dr Madden was twice to New York in search of documents for his history. I wonder he did not apply to me. I never heard of him until I saw his book advertised.'

It required a woman, Helena Concannon, to write the details of the mothers, the wives, the sisters and the sweethearts of the principal players in the events of '98, but it is not only these few upper-class women, who, because of their connections with the male martyrs, should be remembered.[3] The women who fought in 1798 were, for the most part, low on the social scale and all too often their contribution is alluded to in the vaguest terms. It is not intended here to take a romantic view of the women of '98 but rather to look afresh at their contribution and its subsequent interpretation.

While there is no record of the number of women sworn into the United Irish Society there is certain evidence that they were. The alarmist William Colthurst declared before the Secret Committee of the House of Lords that every woman from Tinnahinch Bridge to Roundwood was 'an United Irishman'. There were, however, a variety of oaths and the Secret Committee of 1797 received evidence that 'many [had] taken the oath of secrecy who [had] not taken the United oath. Upon this principle they swear women and children.'[4]

Robert Dwyer Joyce, who wrote the ballad 'The Boys of Wexford' in 1864, claims that a woman was among the first to join the United Irishmen of county Wexford. The ballad begins with the words:

> In comes the captain's daughter, the captain of the Yeos,
> Saying 'Brave United Irishmen we'll ne'er again be foes
> A thousand pounds I'll bring if you will fly from home with me
> And dress myself in man's attire and fight for liberty

3 Helena Concannon, *Women of 'Ninety-Eight* (Dublin, 1919). Included are the mothers of the Emmetts, Lord Edward Fitzgerald, the Sheares and Teelings; the wives of Theobald Wolfe Tone, Thomas Addis Emmet, Samuel Nielson and Lord Edward Fitzgerald; sisters include Mary Ann McCracken, Mary Anne Emmett, Mary Tone, Lady Lucy Fitzgerald, Julia Sheares, and the misses Byrne, Teeling and Hazlett also Sarah Curran and Anne Devlin. 4 J.T. Gilbert (ed.), *Documents relating to Ireland 1795-1804* (Dublin, 1893); T. Crofton Crocker (ed.), *The Memoirs of Joseph Holt* (London, 1838), p. 50.

Of course in the fashion of the day she was not named and no further information was given about her. Writing in the Belfast nationalist newspaper *The Shan Van Vocht* in 1896, Millicent O'Brien claimed that this woman was 'not the daughter of a yeoman captain but daughter of a captain of an infantry regiment in Her Majesty's service who was retired and living on his Irish estate'.[5]

An altered version of the ballad by Edmund Leamy published in 1898 was more in keeping with the prevailing attitude to women. It includes the verse:

> I want no gold my maiden fair
> To fly from home with thee
> Your shining eyes will be my prize
> More dear than gold to me.[6]

There were, however, those whose memory was recorded for less romantic reasons. One was Margaret (Madge) Dixon of county Wexford, whose notoriously cruel reputation has survived. She was married to Thomas Dixon, of Castlebridge, sea captain and captain in the United Irish Society.[7] Throughout the campaign she served alongside her husband and, in his *Memoirs*, Musgrave described 'the ferocity of her disposition', adding that 'her thirst for Protestant blood was insatiable'. He recounts the story of how the couple contrived to raise the crowd against Colonel Le Hunte of the Shemalier Yeomanry corps. Having raided his home at Artramont, four miles from Wexford, they claimed to have discovered an orange-decorated apartment where the Orangemen had plotted 'for the extirpation of the Roman Catholics'. Taking an orange-painted fire-screen from the house, Captain Dixon bore it aloft as he entered Wexford town on horseback. There the couple attempted to raise a body of people to take Colonel Le Hunte and have his blood. However he was reprieved due to the intervention of Bagenal Harvey, Cornelius Grogan and Matthew Keugh.[8]

During the centenary year, a more charitable explanation of Madge Dixon's fury was given by the Revd Robert Leech of Drumlane, county Cavan in a letter published in *The People*.[9] Leech outlined the for-

5 1864 was a year of great activity for the Fenian scribes. *The Irish People* on 26 March carried an advertisement for a collection of over one hundred ballads, romances and songs by R.D. Joyce published by James Duffy. The pen-name of R.D. Joyce was 'Merulan'; see also *The Shan Van Vocht* vol. i no. 2, 27 February 1896, p. 1. 6 Denis Devereux, *Songs and Ballads of '98* (Dublin, 1898) p. 11. 7 Daniel Gahan, *The People's Rising: Wexford 1798* (Dublin, 1996), pp 196, 218-19. 8 Richard Musgrave, *Memoirs of the Irish Rebellion of 1798*, edited S.W. Myers and D. McKnight (Indiana, 1995), pp 438-9. 9 *The People*, 13 August 1898.

tunes of his wife's grandfather, one of the captives of the Dixons, who escaped death at Wexford Bridge 'by the intervention of Bishop Caulfield'. They escaped a second time by the effort of Wexford's parish priest, John Corrin, and a third time by the rapid advance of the soldiers. Leech continued: 'it is but right to say that ... Dixon's wife, a tall fine-looking woman, had been previously outraged by one of the soldiers and this seems to have been the cause of their fury and revenge'.[10] Such a violation may explain the fury of Captain Dixon and his wife who were particularly noted for their vindictiveness in '98. There is no account of the Dixons' subsequent lives. George Taylor's account of '98 states that 'wherever they secreted themselves they never could be found, though a large reward was offered for their apprehension'.[11]

Equally unfavourable memories have been preserved of women informers. Among these was Mary Savage of Barraderry, who, according to Charles Dickson gave information on Michael Dwyer and John Philpot Curran to Lord Castlereagh.[12] The story of another episode, Bridget Dolan's betrayal of Billy Byrne is discussed elsewhere in this volume. Suffice it to recall Luke Cullen's account of Bridget Dolan:

> This wretch positively commanded the troops and yeomen in Rathdrum. They had her dressed in a lady's beautiful riding habit with beaver hat, and a rich black plume bending a little to one side of her face, gracefully bending and dispelling the wreaths of smoke that arose from a little black tobacco pipe which she almost constantly had in her mouth ... Thus mounted on her charger she led the cavalcade when she pleased ... She led them one day to Knocknamagohill about a mile from the Meeting of the Waters, where two brothers named Byrne were, under the protection of the Amnesty Act, working in their fields. She pointed them out. They were shot.[13]

II

Although most individual heroines had no chronicler, Mary Doyle of Castleboro is especially remembered for her gallant effort at the battle of New Ross, where she prevented the loss of a valuable artillery piece

---

10 Letter dated 10 August 1898 to the Editor of *The Freeman* reprinted in *The People*, 13 August 1898.   11 George Taylor, *Rebellion in Wexford in the year 1798* (Dublin, 1800), p. 193.   12 Dickson, *The Wexford Rising*, pp 157-9.   13 Ronan (ed.), *Insurgent Wicklow*, pp 71, 94.

by the United army.[14] As a result, Doyle is utilised in Patrick Kavanagh's *A popular history of the Insurrection of 1798* which records 'an amazon named Doyle, who marched with the insurgent army and bore
herself as gallantly as the most courageous man'.[15] The sobriquet of
amazon continues to be applied to Doyle, a stark association with the
fabled female warriors of that name who cut off the right breast in order
to draw the bow to its head.

On other occasions Doyle made herself very useful with a bill-hook,
cutting off the cross-belts of the fallen dragoons and handing them to
her comrades. This was a common task for camp followers, many of
them apparently women, as Joseph Holt's *Memoirs* recall the presence of
'several women in the camp' who were engaged in making gun-powder.
In other instances women were used as 'moving magazines'. To Holt's
Memoirs, Thomas Crofton Croker added an account of Suzy Toole, the
daughter of Phelim Toole, a blacksmith of Annamoe in county Wicklow. Aged about thirty years of age in 1798, she was employed with her
father in his forge where she was said to be very dextrous in handling
the sledge. Croker, our earliest source for Suzy Toole, has given us a
rather unflattering description of this valiant woman:

> 5' 8" tall when she stood upright, which was not often for by the
> habit of sledging she had acquired a stoop; but her shoulders,
> though round were broad and her limbs strong and sinewy. Her
> face when young was broad as a full moon and her nose nearly
> flat to her face, having been broken by a stone in a faction fight
> ... and this certainly made her anything but an inviting object.
> Her eyes were black and sparkling. What they would have been
> in a handsome face, with a decent nose between them, I will not
> venture to say. She had an extraordinary ability to change her
> whole appearance ... With her dirty pepper and salt coloured
> frieze cloak, her stoop and dropped jaw, she could appear a
> decrepit miserable baccagh (cripple) scarcely able to crawl, but
> when it was necessary to act with vigour, her powerful muscles
> and brawny limbs made her more than a match for many men. A
> blow from her clenched fist was like the kick of a horse ... She
> was quick in expedients and ready with a reason for all occa-
> sions.[16]

14 Thomas Cloney, *A personal Narrative of those transactions in the County of Wexford in
which the author was engaged, during the awful period of 1798* (Dublin, 1832), pp 41-3. 15
P.F. Kavanagh, *A popular history of the Insurrection of 1798* (Cork, 1898), p. 151; Charles
Dickson, *The Wexford Rising in 1798* (Tralee, 1956), p. 115. 16 *Memoirs of Joseph Holt*,
p. 49.

Toole is remembered as the 'moving magazine', from her ability to provision the United army; she secured ball cartridge and ammunition from disaffected soldiers, but she also provided intelligence on the movements of the King's troops. The performance of similar duties meant several narrow escapes for Rose Mullen, wife of James Hope and Biddy Palmer eulogised by Joseph Holt and Miles Byrne. Less fortunate, however, several women arrested near Dublin on 9 July 1798, but unlike the 'moving magazine' these remain anonymous.[17]

Throughout the summer of 1798 a pall of smoke lay over the landscape of county Wexford from the number of homes put to the torch. In such circumstances, many women and children flocked to the rebels for refuge. Dickson records that on Vinegar Hill 'large numbers of women and children had accompanied the fighting men'.[18] Such women were not content to cower for protection, indeed, Sir Jonah Barrington observed that on Vinegar Hill 'a great many women ... fought with fury'.[19]

Teresa Malone, for example, is remembered for her action in the socalled Battle of Kilcumney – a mopping–up operation by Crown forces. In dense fog at the end of June 1798, the civilian population around Kilcumney was mercilessly treated as active enemies, and the ballad of Teresa Malone tells of how John Murphy's thatched house was torched, while a party of insurgents took refuge within. Among the insurgents who managed to escape was 'the raven haired' Teresa Malone who handled a horse and pistol in expert fashion. Nothing more is known of her except that she is buried in the graveyard of Ballinkillen near Bagenalstown, county Carlow. In a footnote the ballad writer claims that 140 inhabitants of Kilcumney were massacred leaving over 400 children orphaned; one may assume that women were numbered amongst the dead.[20] Another account from Kilcumney tells of a woman named Fitzpatrick, who, with baby in arms, was shot together with her husband Patrick. Thomas Cloney relates how their other five children ran to a neighbour's house crying: 'my Daddy is killed, my Mammy is killed and the pigs are drinking their blood'. An aunt of the children, Joan Kealy, took and reared the children, but having no means of supporting them she was reduced to begging in order to feed them.[21]

Further afield, Molly Weston distinguished herself not only for recruiting United Irishmen, but for her bravery in the Battle of Tara.

17 Concanon, *Women of 'Ninety-Eight*, p. 330; James Collins, *Calendar Almanac* (Convent View Drumcondra, 1898). 18 Dickson, *The Wexford Rising in 1798*, p. 156. 19 P.F. Kavanagh, *A popular history of the Insurrection of 1798*, cent. ed. p. 208. 20 *The People*, 26 November 1992. 21 Thomas Cloney, *A Personal Narrative of 1798* (Dublin, 1832), p. 85.

Born and reared at Worganstown, near Oldtown, county Meath, her family occupied an extensive farm. She was described as 'handsome and vivacious, quick in mind, active in body … a daring and accomplished horse-woman'. Details of her dress have been preserved in folk memory. She was said to wear a green riding costume, with gold braid in the manner of a uniform and a green cocked hat with a white plume. She was armed with sword and pistols and was accompanied by her four brothers as she rode out to battle. Weston rallied and regrouped the stricken pikemen; she placed herself at their head and led repeated charges against the Reagh Fencibles. In one instance, according to a ballad, a loaded field piece was captured by the insurgents. Molly Weston swung the gun around and 'eleven petticoat rascals she killed upon the spot'.

Although survivors brought home accounts of the deaths of her four brothers, Molly Weston was never seen again. According to Patrick Archer, writer of *Fair Fingall*, the only recognition of her part in the engagement at Tara was by an unnamed English historian, who tells that after the conflict a dead charger, equipped with a lady's side-saddle was found on the battlefield. In the folk memory of the people of Meath, Molly Weston is perceived in 'the role of leader'. The ballad 'The Muster in Fingall' 1798 tells:

> And westward as they marched away
> Shanbaile joined the brave array
> While Ballygara and Dunreagh
> Sent forth their pikemen tall
> And with them Molly Weston came
> To Worganstown belongs the fame
> Of her who fought in Freedom's name
> With thy brave sons, Fingall.[22]

A number of ballads celebrate heroines of Ballinahinch, where the United army under Henry Munroe engaged the British troops under Generals Nugent and Barber. *The Battle of Ballinahinch* tells that after General Munroe's arrest his sister entered the battle:

> Then in came his sister well clothed in green
> with a sword by her side, both long sharp and keen
> They gave her three cheers and away she did go
> Crying 'I'll have revenge for my brother Munroe'.[23]

22 Patrick Archer, *Fair Fingall* (An Taisce, second ed. 1975), p. 88. 23 *The Shan Van Vocht*, 7 June 1897, p. 102.

More famous still, however, was Elizabeth Gray, celebrated as 'Ulster's Joan of Arc'. Reputedly, she fought beside her brother George and her lover William Boal, both leading United Irishmen, with a sword in the thick of battle. Their division bore a full share in the disasters of the day, and many of their number fell in the retreat; no quarter was given and no prisoners taken. In the retreat from Ednavady Hill on 13 June, Betsy Gray was cut down, her hand was cut off by a stroke of a yeoman's sword and she died from a shot through the eye.[24] The event was recorded by the balladeer;

> Now woe be on thee, Anahilt,
> And woe be on the day,
> When brother, lover, both were slain,
> And with them Bessie Gray.[25]

Another account of her was provided by Wesley Greehill Lyttle whose novel, *Betsy Gray, or the Hearts of Down*, was published in 1886. He described her as a highly educated young lady, daughter of a prosperous farmer of county Down. She was buried, with her brother and her lover, in the vale of Ballycreen about two miles from Ballynahinch. Later her American grand nephew erected a granite monument on her grave, which, in time, became a place of pilgrimage.[26]

Perhaps the definitive embodiment of stoic heroism of the period is to be found in Anne Devlin. A first cousin of Michael Dwyer and Hugh Vesty Byrne, Anne was born in 1781, the second child of seven born to Bryan and Winifred (*née* Byrne) of Cronebeg, county Wicklow. Her father was arrested in the general rounding up of Dwyer's men following the attack on outposts of Rathdrum on 16 October 1798, but Anne 'was constantly employed carrying dispatches to and from Michael Dwyer the rebel outlaw'.

In time she became housekeeper to Robert Emmet and she was arrested when his house was raided on 26 July 1803. Though threatened and tortured she persisted in her total ignorance of her master's movements. Anne was sentenced to hang and was suspended by the neck on a rope from the tilted shafts of a cart. She was tortured and prodded with bayonets until covered in blood, but she revealed nothing – similarly she resisted a more subtle offer of £500 and was unmoved by

24 McCormick, *The Irish Rebellion*, p. 17. 25 Cited in A.T.Q. Stewart, *The Summer Soldiers: The 1798 Rebellion in Antrim and Down* (Belfast, 1996), p. 227. 26 Devereux, *Songs of '98*, p. 26; *The Shan Van Vocht*, September 1897, NLI, M/F Reel 1, pp 97–8; A.T.Q. Stewart, *The Summer Soldiers: The 1798 Rebellion in Antrim and Down* (Belfast, 1996), p. 227.

unfounded information that her associates had confessed. She was taken to Kilmainham where she was placed under strict observation in an effort to discover any communication between herself and the male prisoners. She was treated with incredible harshness and cruelty by Dr Trevor and Major Sirr. Anne spent nearly three years in various prisons, mostly in solitary confinement. She often spent months in a cold, damp cell until at last as she herself stated, she became 'more the shape of a cow than that of a human being'. In 1806 there was a movement to release state prisoners, all of whom were confined in Kilmainham. Habeas Corpus writs were issued and a nominal roll of the prisoners was compiled but before it was completed, Anne Devlin was temporarily removed by Dr Trevor from Kilmainham to Dublin Castle and by this means her name was omitted from the list. She remained incarcerated for many more weeks until her release was secured through the intervention of a prison wardress who petitioned the Chief Secretary.

When Anne's health improved, she earned her living as a housekeeper. She later married a Campbell and lived in John's Lane Dublin. Her husband died in 1845 and for the last few years of her life she and an invalid daughter appear to have been supported from the scanty earnings of her son. By this time her sight had failed. In 1842 Dr Madden found Anne Devlin-Campbell, living in great poverty in a stable yard off John's Lane. She died in extreme poverty in the garret of a house at Little Elbow Lane off the Coombe, on 18th September 1851 at the age of seventy and is buried in Glasnevin Cemetery.[27]

III

Throughout 1798 female sympathisers and family members provided invaluable support to the insurgents in their capacity as under-cover agents. Many had performed this function before the outbreak of hostilities. Rose McGladdery, 'a sworn United man', for example, brought information in and out of Kilmainham where her husband William McCracken and his brother Henry Joy, were imprisoned for thirteen months from September 1796.[28] A similar function was discharged by Mrs Oliver Bond, who enabled State Prisoners maintain contact with the outside world by hiding writing materials, newspapers and commu-

27 Charles Dickson, *The Life of Michael Dwyer, with some accounts of his companions* (Dublin, 1944), p. 350; Ronan (ed.), *Insurgent Wicklow 1798*, pp 50, 115; Concannon, *Women of 'Ninety-Eight*, pp 286, 352; Ruan O'Donnell, 'The Rebellion of 1798 in County Wicklow', in Ken Hannigan and Wm Nolan (eds), *Wicklow History and Society* (Dublin, 1994), p. 371. 28 Concannon, *Women of 'Ninety-Eight*, p. xiii.

nications from friends beneath the crust of freshly baked pies which she personally delivered to the jail.

It would be mistaken, however, to reduce Mrs Bond's contribution to this clever device. Indeed, during the centenary celebrations a grand-niece of Oliver Bond's, Kathleen Bond of Botanic Avenue, published a letter in the *Belfast Newsletter* which described Mrs Bond as 'a rampant rebel ... [whose two] brothers, named Jackson, were hanged for high treason'.[29] Kathleen Bond's letter was an obvious attempt to distance the Bond family from association with the rebellion a century earlier, asserting that

> it was against the wishes of Oliver Bond that his wife held United Irish meetings on his property and that when arrested he was shielding his wife and on that account went to prison where he died mysteriously at the hands of two unknown men.

In any event, once the rebellion began, many courageous women acted as couriers to the United army. Miles Byrne tells that in the beginning of May 1798 all United men were obliged to leave their homes and hide themselves as best they could, awaiting orders to rise. He makes frequent mention of his brave sister who brought information of events elsewhere: 'the people were rising in every direction and had already defeated the troops ... She saw me depart with joy and delight for she had set her heart and soul on the success of our undertaking.' On another occasion, Byrne returned to his mother's house and found that she had gone to Gorey to try to get their step-brother Hugh, out of prison.[30]

Similarly, Mrs Gallagher, wife of Lord Edward Fitzgerald's body-guard, carried out a daring rescue operation while her husband, Patrick, was on board a prison ship awaiting transportation from Dublin Bay. Visiting him to say goodbye, she concealed a coil of rope beneath her cloak, one end of which she passed to her husband. Minutes after her departure, Gallagher leaped into the water and was towed by his gallant wife who rowed ashore. The couple subsequently escaped to France, where they were well-known to Miles Byrne.[31]

IV

The enduring treatment of the women of '98 has, however, tended to focus simply on their supporting role, as mother, sister, or sweetheart of

29 *Belfast News Letter*, 5 January 1898. 30 Byrne, Miles, *Memoirs* (New York, 1863), I, p. 25. 31 Concanon, *Women of 'Ninety-Eight*, p. 319.

the United men. Luke Cullen and P.F. Kavanagh, for example, tend to group the more proactive women together under the pejorative Amazonian tag. Within this frame, Luke Cullen payed a barbed compliment to a group of Protestant women who attacked yeomen at Newcastle county Wicklow in order to halt the dragooning of Michael and Patrick O'Neill:

> Mrs Jones and a few of her Amazonian neighbours plied the found shot of the road with such unerring effect that the no-quarter heroes gave the youth his liberty and life.[32]

Passive feminine patriotism was clearly more acceptable in nineteenth-century Ireland, on the basis of stories like that of the Widow Hill of Castlecomer, county Kilkenny. The stylised account of the arrest and torture of her brother and son was recorded in *The Irish Magazine*, edited by the veteran United Irishman, propagandist Watty Cox. This account records how young Hill's captors promised him peace and his life if he would turn informer. He agreed but his mother visited him before he presented his information. The poor widow was suspicious, and she asked the boy if he had contemplated becoming an informer. Distraught at her son's candid response, she fell on her knees and begged him to consider the consequences of such betrayal. She implored him to resist – he took her advice and the next morning he was executed along with his uncle.[33]

This theme was also taken up by Mrs K.I. O'Doherty in her poem *The Patriot Mother*:

> A leanbh, a leanbh, the shadow of shame
> Has never yet fallen on one of your name
> And oh! may the food that from my bosom you drew
> In your veins turn to poison, if you are untrue.[34]

This portrayal of the courage and determination of the women of '98 was also evident in the way they sought out their loved ones amid the carnage on the battle-fields, to ensure that at least they might have a decent burial.

One such account centres on the infamous massacre of surrendering rebels at Gibbet Rath, county Kildare, where 350 unarmed men were killed as they surrendered. Tradition recalls that when Denis Downey's riderless horse returned home, his wife went to the place and found it

32 Myles Ronan (ed.), *Luke Cullen Insurgent Wicklow 1798* (Dublin, 1959), p. 31.   33 Story from *The Irish Magazine*, November 1811, reproduced in McCormick, *The Irish Rebellion*, p. 22.   34 Devereux, *Songs and Ballads of '98*, p. 7.

littered with corpses. She turned over 200 dead bodies before she discovered her husband's body. She laid him on a cart, covered him with straw and a quilt and proceeded to the house of a relative to wake him. However the wake could not be held for fear of reprisal and she had to wrap the body in a sheet and lay him in a hastily made shallow grave.[35] A similar tale of mourning, published in the *Free Press* in 1898, centres on a Mrs Dawson who, reputedly, went to Tullow to search out the remains of Father John Murphy. Mrs Dawson, who was commonly called Aunt Molly in the Murphy family circle, is said to have collected his head and ashes and taken them to Ferns where they were buried in the grave of Dr Andrew Cassin, parish priest of Ferns.[36] The veracity of this account, however, is questioned by Father Murphy's biographer.[37]

Mary Ann McCracken's radical political outlook has been discussed by Gray but her popular reputation stems from the devoted way in which she cared for her brother 'Harry'. Mary Ann gave her own account of his last days. While he was in hiding she regularly visited, by night, the hills where her brother was concealed, taking with her food, clothes and money. She sat by his side during his hopeless trial and walked, arm in arm, with him to his execution. She tried unsuccessfully to resuscitate his body which she accompanied to its last resting place. She later recalled her sense of duty to prevent misrepresentation, and to 'put it out of the power of my brother's enemies to injure his character while living or his memory when dead'.[38] Mary Ann's love for her brother continued in the care she devoted to his illegitimate daughter Maria, who in time grew up to become her constant companion.

V

The life experience of ordinary people was generally neglected in historiography and the practice of using history in order to further their own aims, by politicians and churchmen, reinforced the relegating of women to 'Kinder, Kuchen und Kirche' roles. This continued into the early twentieth century where the traditional attitude was that above all women should be prized male possessions. The Wexford Franciscan P.F. Kavanagh, whose propagandist history of the 1798 rebellion became the accepted orthodoxy, wrote a poem called 'My Friend' which

35 Mrs Downey was the grand-mother of Canon O'Hanlon, the distinguished hagiologist; Holt, *Memoirs*, p. 314; see also Concannon, *Women of 'Ninety-Eight*, p. 313. 36 *Free Press*, January 1898. Letter written by 'the grandson of a rebel'. 37 N. Furlong, *Father John Murphy of Boolavogue, 1753-98* (Dublin, 1991). 38 McCormick, *The Irish Rebellion*, p. 13.

deals with some of the activities of the suffragettes and is fairly telling of what was expected of women at that period:

That women should not have a vote I do not mean to say
But let them urge their claim, if just, in some more peaceful way
But God Bless these kindly gentle women, the honoured of our land
Who obey and love their husbands – because this is God's command.[39]

There was a fine line where a woman could 'overstep the bounds of womanhood' and clearly women were not the instigators of the insurrection. However they fully supported the ideals of 'liberty and equality' which, had they but known, did not apply to women. It is inappropriate to use male norms of power as a standard by which to judge the activities of women in 1798. Perhaps a study of the political and economic forces impinging on the interrelationships of men's and women's lives would give a better understanding of their experience. Despite not being reckoned in 1798, women were involved in the Insurrection and this involvement is recorded in story and ballad. While they are shown to have played a part in the fighting, the daring and the suffering the question remains: was that role more important on a human level than the role played by women who did the grieving, the nursing, the feeding, the sheltering, the supplication and the caring?

39 P.F Kavanagh, 'My friend' in *The Wexford Rebel and other poems* (Dublin, 1917), p. 14.

Select bibliography

Bartlett, Thomas, 'An end to moral economy: The Irish Militia disturbances of 1793' in *Past & Present*, lxc (1983), pp 41-64.
—, *The Fall and Rise of the Irish Nation: The Catholic Question 1690-1830* (Dublin, 1992).
—, 'Nationalism in Eighteenth-Century Ireland' in O'Dea and Whelan (eds), *Nations and Nationalism*, pp 79-88.
—, *Theobald Wolfe Tone* (Dundalk, 1997)
Burke, Edmund, *The Works of the Rt. Hon. Edmund Burke* (2 vols, London, 1834).
—, *The Writings and Speeches of Edmund Burke*, vol. iii; *The French Revolution*, edited by L.G. Mitchell, (Oxford, 1989).
Byrne, Miles, *Memoirs of Miles Byrne, Chef de Bataillon in the Service of France, edited by his Widow* (2 vols, Paris, 1863).
The Tryal of William Byrne of Ballymanus (Dublin, 1799).
Concannon, Helena, *The Women of 'Ninety-Eight* (Dublin, 1919).
Caulfield, James, *The Reply of the Rt. Revd. Dr Caulfield, Roman Catholic Bishop and the R.C. Clergy of Wexford to the Misrepresentations of Sir Richard Musgrave, Bart* (Dublin, 1801).
Cloney, Thomas, *A Personal Narrative of those Transactions in the County of Wexford in which the author was engaged at the awful period of 1798* (Dublin, 1832).
Colley, Linda, *Britons: Forging the Nation 1707-1837* (New Haven, 1992).
Cullen, L.M., *The Emergence of Modern Ireland 1600-1900* (London, 1981).
—, 'The 1798 Rebellion in its Eighteenth-Century Context' in P.J. Corish (ed.), *Radicals, Rebels and Establishment* (Belfast, 1985) pp 91-113.
—, 'The 1798 Rebellion in Wexford: United Irish Organisation, Membership, Leadership' in Whelan (ed.), *Wexford: History and Society*, pp. 248-95.
—, 'The Political Structures of the Defenders' in Gough and Dickson (eds), *Ireland and the French Revolution*, pp 117-38.
—, 'The Internal Politics of the United Irishmen' in Dickson, Keogh and Whelan (eds), *United Irishmen*, pp 176-96.
—, 'Politics and Rebellion in Wicklow in the 1790s' in Ken Hannigan and William Nolan (eds), *Wicklow: History and Society* (Dublin, 1994), pp 411-501.
Curtin, Nancy, 'The transformation of the Society of United Irishmen into a Mass-Based Revolutionary Organisation 1794-96 in *I.H.S.*, xxiv (1985), pp 463-72.
—, *The United Irishmen: Popular Politics in Ulster and Dublin 1791-1798* (Oxford, 1994).
—, 'Women and Eighteenth-Century Irish Republicanism', in M. MacCurtain and M. O'Dowd (eds), *Women in Early Modern Ireland* (Dublin, 1991), pp 133-47.
Dickson, David, Introduction to Richard Musgrave, *Memoirs of Various Rebellions in Ireland* (repr. Fort Wayne, 1995).
—, Keogh, Dáire and Whelan, Kevin (ed.) *The United Irishmen: Radicalism, Republicanism and Rebellion* (Dublin, 1993).
Elliott, Marianne, *Partners in Revolution: The United Irishmen and France* (New Haven, 1982)
—, 'The Defenders in Ulster' in Dickson, Keogh and Whelan (eds), *United Irishmen*, pp 222-33.
Farrell, William, *Carlow in '98: The Autobiography of William Farrell*, ed. Roger McHugh (Dublin, 1949).
Froude, James Anthony, *The English in Ireland in the Eighteenth Century* (3 vols, London, 1872-74).

Furlong, Nicholas, *Father John Murphy of Boolavogue 1753-1798* (Dublin, 1991).

Gahan, Daniel, 'The Military Strategy of the Wexford United Irishmen in 1798' in *History Ireland*, no. 4 (1993), pp 28-32.

—, *The People's Rising, Wexford 1798* (Dublin, 1995).

Gordon, James, *History of the Rebellion in Ireland in year 1798* (Dublin, 1801).

Gough, Hugh and Dickson (eds), *Ireland and the French Revolution* (Dublin, 1990).

Graham, Thomas, 'An Union of Power: The United Irish Organisation' in Dickson, Keogh and Whelan (eds), *United Irishmen*, pp 244-55.

Hay, Edward, *History of the Insurrection in the County of Wexford, A.D. 1798* (Dublin, 1803).

Holt, Joseph, *Memoirs*, ed. T.C. Croker (2 vols, London, 1838).

Kavanagh, Patrick, *A Popular History of the Insurrection of 1798* (Dublin, 1870).

Keogh, Dáire, *The French Disease: The Catholic Church and Radicalism in Ireland 1790-1800* (Dublin, 1993).

—, and Nicholas Furlong (eds), *The Mighty Wave: The 1798 Rebellion in Wexford* (Dublin, 1996).

Lecky, W.E.H., *History of Ireland in the Eighteenth Century* (5 vols, London, 1892).

Madden, R.R., *The United Irishmen, their Lives and Times* (7 vols, London, 1842-46).

McNeill, Mary, *The Life and times of Mary Ann McCracken, 1770-1866* (Dublin, 1960).

O'Dea, Michael and Whelan, Kevin (eds), *Nations and Nationalism: France, Britain, Ireland and the Eighteenth-Century Context* (Oxford, 1995).

Power, T.P. and Whelan, Kevin (eds), *Endurance and Emergence, Catholics in Ireland in the Eighteenth Century* (Dublin, 1990).

Ronan, M.V. (ed.), *Personal Recollections of Wexford and Wicklow Insurgents of 1798 as collected by the Rev. Luke Cullen 1798-1859* (Enniscorthy, 1958).

Russell, Thomas, *Journals and Memoirs*, (ed.) C.J. Woods (Dublin, 1991).

Smyth, Jim, *The Men of no Property: Irish Radicals and Popular Politics in the late Eighteenth Century* (Dublin, 1992).

Stewart, A.T.Q., *A Deeper Silence: The Hidden Origins of the United Irishmen* (London, 1993).

—, *The Summer Soldiers, The 1798 Rebellion in Antrim and Down* (Belfast, 1995).

St Mark, J.J., 'Matilda and William Tone in New York and Washington after 1798', *Eire-Ireland*, vol. 22, no. 4 (winter 1987) pp 4-10.

Thuente, Mary Helen, *The Harp Restrung: The United Irishmen and the Rise of Irish Literary Nationalism* (Syracuse, 1994).

[Tone, Theobald Wolfe], *An Argument on behalf of the Catholics of Ireland* (Dublin, 1791).

Veritas, *The State of His Majesty's Subjects in Ireland professing the Roman Catholic Religion* (2nd ed. Dublin, 1799).

A Vindication of the Roman Catholic Clergy of the Town of Wexford during the Unhappy Rebellion (Dublin, 1799).

Walsh, Walter, 'Religion, Ethnicity and History: Clues to the Cultural Construction of Law' in Ronald Bayor and T.J. Meagher (eds), *The New York Irish* (Baltimore, 1995) pp 48-69.

Whelan, Kevin, 'Politicisation in County Wexford and the origins of the 1798 Rebellion' in Gough and Dickson (eds), *Ireland and the French Revolution*, pp 156-78.

—, *The Tree of Liberty: Radicalism, Catholicism and the Construction of Irish Identity* (Cork, 1996).

Wollstonecraft, Mary, *A Vindication of the Rights of Women* (London, 1792).

Zimmermann, G., *Songs of Irish Rebellion: Political street ballads and rebel songs, 1780-1900* (Dublin, 1967).

Contributors

THOMAS BARTLETT, MRIA, Professor of Modern Irish History, National University of Ireland, Dublin.

JOHN D. BEATTY, Allen County Library, Indiana.

ELEANOR BURGESS, Council Member of British Association for Irish Studies and editor of Journal of the Butler Society.

NANCY J. CURTIN, Associate Professor of History, Fordham University, New York.

JOHN GRAY, Librarian, The Linen Hall Library, Belfast.

ANNA KINSELLA, local historian and regular contributor to Wexford historical journals.

MAUREEN MURPHY, Professor of English/Secondary Education at Hofstra University, New York.

RUAN O'DONNELL, Lecturer in history at St Patrick's College, Dublin City University.

KEVIN O'NEILL, Associate Professor of History, Boston College.

MARY HELEN THUENTE, Professor of English, Indiana University/Purdue University, Fort Wayne.

EDITORS

NICHOLAS FURLONG is President of the Wexford Historical Society.

DÁIRE KEOGH, Lectures in the History Department at St Patrick's College, Dublin City University.

Index

Adams, Abigail 45
Adams, Jane 129-33, 135, 187
Adams, Revd Tobias 130
'Adversity's Cot' 17
Aghavannagh, Co. Wicklow 97
Annals of Ballitore 140, 157
Anthologia Hibernica 16, 17
Antrim 55
Archer, Patrick 193
Archer, Thomas 102, 108
Arklow, Co. Wicklow, 96, 98
Aughrim, Co. Wicklow, 97

Ballad Poetry of Ireland, The 22
Ballinacor, Co. Wicklow 94
Ballinahinch, Co. Antrim 193, 194
Ballinamuck, Co. Longford 102, 178-
   82, 185
Ballinkillen, Co. Carlow 192
Ballitore, Co. Kildare 139-40, 141,
   148, 159
Ballymanus, Co. Wicklow 97
Ballynahinch, Co. Down 67
Ballyrahan Hill, Co. Wicklow 98
Bantry, Co. Cork 158
Barber, Jane 121-3, 134, 187
Barber, Samuel 121
Barker, Capt. William 121, 127, 134
Barrington, Sir Jonah 152, 156, 192
Barry, J. 23
Bayly, Revd Edward 103
Beale, J. 154
Belfast Newsletter 196
Belfast 15, 39, 57, 61
Bennet, William 159
Betsy Grey, or the Hearts of Down
   194
Bewley, John 154
Bewley, Mary 156, 157
Bewley, Molly 151
Bewley, Thomas 151

Billy Bluff and the Squire 12, 13, 17
'Billy Byrne of Ballymanus' 88, 106,
   111
Bligh, Colonel 127
Boal, William 194
Bodenstown, Co. Kildare 35
Bonaparte, Lucien 41
Bond, Kathleen 196
Bond, Oliver 196
Botticelli, Sandro 184
Boyd, John 124
Brady, John 98
Brownrigg, John 123
Brownrigg, Mrs 123-5, 134
Bruce, Revd William 51
Bulger, Mat 159
Bunbury, Sir Charles 168
Burk, John Daly 11, 20, 23
Burke, Edmund 147
Butler, Hubert 163
Butler, Laurence 130
Byrne, Ann 101
Byrne, Bryan 194
Byrne, Charles 105
Byrne, Garret 95, 105
Byrne, Hugh 'Vesty' 112, 194
Byrne, Mary 117, 118
Byrne, Michael 'Vesty' 109, 112
Byrne, Miles 68, 108, 113, 179, 192,
   196
Byrne, William 88, 92, 94, 95, 97,
   104-5, 106, 190

Caldwell, Lieut-Col. 93
Camden, Lord 172
'Carolan's Receipt' 11
Carty, Patrick 182, 184
Casey, John Keegan 7
Cassin, Dr Andrew 198
Castlebar 177, 178

Castlereagh, Robert Stewart,
    Viscount 169, 170-1
Castletown, Co. Kildare 163, 167,
    168, 171, 175-6
Cave Hill, Belfast 52
Celbridge, Co. Kildare 168, 170
Charles II 163
Chaytor, Thomas 145
Clare, John Fitzgibbon, 1st earl of
    172
Cloney, Thomas 69, 113, 192
Cloone, Co. Leitrim 178
Clovass, Co. Wexford 121
Colthurt, William 94
Columb, Michael 181
Concannon, Helena 188; *see also The
    Women of 'Ninety-Eight*
Conolly, Lady Louisa 163-76
Conolly, Thomas 163, 164, 165, 174
Conolly, William 164
Coope, John 70
Cope, Revd Charles 102, 103
Cork 70
Cornwallis, Charles, 1st Marquis of
    67, 68, 88, 108, 174, 177
Corrin, Fr John 117, 190
Cox, Watty 197; *see also Irish
    Magazine and Monthly Asylum*
Cranach, Lucas 184
Crawford, Captain Dukey 181
Crawford, Colonel 178
'Crazy Jane' 25
Croker, Thomas 191
Cullen, James 109
Cullen, Br Luke 68, 89, 92, 100, 110,
    197
Curran, John Philpot 190
Curtin, Nancy 56, 67

da Castelfranco, Giorgione 184
Dale, Catherine 115
Daniel, William 126
Davis, Mathew 106, 110
Dawson, Mrs 198
de Kerouaille, Louis 163

Delany, Malachi 155, 159, 161, 162
Delany, Peter 155, 159
Devereux, John 128
Devlin, Anne 65, 194, 195
Dickson, Charles 111, 190
di Giovanni, Matteo 184
Dixon, Margaret 'Madge' 111, 189
Dixon, Thomas 124, 189
Dolan, Bridget 'Croppy Biddy' 70,
    87-113, 190
Doornen, Michael 108
Doré, Gustave 184
Dorson, Richard M. 180
Douglas 35
Downey, Denis 197
Downpatrick, Co. Down 60
Doyle, Fr James 126
Doyle, James 106
Doyle, John 108, 110
Doyle, Mary 190
Doyle, Patrick 93
Drennan, William 10, 32, 34, 59
Dublin Penny Journal 186
Dublin 38, 39, 57, 60, 178
Duffy, Charles Gavin 22
Dungannon, Co. Tyrone 70
Dwyer, Mary 100-1
Dwyer, Michael 99, 106, 190
Edgeworth, Maria 179
Elizabeth I 16-17
Ely, Lord 123
Emmet, Robert 10, 11, 23, 65, 194
Emmet, Thomas Addis 26, 47
Enniscorthy, Co. Wexford 127, 128
'Erin' 18

Fair Fingall 103
Fallon, James 108
Fenlon, Martin 127, 134
Finn, Owen 160
Fitzgerald, Emily 163, 164, 167, 169,
    173, 174-5
Fitzgerald, Lady Pamela 65, 169-171
Fitzgerald, Lord Edward 65, 70, 124,
    164, 169

Fitzpatrick, W.J. 89
Flynn, Jack 99
Fort George 65
Fourth Reading Book 186
Fowler, John 109
Fox, Caroline 163, 164
Fox, Henry (Lord Holland) 163, 168
Free Press 198
French Revolution 142, 149

Gallagher, Mrs 196
Gallagher, Patrick 196
Gellner, Ernest 27
Gentileschi, Artemisia 185
George II 168
Geraghty, Michael 70
Gill, Robin 180, 181, 183
Glassealy, Co. Kildare 115
Glenarm, Co. Antrim 69
Goddard, Eliza 69
Godwin, William 55, 147
Goff, Dinah 118-21, 134, 187
Goff, Elizabeth 118
Goff, Jacob 118
Gordon, James 115
Gordon, Lord William 168
Gorey Hill, Co. Wexford 96, 97
Granard, Co. Longford 177
Granu Wale 16-18
'Granu's Advice to her Children' 18
'Granu's Call' 18
'Granuweal – An Old Song' 17
Greenfeld, Liah 27, 28
Grey, Elizabeth 'Betsy' 67, 194
Grey, George 194
Griffith, John 70
Grogan, Cornelius 189
Grubb, Elizabeth 146, 151, 154, 156,
    157, 158
Grubb, Robert 149, 150, 152-3, 154
Grubb, Sarah 149, 150
Gunning, John 69

Halpin, Thomas 111
Halton, William 117

Hanna, Hugh 62
Hart, Charles 44
Hart, Mrs 183
Harvey, Bagenal 123, 124-5, 189
Haughton, Hannah 142, 143
Heber the Kentel 183
Hill, Mrs 197
Hobsbawn, Eric 27
Holofernes 184
Holt, Hestor 99
Holt, Jonathan 99
Holt, Joseph 95, 98, 100, 101, 191,
    192
Holt, William 99
Hope, James 192
Hope, Jenny 63
Hope, John 98
Hughes, James 96
Hughes, John 109
Humbert, General 177
Hume, William Hore 109

Iconologia 11, 14
Irish Legacy, The 22
Irish Magazine and Monthly Asylum,
    The 23, 197
Irish Melodies 10

Jackson, Revd William 38
Jacob, Dr Ebenezer 123, 124
Jael 183-4
James, John 97
Joan of Arc 185
Jobit, Jean-Louis 178
Joy, Grisel 57
Joy, Henry 49, 50, 54, 57-8
Joyce, Robert Dwyer 188
Judith 184, 185

Kavanagh, James 111
Kavanagh, Patrick 191, 197, 198
Kavanagh, Peter 101
Kavanagh, Thomas 96
Keally, Michael 108
Kealy, Joan 192

Kearney, William 131, 135
Kearns, Catherine 95
Kearns, George 98
Keugh, Matthew 125, 131, 189
Kilcavan Hill 97
Killala Bay, Co. Mayo 177
Killaligan, Co. Wexford 125-8
Killynure, Co. Down 69
Kilmainham Jail 54
King, Thomas 102, 103, 110
Klimt, Gustav 185

Lake, General 178
Langrell, Isaac 97, 106-7
Leadbeater, Mary Shackleton 137-62,
    187
Leadbeater, William 140, 142, 153,
    155, 160
Leamy, Edmund 189
Lecky, William 145
Leech, John 69
Leech, Revd Robert 189
Le Franc, Martin 185
Le Hunt, Colonel 189
Leixlip, Co. Kildare 170
Le More, Ellen *see* Le More, Mary
Le More, Mary 20, 22-7
'Leo' (John Keegan Casey) 7
Lett, Barbara 125-8, 134, 135, 187
Lett, Joshua 126
Lett, Mary 126
Lett, Newton 126
Lett, Stephen 126
Lettergeragh, Co. Mayo 183
Lettergullion, Co. Longford 183
Lewins, Thomas 103
Libertas 14
Little Warbler 22
Locke, John 28
Lough Swilly, Co. Donegal 40
Lyster, John Henry 123
Lyttle, W.G. 67, 194

McCann, Betty 69
Macartney, Revd Arthur 63

McCormick, William 92, 93
McCracken, Henry Joy 28, 47, 49,
    50, 52-6, 195
McCracken, John 50
McCracken, Margaret 50, 52, 55
McCracken, Mary Anne 28, 47-63,
    66, 198
McCracken, William 50, 53, 195
McDowell, R.B. 48
Mac Eoin, Sean 185
McGladdery, Rose 195
McGuire, John 129
McHenry, James 12, 23
McHenry, Mary 69
McKenna, Theobald 145, 146, 151
Maclise, Daniel 10
MacNeill, Eoin 9
McNeill, Mary 48, 54, 57-8
MacNeven, Dr 187
MacNeven, William James 26, 70
Macpherson, James 24
McQuade, Art 180, 181
McSkimmin, Samuel 69
McStravick, Jane 69
McTier, Mrs 59
*Madden's Literary Remains of the
    United Irishmen of 1798 and
    Selections from Other Popular
    Lyrics of their Times* 14, 18, 22
Magee, Gunner 180
Magee, William 50
Malone, Teresa 192
Manders, Hanah 115
Manning, William 104
Manson, David 49
Mantegna, Andrea 184
Marsillac, Jean 153
Martin, Eliza 35
Martin, Molly 121
'Mary, A Doggrel Poem' 23
Maynooth, Co. Kildare 34
Memoirs of the Irish Rebellion 64, 70
Miles, Rosalind 62
Montesquieu 30, 33
Moore, James 70

Moore, Major-General John 105
Moore, Thonas, *see Irish Melodies* 10, 24
Moreton, Henry 103
Mullen, Rose 192
Munroe, Henry 193
Murphy, Fr John 198
Murphy, John 115
Murray, Tom 160
Musgrave, Sir Richard 115
'My Emmet's No More' 23

Naas, Co. Kildare 143
Napier, Colonel George 166, 168, 174
Napier, Emily 172
Napier, Lady Sarah 163, 166, 167, 168, 174
Nation, The 188
National Journal 10, 16
Neal, Samuel 149
Neil, Edward 108
Neilson, Samuel 53, 54
New Monthly Magazine 43
Newland, Sarah 152
News Letter 49
Northern Star 13, 15, 24, 50
Nowlan, John 107, 108

O'Neill, Michael 197
O'Brien, Jack 122
O'Brien, Millicent 189
O'Connor, Fr Roderick 133
O'Connor, Laurence 148
O'Keefe, Lawrence 100
O'Connell, Daniel 43, 61
O'Doherty, K.I. 197
O'Faolain, Sean 9
Ogilvie, William 169, 170
O'Malley, Grace, *see* Granu Wale
O'Neill, Patrick 197
O'Tuairisc, Eoghan 181
Owen, Revd Roger 130, 131

Paddy's Resource 9, 11, 14, 15, 17, 18, 20, 21

Paine, Tom 32, 51
Palmer, Biddy 192
Paris 42, 43
Patrick: A Poetical Tale of 1798 23
Patriot Mother, The 197
Patriot Soldier, The 15
Pearse, Patrick 25, 44
People, The 189
Philadelphia 39
Phillips, Tom 104
Pike, Richard 152
Political Justice 147
Popular History of the Insurrection of 1798, A 191
Pounden, Alicia 128-9, 135
Pounden, John 128, 129
Press, The 14, 18, 24, 93
Princetown, New Jersey 39

Raphael 184
Rathaspick, Co. Wexford 114
Rathdrum, Co. Wicklow 104, 107
Rebellion Act of March 1799 102
Redmond, James 110
Redmond, John Cooke 117
Redmond, Michael 117
Reliques of Ancient English Poetry 24
Rembrant 185
Researches in the South of Ireland 130
Richards, Elizabeth 116-18, 136, 187
Richards, Thomas 116
Ripa, Lescre, *see Iconologia*
Roundwood, Co. Wicklow 94
Rousseau 33
Rubens, Peter Paul 185
Russell, Thomas 38, 39, 44, 47, 48, 52, 53, 58-9, 60

Sampson, William 42, 43
Sarazin, General 178
Saunder's News-Letter and Daily Advertiser 178
Savage, Mary 190
Scott, Job 149, 150, 156
Shackleton, Abraham 155

Sham Squire; and the informers of 1798, The 89
Shan Van Vocht, The 189
Sisera 183-4
'Song of Moira the Maniac' 23
Songs of Ireland 23
Speculum humanae salvationis 185
'St Patrick's Delight' 18
Stewart, A.T.Q. 56
Stone, Benjamin 101
Summerville, Michael 70
Swan, Capt. Thomas 92
Synnott, John 98

Taylor, George 113, 190
Teeling, Charles Hamilton 23
'The Band of Erin' 12
The Battle of Ballinahinch 193
'The Boys of Wexford' 188
'The Exiled Irishman's Lamentation' 19, 22
'The Grave of Russell' 11
'The Liberty Tree' 13
'The Maniac' 21
'The Muster in Fingall' 193
'The Olive Branch' 15
'The Rebel's Grave' 23
Thomas, Debby 144
Tombreen, Co. Wicklow 94
Tone, Matilda 26-46, 67, 188
Tone, Peter 36
Tone, Theobald Wolfe 26, 27, 31, 32, 34-41, 43, 4, 45; *Life*, 3, 7, 39-43

Tone, William Jr 41, 42
Tone, William 40
Toole, Johnny 90
Toole, Patrick 110
Toole, Phelin 191
Toole, Suzy 191
Toole, William 117
Tour in France 138
Trevor, Dr 195
Tuberneering, Co. Wexford 94, 98

Valentine, Rachael 96
Vindication of the Rights of Women, A 50
Vinegar Hill, Co. Wexford 105, 115, 129, 179, 192

Wainwright, Capt. William 102, 103
Walpole, Col. 95
Weston, Molly 192, 192
Wexford 124, 133, 190
Wild Irish Girl, The 12
Wilson, Thomas 42
Witherington, Edward 34
Witherington, William 34
Wollstonecraft, Mary 7, 50-1, 55
Women of 'Ninety-Eight 8, 47-8, 64, 65
Woolaghan, Hugh 103
Wtewael, Joachim Antonisz 185

Yelveton, Lord 108
Young, Arthur, *see Tour in France*